# ABCs *of* RIFLE SHOOTING

**DAVID WATSON**

Published by

Gun Digest® Books, an imprint of F+W Media, Inc.
Krause Publications • 700 East State Street • Iola, WI 54990-0001
715-445-2214 • 888-457-2873
www.krausebooks.com

To order books or other products call toll-free 1-800-258-0929
or visit us online at www.gundigeststore.com

Disclaimer: The techniques and procedures in this book are given for academic study only. It is not the intention of the author, publisher, and distributors of this book to encourage the readers to perform any techniques or procedures herein. Attempting to do so can result in severe injury or death to the firearms user or bystanders. The author, publisher, and distributors disclaim any liability for any loss, claim, damage, or injury of any type, howsoever arising, whether in tort (including without limitation negligence), contract, statute, equity or otherwise, that any reader, bystander or user of information contained in this book suffers as a result of or in connection with the use, misuse, or otherwise of the information and their application to firearms contained herein.

ISBN-13: 978-1-4402-3897-0
ISBN-10: 1-4402-3897-9

Edited by Jennifer L.S. Pearsall
Cover Design by Jana Tappa
Designed by Jana Tappa

Printed in China

# Acknowledgements

A great many people, knowingly or unknowingly, assisted in the writing of this book. To all, thank you. In particular, I would like to thank Wg Cmdr Kirsten Abercromby, Dimitrios Darios, Leigh Heron, John Hall, and Zoe Reynolds for their technical assistance. I would like to thank Ally Rolls, of Ally Rolls Photography, for her artistry, professionalism, and patience with me! I would also like to thank Burris Optics, Barrett Firearms, Accurate Innovations, XLR Industries, Scope Dope, Sniper Tools, Richards Microfit Stocks, JA Enterprises, Stillers Precision Firearms, and Pacific Tool & Gauge for their superb products and inspiration to go above and beyond. I must also thank Jennifer L.S. Pearsall and the team at F&W Media, without whom this book would not be possible. Finally, I would like to thank my wife, Jillian, for her love and support, suggestions, help, and for listening one fateful Saturday morning, when I said "I think I will write a book … ."

# Dedication

*To all those shooters out there, who strive for the best in themselves and seek to make tomorrow better than yesterday, this book is for you!*

# Introduction

This book is intended to instruct the average shooter about what can be accomplished with the shooting equipment such a shooter has on hand. In a heavily commercialized and disposable world, people have forgotten the lost art of working with and making the most of what they have. Too easily, people are inclined to reach for the next best thing, rather than hone their skills and streamline their equipment to achieve the desired results. This book seeks to revive that lost skill in hunters and competition shooters alike and return them to the days of old, when a firearm was purchased and kept for life, to be handed down through the family and to end up as a piece of living history.

Although some shooters may read this book and conclude that many cutting edge techniques and pieces of equipment are absent, this is intentional, as many of those techniques and pieces of equipment are either not relevant to the bulk of shooters, or because the gains available to accuracy would be masked by other, more simple techniques or equipment.

Finally, this book attempts to teach all shooters to respect themselves, their ammunition, and their rifle equally, in the hope that shooters will develop a sense of living history. Enjoy. Enjoy this book, your guns and, most of all, your shooting.

# About the Author

Born "Down Under," in Australia, outdoor pursuits are in David Watson's blood. Introduced to firearms at an early age by his father, David learned to shoot from a grassroots level, using the family .22, later going on to pursuits in both hunting and sporting environments. At the age of 17, David volunteered for service in the Royal Australian Army as an infantry soldier and, subsequently, as an officer, where his shooting skills and his appreciation for all aspects of small arms usage were further honed.

Following his military service, David opened a gunsmithing business that specializes in the optimization of vintage and surplus military rifles to achieve maximum accuracy in competition, and his rifles have won many competitions. David has been heavily involved in civilian sporting clubs and has also participated in law reform programs designed to bring fairer legal outcomes for Australian firearms owners.

David is a collector of classic military rifles and an avid hunter. He spends a great deal of time hunting deer with his wife, Jillian, in the Tasmanian Highlands. Aside from his interests in firearms, David is also a martial arts instructor of feudal Japanese battlefield arts, a recreational pilot flying aerobatics aircraft and hang gliders, and is involved in the development of experimental aircraft.

This book is borne out of questions and conversations David has had with fellow shooters, military colleagues, and gunsmithing customers. This book is also a product of David's desire to achieve the best results out of each and every firearm, to treat every firearm as a treasured possession, and to rekindle that lost sense of pride that every shooter has sometimes had in their rifle.

# The Fundamental Components of Accurate Rifle Shooting

Accurate shooting is built upon and is the product of three fundamental components: the rifle, the ammunition, and the shooter. The three are all equally important and inter-related. Failure to pay respect to any one of the fundamentals will result in poor shooting.

First, the rifle. The rifle must be set up correctly for its shooter, in physical terms. It must be correctly configured with its ancillary equipment such as scope and bipod, and it must also be compatible with the use of good handloaded or match ammunition.

Second, the ammunition. The ammunition must be sized in terms of power, recoil, and caliber to the shooter's abilities, needs, and purposes, and it must be correctly manufactured and optimized for the rifle it is to be fired from.

Third, but not last or least important, is the shooter. The shooter must maintain good physical fitness and operate the rifle correctly, properly maintain their rifle, select the correct ammunition for the shot, and provide a stable shooting platform for the rifle and ammunition.

If any one of the fundamental aspects is overlooked, it will be reflected in the shooter's range score or trophy wall and will prevent the shooter from further honing their skills. Care must be taken and efforts must be made to ensure that all three of these fundamentals are addressed equally and appropriately.

"Beware the man with only one rifle, he probably knows how to use it."—*Anonymous*

# Contents

## PART III: THE SHOOTER

## PART IV: PUTTING IT TOGETHER

## PART V: SHOOTER MAINTENANCE

**CHAPTER ONE**

# An Overview

The rifle and its correct maintenance, use, and employment form the first fundamental component of accurate shooting, and while the rifle may seem to have pride of place as a symbol of a shooter's skill, it is, in fact, no more or less important than the condition of the shooter and ammunition, with regards to accurate shooting.

In a commercialized world, there is a culture or belief of excess creating success in shooting. Many firearms dealers, gunsmiths, and shooters will tell the shooter that the next newest rifle is undoubtedly the best, and that the only way to learn, improve, and succeed is to open their wallet and spend all that they can on that exotic action, specialized scope, or rare breed of rifle. While this may have been true in the 1960s and '70s, where custom built rifles were the only way to go to achieve superior performance, modern manufacturing techniques and the use of CNC lathes and mills have allowed firearm manufactures to build good quality firearms not only faster and cheaper, but also more accurately. The off-the-shelf rifles of today are of the same quality as match rifles of yesterday. That said, many rifles made some 20, 30, or even 50 years ago, providing they are without defect, are capable of providing very good accuracy and, in many cases, will outshoot the majority of shooters, when set up correctly and used in conjunction with good quality commercial or handloaded ammunition.

So what does all this mean? It means that the accurate rifle doesn't have to be the latest and greatest or most expensive. Indeed, the accurate rifle is the rifle that the shooter is willing to put time, effort, and training into, as opposed to pining for what the Joneses have; bear in mind that the Joneses generally believe that the latest and greatest and most expensive rifle will improve their range scores or enable them to take that bull elk. In most cases, it won't help them to do either.

Take another look at what you have in your rifle cabinet or safe. Now, learn to use what you have, to its limits. Too, clearly define what it is you want to achieve, then pursue a rifle, whether it be factory or custom, that will fulfill your needs. Not only will you save money and put the Joneses to shame, you will improve your skill and knowledge as an accomplished shooter.

## THE RIFLE IN OVERVIEW

The typical rifle is comprised of three major components, the action, barrel, and the stock. These three components work in unison and must be treated

*This is 237 years of firearms evolution, from American independence to the present day.*

equally. Any limitation in one particular component will limit the level of accuracy the rifle can achieve.

The principle role of the action is to transfer ammunition from the magazine to the chamber of the barrel and to provide a firing mechanism to the ammunition. It is necessary that the action hold the ammunition in the chamber in line with the center axis of the barrel.

The principle role of the barrel is to contain the explosion inside the ammunition's case during firing and direct the projectile onto the barrel's rifling so that the projectile follows the barrel's center axis as that projectile speeds up and rotates on the rifling to attain

stability and leave the muzzle of the barrel (again, evenly and on the same center axis as the barrel).

Finally, the principle role of the stock is to provide the shooter stable points of contact with both the barrel and action, so that the unit as a whole can be held and aimed in a stable manner.

By breaking a rifle down into these components and roles, it becomes easier to see how the components work, what can be done to improve the components, and what conditions need to be provided by the shooter to attain maximum accuracy. In the next several chapters, let's look at each and all of these facets.

# CHAPTER TWO

# Barrels

Barrels are made, generally, from 4140 chrome-moly steel or 416 stainless steel, both of which are perfectly suited to the rigors of firing pressures. Bores are drilled using specialized deep drilling equipment, and then the rifling is either button drawn, cut, or hammer-forged into the barrel. From there, the barrel "blank" is turned again to make it uniform to the bore, and a tenon, chamber, and crown are cut into the blank, readying it for fitting to an action.

There are many different combinations of barrel weight, length, and rifling twist rate, just as there are many styles of rifling itself, in terms of the number of grooves and the angles cut onto the lands. Many of these factors are predetermined by the chosen caliber and usage—terms such as "light sporting," "varmint," "target," etc., come into common use—and this is the manner in which commercial rifles are generally marketed. The only time a shooter will really have a say in terms of the particulars of their barrel is if they'll be rebarreling an existing action with a custom-made barrel.

There really is very little difference between an off-the-shelf factory barrel and a custom barrel, though final finish and quality control may vary. The edge a custom barrel provides is that it allows the shooter to tailor the barrel to their purpose. For instance, one can use a barrel of greater length to obtain greater velocities, or manipulate the twist rate to stabilize heavier projectiles, all in the pursuit of gaining accuracy over a particular distance or from a particular caliber. That said, for the majority of hunting and competition, factory barrels are sufficient. If the shooter wishes to compete at a high level or participate in extreme-range hunting, then a custom barrel may be appropriate for those intended uses.

## INSPECTING AND ASSESSING RIFLE BARRELS IN USE

Whether you plink a few targets a couple times a month (or a couple times a year), are sighting in for a long-awaited hunt, or are on the range every hour your free time permits, you're going to need to thoroughly and objectively assess the condition of your barrel, to keep you and your rifle in top shooting form. Though it's a common practice, it is not really sufficient to merely remove the bolt from the rifle and hold up the barrel to the light and peer through it (although, with a trained eye, one can perhaps get away with this for an initial inspection, as severe defects are obvious to the eye).

First, look at the crown and ensure there are no chips, gouges, shavings, or other damage at the edge of the crown, where it turns onto the rifling. Ensure, too, that the rifling is not rounded at the corners of the lands and grooves where they meet the crown. Next, taking a very bright light, inspect the first

PHOTO COURTESY WIKIPEDIA

*From raw steel to precision instrument, barrel making is an art form.*

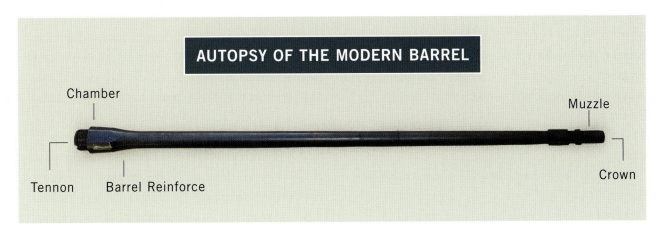

## AUTOPSY OF THE MODERN BARREL

Chamber

Muzzle

Tennon

Barrel Reinforce

Crown

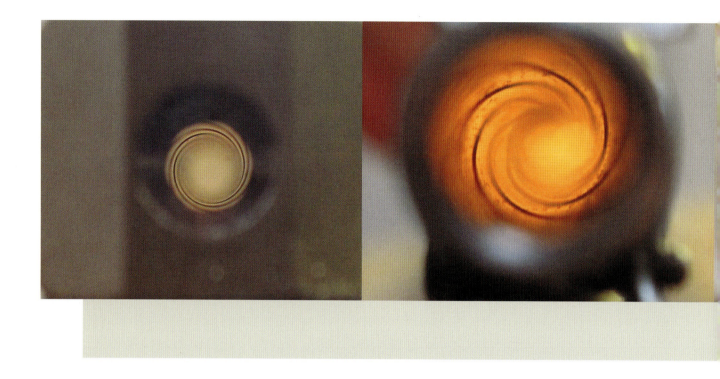

few millimeters of the bore at the crown, looking for discoloration or traces of copper. Look also for evidence of pitting in the bore.

The next step is to look at the "throat," that part of the bore where the chamber leads onto the rifling. Look also, using a very bright light, for evidence of pitting both in the chamber and at the end of the chamber where the rifling starts. At the start of the rifling, there should be a short section that appears like a ramp leading up to each land on the rifling. This ramped section is the "throat," and it should be even and consistent for each land; it should not show any signs of erosion.

Finally, and if possible with benefit of a borescope, the rifling must be inspected. First, look for misformed rifling, particularly on the corners of the lands. Second, look for areas of pitting and/or concentric rings that could indicate a possible bulge in the barrel (a fairly terminal condition, by the way). Finally, having removed the borescope, hold the barrel up to the light and try to assess the reflectivity of the bore. Is it mirror shiny, or greyed out or darkly pitted?

A last and somewhat dubious test is the use of bore gauges to "measure" the diameter of the bore. While this method may be okay for performing a quick assessment at a gun show, for instance, it really tells very little about the true condition of the bore.

## THE BORE REVEALED

Having completed the inspection of the bore, the shooter can then take a deeper look at what problems have been discovered and decide what to do about them (if anything).

Again, let's look at the crown first. Chips or uneven wear are generally caused by improper use of cleaning rods, particularly the segmented steel variety. Another source of damage comes through having dropped the rifle—although only the very honest will admit to that! Wear that is even in nature and that has rounded the rifling at the crown is generally associated with prolonged usage. In and of itself, this is no great problem, provided the barrel has been properly cleaned and cared for. But, if the even rounding also has minor pitting associated with it, it's a fair indicator that the rifle has been neglected.

If copper streaks are seen just inside the crown or there is a grey or black flaky residue present, the barrel requires cleaning in order to assess its condition further. No matter the cause, a damaged crown is by no means a terminal condition. Re-crowning

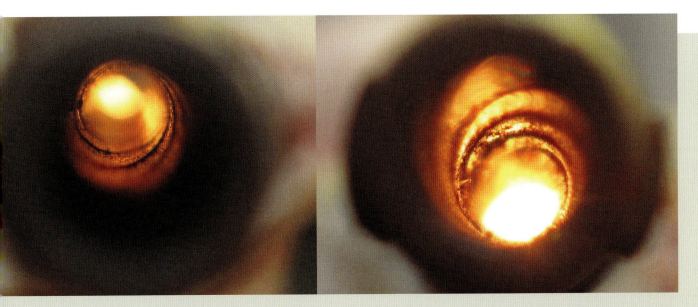

*Barrel condition, the good, the bad, the ugly—and the unbelievable! Don't let a dirty bore turn you off, though. Always clean before looking and assessing.*

is a simple process and is normally conducted by a gunsmith on a lathe, though it is perfectly possible for the shooter to do at home. The process requires only a crowning hand tool. Re-crowning a barrel will remove about 3mm ($1/_8$-inch) in most cases, which is not enough to appreciably affect muzzle velocities.

Looking next at the throat and chamber, if the "ramps" where the projectile is led onto the rifling are not sharp and clearly defined or they are rounded off, you have uncovered a sign of throat erosion. Throat erosion may allow the projectile to potentially proceed slightly off axis to the bore, as that projectile exits the case neck and enters onto the rifling. The projectile going off axis is generally random both in direction and occurrence, and it is generally highly detrimental to accuracy. A small exception to this is when the level of throat erosion is similar to the condition of the rifling and muzzle. In this latter case, the tendency of experiencing "fliers" (occasional projectiles that miss the point of aim significantly), is lessened, due to the larger group size a barrel in this condition will generally shoot.

Looking at the chamber itself, there really shouldn't be any damage here, no matter how badly the rifle has been treated, which is good, because, ultimately, there is no way to repair a chamber or throat. This does not mean the barrel should be consigned to the trash can. A worn or damaged chamber and throat can be recut, a process known as "rechambering." This can be accomplished in one of two ways. In the first, the barrel is removed from the action and a fresh chamber is cut, using a cartridge-specific tool known as a "chambering reamer" (this tool will be crafted in the original caliber and cartridge for the particular rifle). Once the chamber is recut, the barrel is shortened at the chamber end and refitted to the action. In the second method, the barrel can be rechambered for a different cartridge, so long as it is compatible with the action and bore dimensions.

Next up for inspection is the rifling itself, preferably with a borescope. If there is discrete damage to the rifling or a dark ring is apparent (indicating a bulge in the barrel), this is generally the result of some sort of misfire or, heaven forbid, the "shooting out" of a jammed cleaning rod (yes, people do that). Unfortunately, this type of damage is irreparable in a barrel; in fact, it's terminal. That said, you'll hear anecdotal evidence to suggest that, every now and then, a bore with this type of damage "shoots just fine," although such is rarely the case.

If there are areas of fine pitting in the bore, sometimes this can be remedied by bore lapping or polishing, although it should be noted that this process will not remove the pitting, just help to limit its effects on the projectile and detriment to accuracy. It should also be noted that bore lapping and polishing might help the bore and it might not. Fire lapping is a better alternative (this is identical to the "running in" process described later in this book).

Having searched for discrete damage in the bore and, perhaps, found none, the shooter then needs to look at the reflectivity of the bore. A bright and shiny bore can be an indicator of either a little used bore or one that has been properly cared for. A greyed bore indicates one that has seen the beginning of the formation of uniform pitting—again, not a terminal condition in its own right, but something to keep in mind as you continue to take the rifle afield. A darkly pitted bore, on the other hand, speaks for itself.

Through all this process, it would be quite easy to be too hard on the condition of a particular barrel, and a shooter could dismiss many barrels unnecessarily. It should be clearly noted that a barrel with an undamaged but worn crown, a slightly eroded throat, and a greyed-out bore will still shoot reasonably well and, in some cases, may shoot very well. In cases such as these, it is not necessarily the accuracy that may suffer directly. It is more the case that a barrel in such condition will take more fouling shots to group well, but, at the same time, will also foul faster and have its accuracy degrade faster between cleanings than a barrel in better condition.

If the shooter should feel that their barrel is on its way to being worn out, stop, give it a good cleaning, and objectively assess it. If the wear is even throughout all the components, it's likely the bore still has life left in it.

## CUSTOM BARRELS

Custom barrels are the product of specialized barrel makers. In such a barrel, the shooter can specify the caliber, twist rate, length, weight, style of taper, style of crown, number of grooves, style of grooves, number of flutes (if desired), and the barrel steel to be used. The shooter's best friend here is the barrel maker, who, when presented with a clear definition of the barrel's use, will be able to produce a barrel to meet those needs.

It is the responsibility of the shooter to provide a definition of the rifle's intended use to the barrel maker. Is the barrel for a lightweight mountain stalking rifle or a Palma match rifle? Will the barrel be used in conjunction with a scope or with iron sights? What type of action will the barrel be required to mate to? These are all important questions to which the barrel maker will need answers. A good barrel maker will also ask the shooter to specify what ammunition will be used, in order to determine the correct twist rate and best length. These are the questions from which extra performance in custom barrels can be derived. That said, many shooters believe that the benefits of a custom barrel lie in the quality of the product. Although some barrel makers produce barrels of such fine tolerances that their barrels perform significantly better than one commercially produced, it is more often the case that most custom barrels derive their performance from the exacting specifications, rather than the exacting quality of the barrel itself. As with all such things, though, if the shooter is going to these lengths when choosing a barrel, they will need to pay the same amount of attention to the action and stock, as well. Performance will always be limited by the weakest link or, in our case, the most inaccurate part.

## BARREL LENGTH AND WEIGHT

Barrel length and weight, when ordering a custom barrel or assessing factory options on an off-the-shelf rifle, should be driven by the shooter's purpose for the rifle. That said, it is critically important for the shooter to have a firm understanding of the effects of different barrel lengths and weights.

Looking first at barrel length, in essence, the longer the barrel, the greater the muzzle velocity for the shooter's ammunition. This is because the projectile is exposed to the propulsive force of the cartridge being fired for longer. Likewise, a shorter barrel will result in less velocity from the same cartridge. This general rule does have limitations. As a barrel gets longer, the velocity gains become less until, ultimately, in a very long barrel, the projectile will, in fact, begin to slow down before it reaches the end of the barrel.

The key here is choosing the right length for two factors. First, the barrel length needs to be appropriate for the caliber and cartridge. Second, the barrel length needs to be chosen so that the harmonics are correct for the projectile. The former is an easy choice. The latter is extremely complicated and goes well beyond the boundaries of this text. Without writing the necessary book on that subject, just

know that, with barrel harmonics, barrel length is related to barrel weight.

When considering what barrel length the shooter needs for a particular caliber, the shooter need only look at the amount of powder being burnt during firing. This can be broken down into several categories. Small-caliber rifles such as .223 and .22-250 need only have 16- to 22-inch barrels. Larger centerfires such as 7.62x39 and .308 are best served with barrels in the region of 20 to 24 inches, while larger calibers or magnum cartridges such as .300 Winchester Magnum and .338 Lapua Magnum are best served with barrels in excess of 26 inches. These barrel lengths will see that the bulk of the energy from the

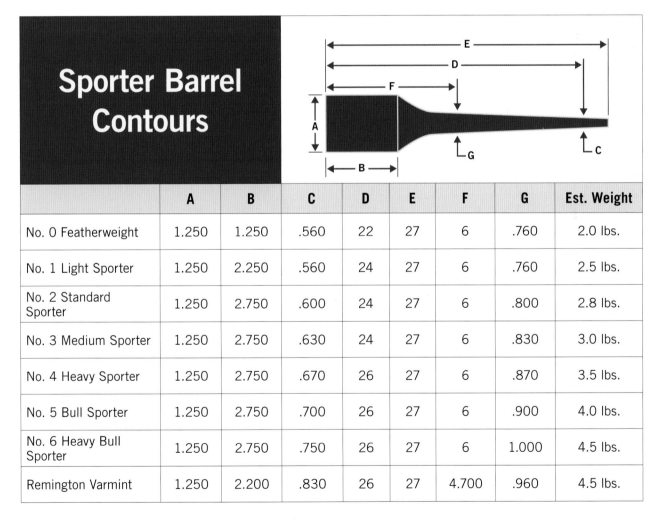

| | A | B | C | D | E | F | G | Est. Weight |
|---|---|---|---|---|---|---|---|---|
| No. 0 Featherweight | 1.250 | 1.250 | .560 | 22 | 27 | 6 | .760 | 2.0 lbs. |
| No. 1 Light Sporter | 1.250 | 2.250 | .560 | 24 | 27 | 6 | .760 | 2.5 lbs. |
| No. 2 Standard Sporter | 1.250 | 2.750 | .600 | 24 | 27 | 6 | .800 | 2.8 lbs. |
| No. 3 Medium Sporter | 1.250 | 2.750 | .630 | 24 | 27 | 6 | .830 | 3.0 lbs. |
| No. 4 Heavy Sporter | 1.250 | 2.750 | .670 | 26 | 27 | 6 | .870 | 3.5 lbs. |
| No. 5 Bull Sporter | 1.250 | 2.750 | .700 | 26 | 27 | 6 | .900 | 4.0 lbs. |
| No. 6 Heavy Bull Sporter | 1.250 | 2.750 | .750 | 26 | 27 | 6 | 1.000 | 4.5 lbs. |
| Remington Varmint | 1.250 | 2.200 | .830 | 26 | 27 | 4.700 | .960 | 4.5 lbs. |

*The profile of a barrel will determine its weight and taper. Although standard profiles are set, in truth, the shooter can order almost any taper imaginable. (Note: Measurements A-G here and in the charts on the following page are in inches.)*

# Varmint and Match Barrel Contours

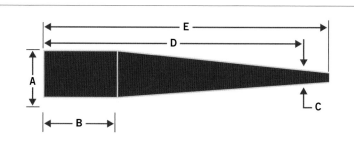

| | A | B | C | D | E | Est. Weight |
|---|---|---|---|---|---|---|
| No. 7 Light Target | 1.200 | 2.750 | .750 | 26 | 27 | 5.5 lbs. |
| No. 8 Standard Target | 1.200 | 2.750 | .820 | 26 | 27 | 6.0 lbs. |
| No. 9 Heavy Target | 1.250 | 2.750 | .875 | 26 | 27 | 6.5 lbs. |
| No. 10 MTU | 1.250 | 2.750 | .930 | 26 | 27 | 7.0 lbs. |
| No. 11 Straight Blank | CM 1.300/SS 1.250 | — | CM 1.300/SS 1.250 | 28 | 29 | 10.0 lbs. |
| No. 12 SS Oversize OD | 1.450 | — | 1.450 | 28 | 29 | 13.0 lbs. |
| No. 12 CM Oversize OK | 2.000 | — | 2.000 | 28 | 29 | 23.0 lbs. |
| No. 13 50BMG | 2.000 | — | 2.000 | 36 | 37 | 32.0 lbs. |
| No. 17 Heavy Varmint | 1.250 | 5.000 | .900 | 28 | 29 | 7.0 lbs. |
| No. 18 Light Varmint | 1.200 | 5.000 | .875 | 28 | 29 | 6.5 lbs. |
| No. 19 Hunter | 1.250 | 4.000 | .750 | 26 | 27 | 6.0 lbs. |

# Palma Barrel Contours

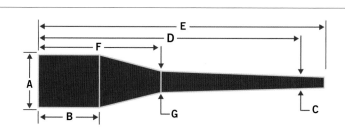

| | A | B | C | D | E | F | G | Est. Weight |
|---|---|---|---|---|---|---|---|---|
| No. 14 Heavy Palma | 1.250 | 2.50 | .900 | 30 | 31 | 5 | 1.000 | 6.5 lbs. |
| No. 15 Standard Palma | 1.250 | 2.50 | .820 | 30 | 31 | 5 | 0.920 | 5.5 lbs. |
| No. 16 Light Palma | 1.250 | 2.50 | .750 | 30 | 31 | 5 | 0.900 | 4.5 lbs. |

cartridge being fired will act upon the projectile to have the desired ballistic performance.

There are exceptions to these rules, and those exceptions rely purely on the purpose of the rifle. An 18-inch barrel on a .308 will make a very handy, lightweight, and convenient scout rifle with good medium range potential. A 30-inch barrel on a .300 Remington Ultra Magnum will make an excellent long-range target or stationary hunting rifle.

Hand in hand with barrel length is barrel weight. Ultimately, the barrel weight will be specified as a "taper pattern," from the chamber end of the barrel tapering down to the muzzle. There are many different types of taper available, ranging from "light" tapers, where the outside muzzle diameter may only be .5-inch, through to heavy bench tapers, where the muzzle is 1.25 inches or greater in diameter. The only real rule here is that lighter taper barrels will warm up faster and cool down faster, factors that increase the chance that the point of aim may change. Heavier taper barrels take longer to warm and cool, thus, in a competition serial where 20 rounds may have to be fired within an allotted time period, the point of aim is less likely to change. So, the taper chosen will depend on the purpose for the rifle. If the shooter is looking for a taper suitable for backpack hunting, where the maximum range is perhaps 200 to 300 yards, a lighter taper is perfectly suitable. If the shooter is looking for a target rifle-type taper, where the rifle may be expected to fire 40 rounds with consistency, then a heavy taper is more appropriate.

The only caveat to the discussion of barrel length and taper is the question of harmonics. Without going into extensive detail, lighter barrels resonate at a higher frequency, heavier barrels at a lower frequency. The higher the frequency, the greater the opportunity for the projectile to exit the barrel while the muzzle is in motion. Again, this subject goes beyond the realms of this book, but the shooter must be aware of its presence. Likewise, it should be noted that, as a barrel is manufactured, stresses are introduced to the structure of the steel on the machined surfaces. These stress lines have the capacity to pull

the barrel in a particular way, both as the barrel heats up and during firing itself. Unfortunately, the affects of these stresses are unpredictable.

Lightweight barrels are more susceptible to being affected by these factors, due to the lower ratio between surface area and total amount of steel contained within the barrel. This is the main reason lightweight barrels are bedded at the tip of the fore-end of the stock, as this type of bedding does provide support for the barrel at its midpoint and can dampen abnormal resonance. This problem can also be cured by heat-treatment of the finished barrel, most commonly by cryogenics or freezing of the barrel, to stress-relieve it (though this process is fairly hit and miss). Interestingly, it is generally unknown that the same effect can be achieved by leaving the finished barrel exposed to natural heating and cooling from the environment over a very long period, say 10 years. Like I said, that's pretty interesting, but also fairly impractical!

## TWIST RATES

"Twist rates" refer to the rate at which the rifling winds its way along the bore of a barrel. The twist rate is expressed as the length of barrel in which there exists one full revolution of the rifling within the bore. An example of a twist rate would be (for a .223) is 1:14, meaning there is one full rotation of the rifling in 14 inches of barrel length. Twist rate is important, because projectiles require a certain speed of rotation in order to stabilize. A projectile that has not stabilized will characteristically "keyhole"—the projectile will hit the target sideways. Conversely, a projectile that is over-stabilized (rotating too fast), may disintegrate before impacting the target!

The correct amount of bullet rotation and its required twist rate is dependent on the length of the projectile (longer projectiles need faster twist rates in the rifling), the speed of the projectile (faster projectiles need slower twist rates in the rifling), the diameter of the projectile, and the specific gravity of the projectile. This data and its use in the Greenhill formula can provide an adequate rule of thumb as to

| Caliber | Twist Rate (expressed one turn:inches) | | | | | | |
|---|---|---|---|---|---|---|---|
| | 1:7 | 1:8 | 1:9 | 1:10 | 1:11 | 1:12 | 1:14 |
| .204 Ruger | | | X | | | X | |
| .223 Remington | X | X | X | X | X | X | X |
| .243 Winchester | X | X | X | X | X | X | X |
| .270 Winchester | | X | | X | | X | |
| .284 Winchester | | X | X | X | | X | |
| .308 Winchester | | X | X | X | X | X | X |
| .303 British | | | | X | | | |
| .323 Mauser | | | | X | | | |
| .338 Lapua | | X | | X | | X | |

the required twist rate. Generally speaking, in .223 rifles, a twist rate of 1:14 is adequate to a 55-grain projectiles, while a 1:9 is required for 65-grain and heavier projectiles. In .308 rifles, 1:12 is fine for projectiles up to 168 grains, and 1:9 is required for projectiles over the 200-grain mark.

## RIFLING

Looking beyond the twist rate, the shooter can consider the style of rifling to be used. Although there are several available, which use different numbers of grooves, there are really only three styles that stand out against the plain-Jane, four- to six-groove 90-degree land-to-groove rifling.

First there is "5R rifling," which was developed for a military application. Rifling that is 5R is essentially the same as any other and can use any number of grooves. The real difference lies in the corners. The corners of 5R rifling are rounded, and this allows the rifling to grip the projectile without cutting into its jacket. This leads to less fouling, and also a better gas seal on the projectile. A further advancement of 5R rifling is that the rifling tends to be staggered, so

that each land is opposite a groove. This effectively squeezes the projectile without pinching it, again, reducing fouling and enhancing the gas seal.

"Lilja-styled rifling" consists of using three lands and grooves. The benefits are essentially the same as with 5R, but the fewer grooves in a Lilja-rifled barrel can lead to an enhanced surface finish within the bore once hand lapped (prior to installation). Further, wear can be reduced, because there is a greater mass of steel within each land to absorb the heat and pressure stresses the rifling is exposed to when fired.

A final type of rifling is known as "polygonal rifling." This style of rifling was one of the first types invented—and then essentially forgotten about. More recently, this type of rifling has been adopted by many handgun manufacturers. Polygonal rifling is generally shaped like an octagon with rounded corners, and this shape rotates through the bore to create the rifling and twist rate. Polygonal rifling, therefore, does not have distinct lands and grooves. Proponents claim this is a more accurate style of rifling, because it disturbs the projectile less than conventional riflings, which tend to cut into the projectile. While this may be the case for slow projectiles, a high-velocity projectiles might tend to "slip" against the rifling surfaces as it leaves the case neck, because the rifling is unable to sufficiently bite in and grip it. That said, higher velocities are achievable with polygonal rifling, due to there being less friction.

## THROAT ENHANCEMENTS

The only time the shooter will ever need to specify the twist rate is when ordering a custom-made barrel, and the barrel maker will best guide the shooter as to the correct twist rate for the shooter's purpose. Further to the twist rate, the shooter can also elect to chamber the rifle with a "tight throat." Essentially, this process decreases the diameter of the throat area of the rifle, making it a near to perfect fit with only 0.002- to -0.003-inch clearance between the case neck and the wall of the chamber. This process helps to ensure that the projectile does not go off axis as it moves from the case neck into the throat and onto the rifling.

Although this process can improve accuracy over a standard chamber, it does require that the shooter only use handloaded ammunition specific for that specific rifle. If the chamber and throat are tighter, the less room

*Styles of muzzle crown vary, from the 11-degree target crown, the typical factory radiused crown, typical military crown, semi-radiused crown, and the vintage crown. All have their place and purpose.*

there is for slight variations in ammunition. In many cases, the shooter will have to size the necks of cases accordingly, and also turn the necks to ensure that they are concentric. This setup is not recommended for big-game or dangerous-game hunting firearms, due to the precise requirements in ammunition; off-the-shelf ammunition will seldom even chamber in a tightly throated firearm.

## CROWNS

The crown forms the very end of the rifling at the muzzle and is of critical importance. As the last point of contact between the rifle and the projectile, the crown must ensure the projectile is not turned off axis to the bore as it leaves the muzzle. Traditionally, the style of crown has had a second function, and that is to protect the true crown from damage by cleaning rods or by dropping the rifle.

First and foremost, the crown must be even, in terms of being concentric to the bore and also in terms of the angle at which the crown is set to the bore. A crown that is uneven or damaged will allow gas to escape underneath the base of the projectile on one side. This will angle the projectile as it leaves the muzzle, thereby ruining accuracy.

A regular or traditional crown is formed on the muzzle with a cutting tool that yields a radius from the outside edge of the barrel to the inside edge of the rifling on the same side of the barrel. This style of crown will generally provide $1/8$-inch of metal protruding past the crown to protect the crown. Though effective at preventing damage, and while the angle at which the crown is set is adequate, it is not the best for accuracy. Testing has shown that an angled but flat-faced crown of 11 degrees (known as a "target crown"), will provide the optimum angle for gas to escape from underneath an emerging projectile. The downside is that an 11-degree target-style crown is more susceptible to damage. Crowns are difficult to assess, when it comes to minuscule damage that can be invisible to the human eye and still have a dramatic effect. In fact, many shooters advocate re-cutting the crown on their rifles every 500 to 1,000 rounds. Although this may be overkill, particularly for a shooter who treats their rifle properly, it does rule out a likely but difficult to detect source of inaccuracy. Crowns are generally cut with a hand tool or on a lathe, and it is a simple job for a gunsmith. It can even be done at home.

## FLUTING

Fluting is the process of grinding lengthwise grooves in the exterior of a barrel. The purposes of flutes in a barrel are, principally, to reduce the weight

*Fluting can add style and character, as well as stiffness to a barrel. It can also add stress and introduce inaccuracy. Flute your barrel for the right reasons and get it done correctly!*

of a barrel, while increasing the rigidity of the barrel and enhancing heat dissipation from the barrel by increasing its surface area. The barrel, having been fluted, will appear like a roman column of sorts, and because the flutes provide sharp, lengthwise angles on the barrel, the barrel will be more stiff. This has an effect on harmonics and can improve accuracy in some cases where light taper barrels are used.

All this does come at a cost. The grinding of the flutes imparts great heat and stress into the steel of the barrel at the molecular level. If done improperly, the barrel can warp, either when the flutes are cut into it or when the barrel heats up during firing. Many gunsmiths advise against fluting, because of its unpredictable and, in some cases, destructive effects on barrels. Organizations that specialize in fluting generally seem to carry out stress relief of the barrel either by heating or cryogenic treatment.

An advancement of regular fluting is that of "spiral" fluting. In this process, the barrel is indexed and rotated at a specific rate. The flutes are then ground in while the barrel rotates, resulting in a spiral about the axis of the barrel. The benefits of this are that first, as the individual flutes are longer, more metal is removed and the surface area is further increased over standard fluting. Second, as the flutes are cut as a spiral, there is less opportunity for the barrel to exhibit harmonic or stress-related problems, because the flutes do not run along the axis of the barrel.

In truth, the only place for fluting is on heavy weapons for the obvious weight reduction, or with rapid-fire weapons where heat buildup is an issue. There is no true need for fluting on competition or hunting rifles, except in extreme cases, and fluting should be carried out only by professional barrel makers.

# CHAPTER THREE

# Stocks

The role of the stock is to transfer the stable shooting platform the shooter creates to the rest of the rifle. The stock must achieve this without applying any incorrect pressure to the barreled action, which could alter the point of aim. Further, when exposed to different temperatures or humidity, the stock must not warp or change its form, so as to apply incorrect pressures to the barreled action.

There are a great many styles and types of materials available in stockmaking today, and a number of ways in which a stock can actually be fitted to a barreled action. Although stock design varies greatly, most rifle stocks will follow the general form of a butt for the shoulder, a long hand or pistol grip, and a fore-end for the secondary hand to grasp. There is an almost limitless combination of lengths and angles of the various parts of a stock with which to achieve particular needs, however, the commercial firearms manufacturers have taken most of these details out of the equation by producing stocks for their rifles that "fit" the majority of the population; many may require only a minor length adjustment of the butt. To that end, many manufactures now supply spacers with their rifles to achieve just that.

Despite the consistent factory products available today, custom stockmaking is a thriving field, and even with the advent of composite stocks, which, by virtue of their construction methods, have done away with much of the specialized skills required in stockmaking. Traditional stockmakers are still

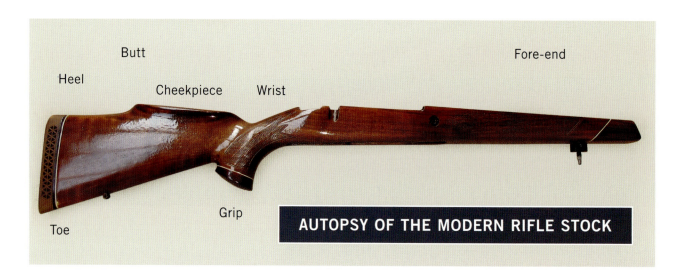

Butt · Fore-end · Heel · Cheekpiece · Wrist · Grip · Toe

**AUTOPSY OF THE MODERN RIFLE STOCK**

*Stocks have evolved through time in terms of materials, construction, and functionality, yet their purpose remains the same.*

available to satisfy high-end, individually tailored stock requests.

Modern technology has also provided us the introduction of two newer types of stock. First is the injection-molded stock, primarily introduced by commercial firearms manufacturers seeking a "budget composite" stock. Second is the chassis system stock, which is generally machined from 7075 aluminum. This type seeks to fill the tactical market via all manner of rails and attachment points.

Given all the different styles and materials, it is very important to note that any stock, correctly bedded, will do its job of providing a stable shooting platform to the barreled action. The only difference between a correctly bedded but old wooden stock and a correctly bedded top of the line carbon fiber stock is that the carbon fiber stock is new. The carbon fiber stock will not make the rifle any more accurate than the wooden stock. (That said, few rifles are correctly bedded and, therefore, show some accuracy benefits from being torqued down into a new stock with or without being correctly bedded.) Make no mistake. All stocks require bedding in order to do their job fully.

## INSPECTING THE STOCK

Although stocks can be made from a variety of materials and using various methods to achieve different shapes and styles, the stressors a stock must endure are the same. That said, damage to any type of stock can generally be characterized as either cracking damage or crushing damage.

When inspecting a used rifle stock, the shooter is best served by removing the barreled action from the stock, allowing the interior to be viewed. Having done this, the shooter must inspect for signs of hammering, whereby a loose action has hammered and crushed the recoil abutment, leading to a poor fit between the stock and the action. The shooter also needs to look for cracks in line with the stock on the front and rear of the action screw holes. Cracking here is evidentce of the action screws carrying recoil loads against the material of the stock, thus cracking the stock with uneven pressures.

Crush damage, particularly in wooden stocks, is characterized by a deep imprint of the action base onto the action platform of the stock. This occurs because of over-tightening of the action screws, which compresses the stock material.

Finally, the shooter can inspect the exterior of the stock, paying particular attention to the wrist, where cracks in line with the stock can spread from the tang rearward, and also cracking at the heel and toe of the stock, the latter generally being caused by poor handling.

It is important that all cracks are repaired and, if there is crush damage, that the stock is bedded properly to the action. Cracks and crush damage can and will affect the accuracy potential of the stock, because this kind of damage works to relieve stress on the stock. The action is designed to be torqued into the stock, and the stock is intended to both carry stress from particular points on the barreled action and, in turn, apply force back to the barreled action. Cracks and crush damage will allow the stock to move and warp, rather than carry stress, thereby loosening or applying incorrect pressures and interfering with accuracy.

It should be noted that many types of damage are perfectly repairable. Really, the defining factor in reparability is not what the damage is, but, rather, what the stock is made from.

## WOODEN STOCKS

Wood is the original, traditional material used in stockmaking. Wood provides a lightweight, durable, and strong stockmaking material that is highly shapeable and, when necessary, easily repairable. Further, with the variety of wood available, particular species can be used for their particular properties. For instance, walnut is often employed for a heavy or decorative use, while some rare varieties of pine are used for their resistance to moisture absorption and warping. For the particular pros and cons of various species of wood, the wise shooter will look to the services of a professional stockmaker.

Wooden stocks do come with some notable disadvantages. The primary disadvantage of a wooden stock that sets it aside from all other types is maintenance. Wooden stocks, if allowed to do so, will absorb and lose moisture, warp with heat, crush with pressure, and be more or less flexible with temperature. All these environmental factors, whether in the field or at the range, have the capacity to degrade accuracy. This doesn't mean that a shooter should only use a wooden stock in a stable environment. A correctly maintained wooden stock will perform just as well as a modern composite or "all-weather" stock.

When looking at the correct maintenance of a wooden stock, the shooter must first consider the finish of the stock. Conventionally, there are two types of finish applied to wooden stocks that must be considered, when the shooter is conducting correct maintenance. First and traditionally is a wax-/oil-based finish. Second is a modern varnish-based finish. Looking first at the wax-based finish, waxes and oils (generally beeswax and boiled linseed oil), are applied to the raw wood of the stock and are hand buffed either periodically as general maintenance, or after shooting as part of the post-shoot cleaning regimen. The wax and oil act as an ablative shield for

the woodwork. As dirt, grime, and moisture collect on the surface of the stock, they are caught in the wax. Hand buffing removes the dirt and restores a fresh, clean surface to the woodwork. Occasionally, or as required, a fresh coat of wax is applied and buffed, renewing the stocks' ablative shield.

The second type of finish is the varnish finish or, in more modern terms, a polyurethane finish. This is a permanent finish applied to the raw woodwork and which, essentially, creates a plastic bag around the woodwork and prevents moisture, dirt, and grime from getting into it. The ability of this finish to do its job properly is solely reliant on the integrity of the finish. Any dings, scratches, or abrasions piercing the finish will allow moisture and, to a lesser degree, dirt and grime, to enter into the woodwork, potentially affecting the stock. Otherwise, though, this type of finish is very hard-wearing and resilient, with

the capacity to last many decades of use. Correct preventative maintenance for both finishes applied to wooden stocks will be covered later in the section dealing with post-shoot cleaning and maintenance.

The second major disadvantage of a wooden stock is its capacity to crack during normal usage. Generally, this is caused by a lack of correct maintenance in one of two ways. First is by allowing moisture to affect the fibers of the stock, causing the stock to warp or set up internal stresses that are relieved by the stock cracking. Second, it can be that inappropriate tensioning of the stock bolts has been introduced, leading to crushing of the wooden fibers underneath the receiver in the region of the recoil lug, or resulting in lengthwise cracks behind the recoil lug or in front of or behind the stock bolt screw holes in the stock.

Although both disadvantages on their faces appear to be severe, they do dovetail perfectly with one of the wooden stock's greatest advantages, and that is the ease with which wooden stocks can be repaired. Wooden stocks can be easily steamed and sanded to relieve the effects of warping, cracks can be pinned or glued, and finishes can be reapplied to make an old stock appear new. This level of reparability in itself bestows a level of reliability, something particularly relevant for backpack hunters a long way from civilization—most damage to wooden stocks can be overcome with a small amount of sandpaper and epoxy glue.

Observant shooters will have noticed that laminated stocks, those made up from strips or wood glued together, have not been discussed in this section. This is because laminated stocks are, technically, a composite stock; they combine the advantages of different layers of wood oriented in different directions and interfacing over an epoxy or other adhesive medium. Laminated stocks will be discussed in the next section.

## COMPOSITE STOCKS

A composite stock, by definition, is one manufactured from several materials that work together, combining their strengths to create another material that possesses greater strengths than the sum of its parts. Composite stocks are a relatively new addition, in terms of firearms history, and yet have been around for roughly 70 to 80 years. Composite stocks have seen a lot of development in this time, including those in materials engineering and advances in the ways in which the materials can be used.

Essentially, composite stocks are made from a matting that is soaked in a glue. The matting provides the structural pathway for stress to be absorbed, while the glue allows that stress to be evenly spread over all the fibers in the mat. Truly, a composite stock achieves its strength from its inherent ability to spread the load.

The toughness of a composite stock is achieved through the glue medium or epoxy system, the epoxy rather forming one large "super-molecule" in the shape of the stock. This creates a very cohesive system that has no weak points or areas that can crack, or that can even possess inherent fracture lines in which

cracks could develop, as is the case with a wooden stock.

Initially, composite stocks were made using hand-laid fiberglass in a polyester resin system. While this method can make very good stocks, they tend to be unnecessarily heavy, due to excess resin, and this actually makes the stock weaker. More modern materials in use today include aramid and carbon fiber in epoxy resin systems. These stocks are made from carbon or aramid textiles that have been pre-impregnated with the perfect amount of resin. These stocks are then vacuum bagged to remove any excess resin (should there be any) and apply pressure to the parts, while they bake in an autoclave or oven at a specific temperature or regime of temperatures for a specific time. This process produces a stock that maximizes the strength available while minimizing the weight.

A composite stock can be made easily to any shape and be very strong, very durable, very light, and very reparable. This isn't to say that composite stocks are the perfect remedy. Composite stocks have several limitations and disadvantages that work hand in hand and should be considered together.

Composite stocks are brittle. This is particularly important to the shooter, given the shock loadings that are placed on composite stocks during firing. If a rifle were to be bolted directly into a composite stock and fired, the shooter would quickly notice that the stock bolt tension would change. This is because the small areas of the stock supporting the recoil of the action are being hammered by the action under firing pressure, and this causes the matrix of fiber and resin to collapse. Accuracy will quickly degrade and the stock will be permanently damaged. To cure this problem, composite stocks are nearly always "pillar bedded," or contain an aluminum bedding platform,

*Composite stocks are available in any size, shape, and color.*

to create a hard, shock loading-resistant surface for the action to recoil against. (It is important to note, at this juncture, that although these systems are referred to as "bedding," they do not actually carry out the true function or provide the real benefits of action bedding. These will be discussed later. The aluminum parts of pillar bedding simply prevent the stock from being damaged during firing.)

Further to their brittle nature, composite stocks are also susceptible to abrasion and chipping in the same ways as wooden stocks. While this may not prove to be a concern in terms of accuracy *per se*, composite materials are subject to the phenomenon of "wicking," whereby a small nick is put into the stock and exposes some part of a fiber. This will allow moisture to "wick" into the fiber matrix. In yachting circles, this condition is known as "boat pox" and is considered to be the rust of composite materials. Too, though this is a highly noticeable condition, moisture can collect quite easily in the internal recesses of the

stock. In humid conditions, moisture may collect on the metal parts and then run into the recesses of the stock. Perhaps not a dire consideration, but certainly one to consider, when thinking about maintenance.

Putting these pluses and minuses into context, composite stocks offer significant advances and advantages over more traditional stocks. Though the scale of these advantages does exceed the requirements of most shooters, they are still a valuable addition to rifles in most cases.

I briefly mentioned laminated stocks before. It is important to recognize the position and role of these stocks, so let's have a closer look at them.

Laminated stocks are, technically, a composite stock of the early days. Being constructed from strips of wood glued together in different orientations, a stock of surprising rigidity and strength can result. Laminated stocks generally have the same advantages of other composite stocks, but they lack one particular disadvantage. As a rule of thumb,

laminated stocks don't require aluminum bedding pillars or a bedding block to protect the recoil areas of the stock. The impact resistance of the wood, acting as the laminate, is sufficient to resist the shock of being hammered by the barreled action. While laminated stocks do their job very well and offer the benefits of a composite stock, with, perhaps, some of the old world charm of a wooden finish, they do exist in a no man's land of application. Nevertheless, in terms of accuracy, a laminated stock would be an excellent upgrade, where a composite stock is out of reach financially.

## CHASSIS SYSTEM STOCKS

Chassis systems are the product of advances in metallurgy and, most notably, machining, particularly CNC machining. Chassis systems are, essentially, a rifle stock that has been very accurately milled, generally from a very strong grade of aluminum such as 7075, to create a one-piece bedding platform and

*Chassis systems tend to look fairly industrial, but they do offer adjustability and the tactical look so popular with today's modern riflemen.*

stock that is a perfect match to the barreled action. Once established, various coatings and accoutrements can be attached to achieve the desired form, functionality, or style the shooter has decided upon.

The one real advantage of true chassis systems is that they do not require bedding. As the barreled action is torqued into the stock and both parts maintain similar hardness, the barreled action is most unlikely to change its position under firing pressures. It is important to note, however, that this advantage is solely reliant on the correct torque pressures being used. If the torque pressure were to change, accuracy, or at least the point of aim, would suffer.

A second advantage of the chassis system is its near completely inert nature. Being a stable metal, it is not affected by environmental considerations such as moisture and temperature in the way wooden stocks are. Although metal does contract and expand with temperature, because both the chassis system and barreled action are metal, the differential in

expansion is limited; they will both expand and contract at similar rates. Looking more closely at the question of moisture, aluminum is protected naturally by a strong oxide layer that forms very quickly after being machined. This layer will prevent aluminum corrosion and, in conjunction with the other coatings used in the firearms industry, make the chassis system extremely reliable in this regard.

The disadvantages of a chassis system, aside from cost, are principally that of weight, and where a chassis system has had all but a skeleton of metal removed, cracking may become evident as the stock ages. Reparability of chassis systems is problematic. Once cracked, in most cases they cannot be adequately repaired. In the few instances when they can, such repairs require specialty equipment, so such fixes could certainly not be accomplished in the field.

An interesting adaptation of the chassis system is a rail gun stock. This is generally only used for competition and is almost always custom made. The rail gun

*Injection-molded stocks offer a price advantage over other stocks, but this generally comes with an accuracy disadvantage.*

stock is a hugely oversized stock, one not intended to be fired from the shoulder, but rather off the bench. These stocks are deliberately made to be heavy, to create better stability.

When considering a chassis system, it would serve the shooter's purpose best to only choose one when that particular system offers the shooter a specific advantage or enhances a critical component of the shooter's goals. Otherwise, the shooter is better served with a wooden, laminated, or composite stock, noting that, with regards to accuracy, all stocks are as accurate as each other, providing they are correctly bedded and correctly fulfilling their intended role.

## INJECTION-MOLDED STOCKS

Injection-molded stocks are the product of commercialization and cost cutting on the part of the large firearms manufacturers. Injection-molded stocks are made from a high-density thermoplastic that's squirted under high pressure and temperature into a steel mould. What comes out of the mould is the stock. These stocks have been available for about 50 years now, and although their usage is quite widespread, they do form the bottom end of performance rifle stocks. The prime advantage of the injection-molded stock is cost. These stocks are extremely cheap to produce, and this allows firearms manufacturers to offer firearms at more reasonable prices. There are also several aftermarket stock manufacturers that produce injection-molded stocks of various types, each sporting "special features" that makes one manufacturer's stock better than its competitors'.

In reality, all injection-molded stocks need to be grouped together, as their disadvantages are the same across the board. While the advantage of injection-molded stocks (other than cost) is their light weight, this advantage also forms their principal disadvantage, that being a lack of rigidity. Injection-molded stocks flex under firing pressure; even the fore-ends will flex when the shooter is in the prone position and using a bipod or other rest. It is noted by their makers that many injection-molded stocks have special skeletons or design features intended to prevent flexing, but my experiences with several commercial and aftermarket stocks counter that notion.

The secondary disadvantage of injection-molded stocks is their lack of strength. Noting that the ability to flex offsets the chance of cracking, these stocks do tend to fail in the recoil areas where small injection-molded surfaces are repeatedly hammered under recoil. Over time, this will permanently damage the stock and significantly affect accuracy.

This is not to say that injection-molded stocks have no place in the shooter's sport. Certain firearms, notably light .22 LRs, work just fine in injection-molded stocks, particularly as the stocks are quite lightweight, thereby providing a small, trim, and convenient firearm. Too, injection-molded stocks can have their disadvantages rectified to allow them to perform admirably in heavier calibers. With action glass bedding and stiffening of the fore-end, such a stock's opportunity to flex, both under firing pressures and in various firing positions, can be reduced. Such remedies, as is often the case, are easier said than done. For instance, the thermoplastic used in the construction of the stock is a natural release agent that aids in separating the stock from the mould. In the same vein, the bedding is as easily separated from the stock, something that will become evident after a short period. In order to bed and stiffen an injection-molded stock, many holes must be drilled at varying depths and angles in the areas bedded or stiffened prior to that work being carried out, in order to anchor the bedding into the stock. Ultimately, this process will help, but its longevity is questionable.

## BEDDING

Bedding is the system by which the barreled action interfaces with the stock. There are four types of bedding: the non-bedded system, skim-bedded system, pillar-bedded system, and the bedding block system. The purpose of bedding is to ensure that there is no independent movement between the barreled action and the stock during firing (or at any other time). This gives the shooter consistency in point of aim, which is critical to accuracy. Failure to bed an action properly will result in a wandering point of impact and the "stringing" of groups; instead of a circular group, the rifle will produce an oval-shaped group or an actual string of shots, as well as the frustrating situation of fliers, wherein a circular group will be achieved except for one shot that will habitually impact somewhere else.

Correct non-bedded bedding involves ensuring the action platform of the stock is level to the action. This style of bedding is common in surplus military rifles and older commercial rifles.

Skim bedding can be performed on just about any barreled action/stock combination and involves filling the action recess in the stock with a suitable epoxy system, thereby closing those voids and making a tight fitting epoxy "shoe" into which the action can be torqued. This bridges the front and rear action screws and prevents the barreled action from moving by filling in any space it could move into.

Pillar bedding involves installation of aluminum columns in the action screw holes of the stock. This allows the action to be tightened down onto the pillars as well as the action platform, and higher torque levels can be achieved without crushing the stock.

The bedding block method is the highest evolution of bedding and involves a custom-made aluminum shoe fitted into the stock. This aluminum shoe allows the action to be torqued into the stock, but also bridges the front and rear action screw holes, leading to greater rigidity. Generally the bedding block forms the backbone of the stock and, when properly utilized, has the effect of making the barreled action and the stock a single, unitary structure.

All these bedding systems have advantages and disadvantages, but, in their basic form, the improved bedding systems only provide longevity and reliability. How do you tell an improved bedding system from a not so improved one? The shooter will notice that the action screws in a properly bedded rifle will tighten very suddenly. This will indicated a lack of any sponginess in the bedding, and bedding that also allows an even pulling down of the action. A poor

bedding system will tighten over several turns of the action screws; ultimately, it will never get really tight. On a final note, it is important to recognize that any bedding system working correctly will be just as accurate as any other. Let's look more closely at the four types.

## NON-BEDDED BEDDING

The non-bedded system, something of a misnomer, allows for a direct connection between the barreled action and the stock material. In most cases, it is found on older commercial rifles and surplus rifles that were intended to be bedded in this way (as opposed to many commercial rifles these days that simply have no bedding). Traditionally housed in wooden stocks, these rifles would have their barreled actions professionally fitted to the stock by a method of test fitting and relieving various sections of the action platform. Ultimately, the barreled action would sit on a level and even platform in the stock, and then would be torque down to about 45 inch-pounds (in-lbs), or 3.75 foot-pounds (ft-lbs; 12 in-lbs per single ft-lb), ensuring that only the correct parts of the barreled action contacted the correct parts of the stock.

This would provide bedding suitable for most applications and, when freshly bedded, this system can work very well. Yes, it would be subject to environmental conditions and would require periodic maintenance in order to ensure that the bedding system was still performing adequately. That said, with the advances of epoxy glues and bedding materials, there are far easier ways to go about bedding a rifle.

## SKIM BEDDING

Skim bedding is a process of creating an epoxy "shoe" for the action to fit into. This bedding system provides rigidity and support for the barreled action by locking it into a pre-determined position, ensuring that only the correct parts of the barreled action contact the correct parts of the stock. This precludes any movement, for there is simply nowhere for the barreled action to move. This process can be performed on any stock, with or without an existing

*Skim bedding provides an excellent interface between the stock and the action, though it is not as durabe as other bedding methods.*

bedding system, and it is very cheap and easy to do. An additional advantage of skim bedding is that it offers bridging of the front and rear action screws.

There are a variety of epoxy systems that can be used for this purpose, and aside from the resin and hardener, there are a number of filling agents available. As a rule, any epoxy can be used, provided it has been stored properly and is not out of date (epoxies generally have a shelf life of 12 months). The filling agents available range from chalk, which is good for making a mirror surface; cotton flock, which adds to strength; or powdered aluminum or steel, which have enhanced hardness. Powdered stainless steel is also available.

There are many premixed kits available from both the firearms industry and the marine industry. Acraglass kits provide an excellent solution for a bedding epoxy compound, and Marine Tex also offers kits that perform very well. It should be noted that epoxy resins and hardeners generally experience a shrink rate of about two percent as they cure. Although this is not critical to the success of the bedding *per se*, it should be noted that, while the bedding is curing, only finger-tight pressure should be used on the action screws to prevent a situation where the cured bedding contracts beyond the tightening range of the action screws. That, of course, would result in a loose bedding.

The success of skim bedding is heavily reliant on it being performed properly. Putting aside the success of the bedding in terms of accuracy gained, if the bedding is not applied properly, then it will crack and fall apart very quickly; the epoxy shoe will be thin in many places, as it is designed to be sandwiched between the stock and the barreled action, as opposed to being a self-supporting structure. When it is performed properly, and in conjunction with a composite or laminated stock, this type of bedding will provide an excellent platform for accuracy that can and will last for a lifetime.

## PILLAR BEDDED

Pillar bedding is something of a hybrid of the bedding block and skim bedding. Pillar bedding can be performed on all stocks, with the exception of those that contain a bedding block.

Having relieved the stock to ensure that only the correct parts of the barreled action contact the correct parts of the stock, the action screw holes in the stock are reamed out and aluminum pillars, or columns, are installed in the resulting holes. These provide a metal tube with which to run through the action screw and, when tightened, allow the action to torque down against them.

Many gunsmiths believe that this is the end of the process. It's not. Stocks must be skim bedded in addition to the installation of pillars, in order to realize the full potential of the bedding system. Remembering that the pillars provide a solid surface for the action to torque down onto, the skim bedding then provides the shoe that prevents the action from moving.

This style of bedding system is best suited to wooden or laminated stocks, to prevent crush damage to the stock. Such bedding also prevents imprecise torque pressures that might otherwise be caused by sponginess of the wood. This bedding system also has application in composite stocks, protecting the brittle surfaces inside the action recess. Pillars are commonly seen in injection-molded stocks, but this cannot be seen as a bedding system. Pillars are present in these stocks, because any real torque pressure could never be otherwise achieved when pulling the action down onto the thermoplastic surfaces inside the stock.

As a last note, the pillars themselves should never touch the action screws. If this occurs, it can form a "secondary recoil lug," which will cause the action

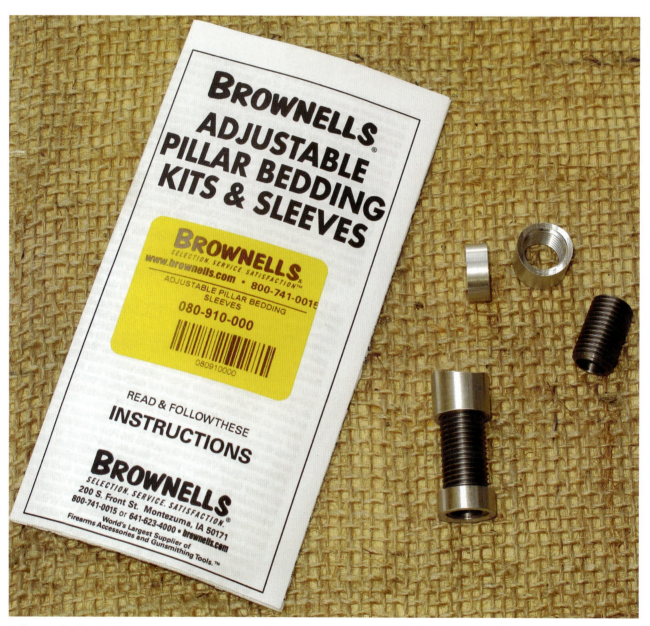

*Pillars and pillar bedding offer the shooter an upgrade opportunity for the non-bedded or skim bedded systems. Pillars offer enhanced crush resistance and permit greater tension on the action screws.*

to flex during firing. Not only will this destroy the bedding system quickly, it will ruin accuracy.

## BEDDING BLOCK

The bedding block is the most advanced and final system of bedding. The bedding block system uses a custom machined block of aluminum fitted into the stock, normally as part of the stock's initial manufacture, where it comprises a structural element within the stock. The bedding block itself is machined as a close-fitting shoe for the action. It should be stressed that the shoe is not a perfect fit and so requires skim bedding to realize the benefits of the bedding block system. Failure to skim bed the bedding block will result in movement of the action during firing. Additionally, the block will slowly be abraded by the harder action, resulting in a looser fit, a problem easily identified as white or grey smudges on the underside of the action. This telltale sign also shows the miniscule contact areas between the bedding block and the barreled action before skim bedding and highlights why the bedding block requires the skim bedding. Correct torque pressures need to be applied to the action screws, and the screws themselves must not contact the bedding block or any other part of the stock whatsoever. If this is allowed to occur, both the bedding system and the accuracy will suffer.

The benefits of the bedding block system relate primarily to the stability of the bedding itself. The bedding block provides a crush-resistant surface with which to torque the barreled action into, thus sandwiching the skim bedding material.

The bedding block system is not affected by environmental effects or temperature, because, similar to the chassis system rifle stock, both the barreled action and bedding block expand and contract at similar rates. The bedding block also bridges the front and rear action screw holes in the stock, and because the bedding block generally exists as a structural element of the stock, it leads to greater strength, due to the unitary structure formed between the barreled action, bedding block, and stock.

*The bedding block is the pinnacle of bedding systems, but it still requires skim bedding to create the perfect fit between the action and the stock.*

There are no real disadvantages of the bedding block system, except perhaps cost. An upside to this is that there are now several manufacturers that specialize in making bedding blocks and putting a stock around them.

An alternative form of the bedding block system is the "V" block system. In a "V" block, instead of locking the action into the stock, the thick barrel shank is locked into the stock and the rest of the barrel and the action are free-floated.

Note that a chassis system stock normally comprises a bedding block in itself. The jury is still out on whether chassis systems need to be skim bedded, but given that the principles are the same for bedding blocks no matter the stock, it would be logical to go ahead and skim bed chassis system stocks, as well.

## ACTION SCREW TENSION

"Action screw tension" refers to the amount of torque that should be used when tightening the action screws that fasten the barreled action into the stock. This is a far more complicated task than many gunsmiths give credit. Not only does the correct amount of torque need to be applied, it must also be

*Correct tension tightens groups!*

applied to the screws in the correct order. Further, in action types that have three screws, special steps need to be taken to ensure that the action is torqued down in a manner to prevent flexing of the action or damaging of the bedding.

The correct (or at least rule of thumb) torque pressures to be used are 45 in-lbs for a wooden or laminated stock and 65 in-lbs for a composite stock or chassis system stock. Many gunsmiths would have the shooter believe that the amount of torque can be felt, and that the screws should be torqued to what "feels right." This is simply not good enough, when the shooter is seeking to achieve the maximum level of accuracy their rifle can provide.

To ensure that the correct torque pressures are applied, a torque wrench must be used and must have a scale in inch-pounds, as opposed to the conventional foot-pounds. There are several low-cost torque wrenches available; one in particular manufactured by Wheeler Engineering fits neatly into a shooter's range toolkit and is a worthwhile addition to any shooter's backpack, whether at the range or in the field.

As an example, looking first at the conventional two-screw system of the Remington 700, the action needs to be placed in the stock, ensuring that it is sitting flat on the bedding. Sometimes that can be difficult to achieve, if the bedding system is very tight. Once the action is properly flat on the bed, the front screw is wound into the action no more than finger tight. The same process is next carried out on the rear action screw. At this point, a torque wrench is set for either 45 or 65 in-lbs, depending on the type of stock used. Once set, it is applied to the front action screw and turned to achieve this torque pressure, followed by the same procedure on the rear action screw.

On a properly bedded rifle, the shooter will discover that the screw will tighten very suddenly. This is normal and indicative that there is little sponginess in the bedding and that the action is being pulled onto the bedding evenly. Many gunsmiths at this point would advocate loosening the rear action screw by a

quarter or an eighth of a turn. The philosophy behind this is that, in order to compensate for poor bedding or a lack of bedding, you'll force the firing loads to be taken on the front of the action, as the rear of the action is loose. In that manner, you'd prevent any flexing of the action (due to the poor bedding), while the rifle was being fired.

Looking at two-screw actions with an unconventional recoil lug, such as some rifles from Ruger, Sako, and Tikka, the same process is adopted, except the action screws are tightened partially and alternately, starting with the front action screw. This partial tightening of front then rear then front then rear, allows for the action to be pulled down and rearwards (noting that the front action screw is on a 45-degree angle), seating the action properly into the bedding. If not done in this manner, the action can get caught up on the recoil lug recess in the stock and begin cutting into the bedding.

Looking at the more complicated case of three-screw actions, such as found on the Winchester Model 70, the role of the third screw is to fix the front of trigger guard to the action. If all three screws are torqued down, the action will flex across its middle, which will enable the action to move under firing pressures. The correct process for tightening a three-screw action is to follow the process for that of a two-screw action, tightening the third screw last, then backing it out until there is little or no torque pressure applied to the screw. Some gunsmiths will even "blind" this screw, using a cir-clip or an "e" clip to secure the screw without allowing it to screw into the action.

Having tightened the torque screws correctly, checking the torque pressures should be built into the regular maintenance program for the shooter's rifle. It should also be noted that, after being bedded, the action screws can be expected to loosen after the first 20 to 50 rounds, requiring re-torqueing. If the action screws are kept correctly tightened, the shooter can expect not only good accuracy from the bedding system and stock chosen, but also good reliability and consistency.

## BUTTPADS AND RECOIL PADS

Buttpads/recoil pads are available with as much variation, in terms of size, material, and shape, as are stocks. Many believe that the prime purpose of butpads and recoil pads is to moderate the felt recoil of the rifle. While this is a benefit, their actual purpose is to augment the length of the buttstock. Ensuring the correct buttstock length for the shooter is a determining factor in augmenting felt recoil and a subject that will be discussed later.

Looking at buttpads and recoil pads in isolation, commercial producers have taken most of the guesswork out of this for the shooter by providing buttpads for their rifles that fit 95 percent of the population. In addition, they are generally manufactured from a medium-density rubber, which does provide a cushioning effect to the recoil during firing.

Many older shooters will remember when rifles were fitted with Bakelite, plastic, steel, and aluminum buttplates. While those pads did/do not provide a cushioning effect, they did/do provide a very rigid platform for the shoulder to brace against. They also help the shooter feel their rifles placed into the shoulder to the same position every time, creating consistency and accuracy. Interestingly, those same old timers probably remember that their rifles of yesterday so equipped with those older-style buttpads didn't kick particularly hard. That would have been due to a better application of correct stock length reducing felt recoil, as opposed to a large, cushioning buttpad taking up the slack.

When considering a buttpad for an accurate rifle, the shooter needs to weigh the potential for reducing felt recoil against a potential accuracy loss. The smaller and harder the buttpad the better, when it comes to accuracy, but that has to be weighed against a sharply kicking rifle, which will eventually have an adverse effect on the shooter and promote a tendency to flinch.

Adjacent to this discussion of buttpads is the adjustable style, which can be adjusted for length, height, and angle. This does give the shooter the ability to fine-tune their rifle's buttstock and also their shooting position. That's all fine and well, but really, the shooter needs to use an item such as this after all the other parameters

*From right to left, steel, standard rubber, and recoil reducing. Buttpads have come a long way in 100 years.*

*The shooter will struggle to achieve the correct eye relief and sight picture, with a stock that is too short or too long.*

are set. Using an incorrect angle on an adjustable butt pad early on can and will influence the position of the scope to the shooter's eye and the position of the shooter's finger on the trigger.

## BUTTSTOCK LENGTH

The length of a rifle's buttstock in relation to the shooter is critical for setting eye relief between the shooter's eye and the rifle's scope, and also setting the shooter's trigger finger on the trigger. Again, manufactures of both commercial rifles and custom stocks have taken the guesswork out of this by producing stocks that fit the vast majority of the population. That said, a stockmaker will measure the shooter before producing a custom stock, confirming or adjusting the measurements as need be.

Although most stocks will fit most shooters, there are fine-tuning steps a shooter can take to get the length set at an optimum measurement for them (and I suggest finding a competent gunsmith to help determine the proper length, or length of pull, as it's usually called). In the case of a buttstock that is too short, all the shooter need do is remove the butt pad and trace it onto a piece of stable, flat material such

*The application of free-floating or fore-end bedding for barrels depends on the barrel, the stock, and the shooter's purpose.*

as aluminum or high-density plastic of the thickness required to move the rifle forward so that the trigger crosses the trigger finger in the right place. Once done, cut out the traced part and fit it between the butt and the buttpad (exactly like the stock spacers so often provided by many of today's manufacturers). If a buttstock is too long, it is best to take it to a stockmaker or gunsmith and have the butt shortened, generally by removing material from underneath the butt pad; this can be complicated, if the end of the butt is curved. Once the correct butt length has been achieved, the shooter will be surprised at how well the adjusted stock shoulders, right along with correct eye relief and improved comfort.

## BARREL FLOATING

The process of floating a barrel is normally carried out when a barreled action is bedded into a stock. Stock material is removed from within the barrel channel, using barrel channel rasps or similar tools, until at least 0.010-inch clearance is obtained. This ensures that, in the first instance, reasonable pressure on the stock will not be transferred to the barrel and, in the second instance, during firing, the barrel is not going to contact the stock through the barrel "whipping."

What barrel floating does is allow the barrel to be unaffected by environmental factors that may impact the stock. Further, it allows the barrel to flex and resonate freely during firing; due to the metallurgical structure of the steel of the barrel, if it is free to flex and resonate naturally, it will flex and resonate the same way each time. Neither of these factors will improve the accuracy of the barrel, but they will improve consistency, and that goes a long way to improving the former.

The floating of a rifle's barrel within the barrel channel, or ensuring that the barrel does not contact the fore-end of the stock, is a contentious issue amongst shooters. Rightfully so, as there are exceptions to the concept of improved consistency. Looking at the case of lightweight barrels, there is a lower ratio of the surface area of the barrel to the amount of metal used in the construction of the barrel, when compared to a heavyweight barrel. When a barrel is made, both the internal and external surfaces are machined, and this can set up uneven stress points along the barrel's length. These stress points have the capacity to alter the way in which the barrel flexes and resonates during firing. While a heavyweight barrel may have the strength and stiffness to resist these uneven stress points, a lighter barrel will be affected and its flexing or resonating altered.

A cost-effective way of alleviating this condition in a lightweight barrel is to provide the barrel with support by the stock at the very front of its fore-end. While the rest of the barrel remains floated, the forward supporting section of stock provides an upward force on the barrel of about seven to 10 pounds. This reduces the barrel flexing and resonating unevenly and introduces greater consistency to the system. There is one caveat to performing this kind of stock work: It should be noted that applying pressure to the barrel can limit the potential of the barrel, so the process should only be carried out on a case by case basis. This method is common with most sporting rifles.

# CHAPTER FOUR

# Actions and Bolts

The specific role of the action, as part of a rifle, is to bridge the bolt and barrel and ensure that the bolt and firing pin mechanism are correctly aligned to the axis of the barrel. Generally speaking, actions also have the secondary functions of supporting the trigger mechanism, supporting the magazine (if fitted), and providing a mounting interface for the stock.

There is a wide range of commercial and custom manufactured actions available on the market today that offer a plethora of features, such as built-in recoil lugs, detachable magazine capability, and integral scope rails. Most of these features are not designed to improve accuracy, so much as set different manufacturers apart from one another and supply solutions to particular shooter needs. In other words, most features of modern actions are commercially driven, not accuracy driven, and most of the decision making involved in choosing an action can be done on the basis of personal preference.

Like many parts of a firearm, a correctly manufactured action that supports the bolt on the same axis as the barrel will do its job just as well as any

other action manufactured to the same standard. It is equally important to note, again, that a rifle will only ever function as well as its least accurate component.

When looking at an action's features, the shooter should recognize that simplicity and adaptability are attributes of an action that lacks extra features, and this can be of great benefit. Take, as an example, the Remington 700. Essentially a tube action and without a fixed recoil lug, it's easy to see that this rifle has provided the wider manufacturing community with an opportunity to produce accessories and aftermarket parts on a scale not seen before. This has allowed the shooter to customize this action almost limitlessly.

Beyond features and accessories, the shooter must consider the accuracy of an action, or the standard to which it is manufactured. In days gone by, to achieve maximum accuracy, the shooter would choose, perhaps, a secondhand action, then take it to a gunsmith for blueprinting and truing. These processes would ensure that the action's critical dimensions were exactly what they were supposed to be and that the action was true, with all critical surfaces on the

*Various rifle actions from the past century. Style and features may vary, but the purposes and roles remain the same.*

same axis. Good examples of this are the Mauser 98s and other commercial actions used extensively for competition during the 1960s and 1970s. These actions were mass-produced on hand-operated tooling and, therefore, could benefit from fine tuning. With the passing of time and the improvements in technology over the last 20 years, manufacturers are now able to produce actions to a higher standard than what was previously commercially possible. The result is that today's off-the-shelf actions are, essentially, of the same standard as competition actions of yesteryear. That said, there is still a market for absolute top-end actions of unparalleled accuracy,

where dimensions are generally measured by laser reflections, and this market is serviced by custom action makers.

Custom action makers generally provide an action and bolt combination that are trued and aligned to within 0.0001-inch or better. These actions are made from top-quality steel, aluminum, or titanium and are expertly hardened and then stress relieved. Actions such as these are only really suitable for the one in a thousand shooter who can make use of this level of precision—so, again, the choice of action, like all parts, should be driven by the needs of the shooter and the purpose for the rifle the shooter has in mind.

## COMMERCIAL ACTIONS

Most commercial actions made today are of very good quality. In fact, it is difficult in this day and age to find a rifle that, due to poor manufacturing, will shoot poorly. Nearly all manufacturers use CNC-based tooling that is self-calibrating and will automatically adjust for tool and machine wear. Likewise, base steels (and other metals) are produced to such fine standards that there is little difference in materials between batches; highly predictable qualities exist across types.

Despite this uniformity, there are still great differences in action styles. As with other components, most of these differences are driven by commercial reasons and have little to do with the accuracy of the end product. Still, there are some differences worth noting.

First is the platform of the action, or its general shape and construction of the action. Take, for instance, the round-bodied action of the Remington 700. This action has no sharp corners (putting aside the action ports and cuts that all actions have), which permits natural and even harmonic vibration under firing pressures. The Remington is a two-screw action, meaning there is a main or front action screw to hold the front of the action in and against the recoil abutment in the stock, and a rear screw to prevent any torsion in the recoil lug via support of the action at its rearmost point. The action is continually supported from the front to the rear, preventing any flexing of the action when tightening the action screws. (It must be noted that there is a susceptibility for the Remington 700 action to flex, under the right conditions.)

Conversely, looking at the Winchester Model 70 and Ruger M77 actions, these actions are cut from blocks of steel and have many angles, platforms, and steps built into them. These actions are intended to be extremely stiff and, as such, have a very short recoil lug that exposes the recoil abutment in the stock to higher loadings. These actions have three screws, and improper tightening of the screws has a marked effect on accuracy. The Winchester Model 70 action also has a protrusion about the rear action screw; under the right conditions, it will act as a recoil lug and interfere with the recoil harmonics of the rifle, producing a detrimental effect on accuracy.

These differences between actions may seem like a comparison of pros and cons, but it is important to note that, when correctly set up, these actions will offer comparable accuracy potential. That said, different actions require different set-ups, and some actions are easier to set up than others!

When considering having an action trued by a gunsmith, the critical surfaces are the face of the receiver where it contacts the barrel shoulder, the threads that the barrel tennon screws into, and the face of the locking lug abutments. If these surfaces are true to the axis of the bore, whether the surfaces are made perfectly perpendicular to or in line with, then the action will be potentially capable of a high degree of accuracy.

It's worth repeating that, when considering commercial actions, the shooter must consider their needs. For instance, if a shooter is building a dangerous-game rifle, then controlled feed to limit the chances for feeding failures is probably important. If the shooter is participating in a timed event, perhaps a detachable magazine is important. A shooter's decision must be guided by their needs, not by what the guy has in the lane next to you!

## CUSTOM ACTIONS

Custom action manufacturers offer top shooters, whether they be long-range hunters or competition shooters, access to precision crafted actions that have been blueprinted and trued and, in most cases, have had additional work done or incorporate extra features to enhance their accuracy potential. Like commercial actions, these custom actions are available with a plethora of features and options. Given the almost limitless array of these features and options, it is difficult to compare the different custom actions and, assuming they are all built to the same standard, there should be little difference, at least in theory, in terms of the accuracy potential that can be achieved.

*Custom action makers focus on precision manufacturing and precision marketing of features. The shooter's decisions here will rely mostly on the features they require.*

When choosing a custom action, the shooter may be better guided by considering the accessories and options available for each, along with what stocks are available for the action. By choosing a custom action, the shooter will eliminate a large number of variables from the accuracy equation, but, in order to realize the full potential of such an action over that of an off-the-shelf commercial action, the shooter must ensure that *all* other parts are manufactured and assembled to the same standard, including the ammunition which, in almost every case, will need to be expertly handloaded.

## ACTION CONDITION

When assessing the condition of an action with a view to perhaps rebuilding it or using it in a hunting or competition rifle setup, very little can be determined when the action is fitted with a barrel. Ideally the action should be disassembled and degreased, allowing the shooter to inspect the critical areas.

When inspecting a disassembled action, the shooter should first look at all the tappings and threads to ensure that none are crossed or damaged. The shooter should then turn their attention to the locking lug abutments inside the action, looking, in particular, for galling on the abutments, or where metal has been pulled away from the abutments, which would indicate that the bolt has been forced closed or the firearm has been actioned with insufficient headspace. Evidence of hammering of the abutments will show as bright, dimpled areas on the face of the abutments and is indicative of overloads or excess headspace. Both problems can be corrected by removing metal from the abutments in a lathe as a refacing of the abutments or as part of a truing process. Keep in mind that, while they can be remedied, these problems can give an insight as to whether the action has had a hard life.

Next, the shooter must inspect the abutments for cracks. This is most easily done with a crack-finding spray, which is a very light solvent and grit mixture that naturally migrates towards cracks and will be highlighted in a black/grey color.

Finally, the shooter can inspect the trueness of the actions by using a depth micrometer to measure the distance from the face of the action to the face of the locking lug abutments at different points around the radius of the action face.

With these inspections complete, the shooter can then look for evidence of any modifications to the action. These may include simple drillings and tappings for various accessories, which cause no problems other than those of an aesthetic nature. Alternately, the action may have already been trued or worked on by a gunsmith, and you'll note that parts such as the locking lug abutments can be refaced only so many times before the abutments are weakened.

Having completed these inspections, the shooter should look all over the action for signs of wear, damage, and repairs, remembering that, if the shooter is at all unsure as to the safety of an action, they must consult with a competent gunsmith.

## BOLTS

Bolts perform a variety of tasks on a firearm. Their primary role is to lock the breech end of the chamber so that the face of the bolt is perpendicular to the axis of the bore and has the correct headspace requirements of the chamber. Secondarily, the bolt must strip rounds of ammunition from the magazine (if fitted) or the loading floor plate, carry the round of ammunition into the chamber, provide a firing mechanism from the trigger mechanism to the primer of the ammunition round, provide a mechanism for extracting an expended cartridge from the chamber, provide a mechanism (in most cases) for ejecting the expended cartridge from the firearm and, finally, provide a handle for the shooter to manipulate the bolt and make all of these processes possible. Dissected like this, it is quite easy to see that bolts are rather complicated pieces of machinery.

Bolts must be very precise pieces of machinery in order to lock the breech end of the chamber perfectly in line with the axis of the bore. It should be noted that, during manufacture of commercial rifles, bolts are matched to actions. Likewise, custom actions are generally provided with a matched bolt. Actions that have a non-matching bolt at least need to be headspaced to ensure the action can be operated safely (it is highly likely there will be a misalignment between an unmatched bolt and an action, leading to a detrimental effect on accuracy).

Given the complexity of bolts and the large number of working parts contained within them, there is a plethora of aftermarket, performance manufactured parts available, such as extended or shaped bolt handles to give the shooter more leverage when actioning, spring kits to increase the speed of the firing pin and shorten lock time (the period of time it takes for the firing pin to ignite the primer after the trigger has been pulled), and different extractors to prevent the possibility of failures. This allows the shooter to customize both off-the-shelf and custom bolts to their specific needs. Even oversize bolt bodies are available, allowing the shooter to match the dimensions of the bolt to the action and create a perfect fit.

## COMMERCIAL BOLTS

Commercial bolts are nearly always matched to actions and serialized so that they cannot be easily mixed up. Commercial bolts are made to the same standard as their parent action, though, as a rule, bolts are made and then fitted to actions, as opposed to being made *for* a particular action.

When considering the truing of a bolt to an action, there are several critical surfaces that must be addressed. First is the rear or load-bearing surface of the locking lugs, which must be perpendicular to the axis of the bore. If they are not, then the lugs will experience different loads under firing pressures, and this will interfere with accuracy.

*Bolts can vary as much as actions.*

Second, the face of the bolt must be perpendicular to the bore. This will allow the cartridge to seat into the bolt face evenly and ensure that the cartridge is delivered to the chamber in a perfectly straight presentation.

Third, the firing pin hole must be within specification or tighter, otherwise there will be an opportunity for the metal of the primer cup to be forced into the firing pin hole under firing pressures (known as "cratering" of the primer).

Finally, the load-bearing face of the locking lugs need to be lapped onto their mating surfaces within the action, on the locking lug abutments. Lapping of the lugs is a process in which an abrasive paste is used to wear down the opposing surfaces against each other. It ensures that there is close to 100-percent

surface contact between the lugs and the abutments and that the contact is even between the lugs. Too, operation of the action will be made much smoother by this process, as the polished surfaces will glide on one another far more easily.

There are many components of a commercial bolt that can be upgraded with aftermarket parts. Many shooters choose to upgrade the firing pin mechanism—striker, firing pin and firing pin spring—with lightweight items and a heavier spring. This allows the shooter to reduce the lock time. Other shooters like to install a heavier extractor spring, to prevent the extractor riding up and over the rim of a case and causing a failure to extract. Another common bolt modification involves fitting of an extended or shaped bolt handle. This allows the shooter to exert greater

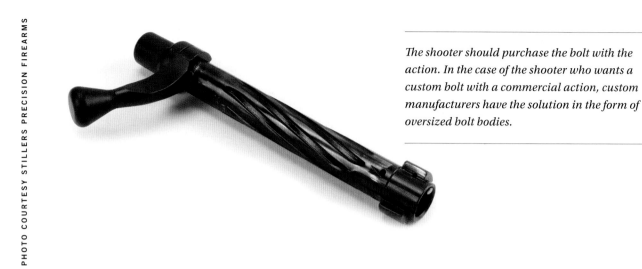

*The shooter should purchase the bolt with the action. In the case of the shooter who wants a custom bolt with a commercial action, custom manufacturers have the solution in the form of oversized bolt bodies.*

torque on the bolt and can make actioning of the rifle easier. This is of particular interest when the shooter is in the prone or prone-supported shooting positions, as it is difficult to action any rifle in this position without momentarily exiting the position and then assuming it again. In most cases, an extended bolt handle will allow the shooter to maintain these shooting positions while actioning the rifle, and this can lead to greater consistency and, therefore, accuracy.

## CUSTOM BOLTS

Custom bolts are generally matched to an action and marketed as a set, though there are manufacturers who supply custom bolts that can be fitted to an existing action. These bolts are made to incredibly high standards and incorporate many features and aftermarket parts, which make them an attractive one-stop shop upgrade for an existing action. Custom bolts, unfortunately, cannot be installed in an action and expected to work at their greatest potential, if at all.

Custom bolts are generally made slightly oversized, so that they must be fitted to the action for the internal dimensions of the action, and then the barreled action needs to be headspaced to the bolt. The winning features of a custom bolt tend to be that they provide a blueprinted and trued bolt coupled with many aftermarket accessories such as an extended bolt handle or an enhanced firing pin system. Many custom bolts are made from exotic materials and include fluting, both straight and spiral, to decrease weight and increase

stiffness. Ideally, the shooter should purchase a bolt and action package produced and matched by the same manufacturer.

## BOLT CONDITION

Assessing the condition of a bolt is relatively straightforward. First, the shooter must look at the rear face of the locking lugs (as with the bolt and action), identifying any signs of galling or hammering. Further, the shooter may look for wear patterns that indicate uneven locking lug contact with the locking lug abutments; this may be a sign of diminished accuracy potential, due to the bolt in the closed position being off axis to the bore.

Having conducted these checks, the shooter can then utilize a crack-finding spray to ensure that there are no signs of cracking on or around the lugs. Next, look at the bolt face for signs of uneven wear and extensive usage. Both will show as wear through the original finish, or a primer ring around the firing pin hole in the bolt face. A primer ring occurs when small amounts of primer gas or sealant escape from around the sides of the primer cup and stain the bolt face. If there are signs of pitting on the bolt face, this is a sure indicator that the bolt has been used with corrosive ammunition and then not appropriately cleaned. Use of corrosive ammunition can also manifest, in some cases, as pitting on the locking lugs.

The next important point is to look at the diameter of the firing pin hole. An oversized hole will allow the primer cup to expand, under high pressure, into this void. Finally, the shooter can look over the bolt body for wear patterns from the bolt being rotated and pushed back and forth within the action.

Having examined the bolt body, the shooter can then turn their attention to the firing pin mechanism. This is best achieved by disassembling the bolt. Once disassembled, the main spring can be inspected and its spring compression tested to ensure it delivers the correct force to the firing pin and striker. Examination of the parts of the bolt that engage with the trigger mechanism for wear and damage can then proceed, noting that the surfaces should be bright, sharp, and smooth. An examination of the extractor and ejector, as well as their springs, can be done with the bolt disassembled, and then the entire bolt group can be cleaned, if necessary.

Having reassembled the bolt, the final check is for firing pin protrusion through the bolt face.

This inspection must be done with the bolt in the un-cocked position. A firing pin that protrudes too far may pierce the primer, causing a blow back of gas and particles towards the shooter. Likewise, a firing pin that is too short, may not transmit enough force to the primer to fire the cartridge.

Fortunately, any problems associated with the working parts of a bolt can be corrected. Springs and small parts can be replaced. New firing pins and strikers can be obtained. Even an oversized firing pin hole can be corrected with the installation and fitting of an oversized firing pin.

Problems with the bolt body itself can be more troublesome. Galling, hammering, and pitting of the locking lugs and bolt face can only really be corrected by removing metal and refacing the surfaces. Of course, such work can be done only so many times. Also, removing metal from these surfaces will require the action to be headspaced again when mated to its barrel.

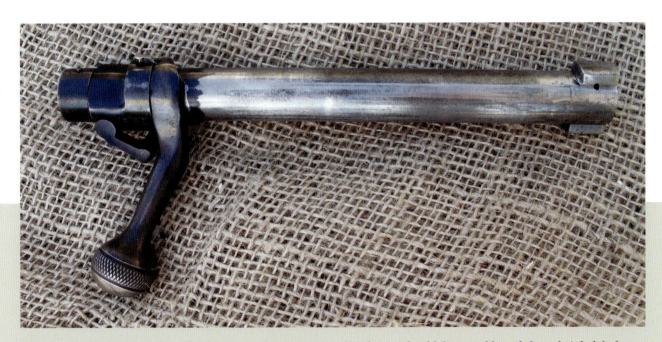

*Bolts are generally neglected in rifle cleaning and maintenance. The shooter should disassemble and clean their bolt before trying to assess its condition.*

# CHAPTER FIVE

# Triggers

Triggers and trigger mechanisms are considered by many shooters to be the province of black magic and chanting. While trigger mechanisms are complicated pieces of machinery that rely on highly polished surfaces, precision springs, and gearing through the use of levers, even the most rudimentary commercial trigger can provide very good performance, provided several basic rules are followed.

Ideally, a good trigger breaks at the same weight every time, without creep, with minimal take-up or movement of the trigger before force is applied to the working parts, and with minimal let-off or rearward movement of the trigger after the trigger has broken. If these three goals can be met, then the shooter has an accurate trigger.

Looking a little closer at trigger weights, in days gone by, bolt-action military rifles generally had two-stage triggers. The first trigger pressure, perhaps set at five pounds, allowed the shooter to "take up" the trigger in a relatively safe fashion, while the second pressure, set around eight pounds, actually allowed the trigger to break. Given that these triggers were set up for wartime conditions and to prevent accidental discharges while the safety was disengaged, it is hardly surprising to understand why they were set to break at such heavy pressures.

In more recent times, commercial hunting rifles are generally marketed with triggers breaking around the four-pound mark, while custom triggers, whether they be aftermarket manufactured or customized commercial triggers, generally hover around the 1.5- to 2.5-pound mark. The lightest are the top-end aftermarket triggers intended specifically for benchrest shooting and adjustable to run as low as eight *ounces*, which is dangerously light for all except highly controlled competition purposes.

Creep in the movement of a trigger's working parts is symptomatic of uneven, rough, or damaged working surfaces within the trigger mechanism. Specifically, creep is the changing force needed to move the working parts against each other to overcome different surface imperfections. The result is a trigger that moves then stops repeatedly until the trigger breaks.

This is highly detrimental to accuracy, particularly because the start/stop movement of the trigger transfers to the rifle as a whole, causing unwanted movement in the point of aim. Beyond this mechanical disturbance is the interruption it causes the shooter, generally making the shooter lose mental focus and drawing their attention away from keeping the crosshairs on the target.

Let-off in a trigger is generally missed by most shooters as an important aspect of trigger control and manipulation. A trigger that has inadequate let-off will have the shooter applying pressure to the firearm as a whole once the trigger has broken and the projectile is traveling up the bore. This can affect accuracy in severe cases. A trigger that has excess let-off will feel imprecise during the follow-through after a shot is taken.

Most commercial triggers these days are adjustable for all three critical points and generally come with a manual for adjustment. In most cases, it is relatively easy to tune out undesirable performance aspects of individual triggers. Of course, these triggers can also be tuned by a gunsmith, who will strip the trigger mechanism and polish the working surfaces of the trigger until a mirror shine is achieved, then set the adjusting screws so that a high-quality trigger mechanism results. Finally, shooters can upgrade to aftermarket trigger mechanisms, which are precision set at the factory in terms of combining parts of different weights and springs of differing compression energy to obtain a trigger mechanism that will reliably break at very low weights.

Although there are many types of commercial and aftermarket triggers, there are two important points that are common to all of them. First, new triggers always seem to come with the internal parts heavily bathed in a thick, dark grease. This lubricant is intended to work like break-in grease in a new vehicle motor. The polished surfaces are lubricated to allow them to bed in against each other and smooth the surfaces to a match finish between the parts over the first 50 or so trigger pulls. This grease is also used to prevent any corrosion on the polished surfaces while the firearm is in transit or at a dealership waiting to be sold.

The issue of the manufacturer's lubricant brings us to the second important point common to all triggers, and that is, unless specifically recommended by the manufacturer, you should *never* lubricate a trigger mechanism. A trigger mechanism that is lubricated will attract dust, grit, and grime, these things mixing

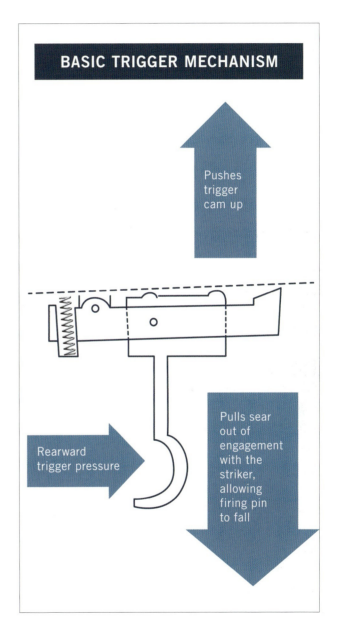

**BASIC TRIGGER MECHANISM**

Pushes trigger cam up

Rearward trigger pressure

Pulls sear out of engagement with the striker, allowing firing pin to fall

*In most trigger mechanisms, the trigger itself holds the spring-loaded sear in place. As the trigger is pulled, it releases the sear, which disengages from the striker. This allows the firing pin to fall.*

All trigger mechanisms are different. Older trigger mechanisms tend to be "open plan" in their design, while modern trigger mechanisms are mostly self-contained and sealed units.

together to form a very efficient abrasive paste that will accelerate the wear on the trigger's parts. Also, in cold climates, lubricants can seize up and freeze, locking the trigger and making the gun unsafe and unreliable.

If the shooter feels they need to lubricate their trigger mechanism, there are dry lubricants such as the Teflon sprays that go on wet and dry like a dust residue, and graphite powder that can be puffed into a trigger mechanism, with the excess blown out with compressed air.

## COMMERCIAL TRIGGERS

Commercial triggers are those that come pre-fitted to off-the-shelf commercial firearms. These triggers

*Nearly all commercial triggers these days are sealed units.*

mechanism must pass three tests (discussed later), before it can be deemed as safe.

There are other adjustments available on some commercial triggers, such as the sear engagement length screw, that should not be attempted by an untrained do-it-yourselfer. This screw, for example, controls internal parameters of the trigger and should only be adjusted by a gunsmith.

Having adjusted the position of any screws on the trigger, the shooter should lock the screws with either Loctite or another similar product (shooters have been known to use nail polish for this task), to secure the screws and prevent them from moving during firing.

## CUSTOM TRIGGERS

Custom triggers are for the very top end of shooting disciplines. Few shooters can truly take full advantage of the precision breaks and incredibly low pull weights achievable with these triggers. To achieve the full potential of such mechanisms, they generally need to be installed by a gunsmith, who will fit and adjust the trigger to the specifications of the shooter. These triggers seldom require further work, such as the polishing of surfaces or the fitting of different springs, to achieve the highest quality break possible. Essentially, these triggers offer the equivalent of a full-house trigger job on a commercial trigger, but have the advantage of also coming equipped with a wide range of adjustments.

## TRIGGER CONDITION

Assessing the condition of a trigger is a fairly straightforward process, yet few shooters do it properly. Most shooters will dry-fire the firearm for a qualitative assessment on how it "felt." Was the trigger creepy? Long to pull? Spongy? Terrifyingly light? This sort of assessment is fine and will give the shooter a good idea of the condition of the working surfaces within the trigger, but there's much more to look at.

To really assess a trigger requires the mechanism to be stripped and inspected. A more important (and generally skipped) inspection is the safety test. There are three parts to this.

are generally made to the same standards as the rest of the firearm and, with the advances in technology, the fit of parts is good enough to ensure that the trigger will perform reasonably well out of the box. That said, there is still much room for improvement.

As I said, these triggers tend to come jam-packed with grease. This should be removed with a degreasing spray and then cleaned with alcohol and allowed to dry. The shooter does have the option to re-lubricate the trigger if recommended by the manufacturer or opt for a dry or non-lubricating system. This simple cleaning process alone will normally improve the performance of a commercial trigger.

Looking a little closer, the shooter can also adjust the trigger for weight, take-up, and let-off. Triggers out of the factories these days seem to have been set by lawyers, not gunsmiths. They tend to be set at fairly heavy weights that, for most shooters, would begin to interfere with the accuracy potential of the firearm. The adjustment range provided is, unfortunately, often fairly limited, but getting a trigger to break at the 3.5- to four-pound mark is normally possible. Note that, if the shooter tries to adjust it further, they are likely to disable the safety or prevent the firearm from cocking correctly, the latter of which can allow the firing pin to run forward on the closing of the bolt. In any event, having made any adjustments or alterations, the trigger

*Custom triggers are usually sealed and generally sport features not found on the commercial market. Further, custom triggers are designed to be far more adjustable than their commercial counterparts.*

Treating the safety test as a first assessment, the firearm must be actioned relatively hard; in the case of a bolt-action rifle, the bolt must be opened, withdrawn, run forward, and rotated in a smooth but fast movement. A trigger that is unsafe may not actually cock the firearm when a bolt is actioned quickly. This may permit a slam-fire to occur, where the firing pin falls as the bolt is closed and fires the round in the chamber, though the chamber may not be properly locked.

The second safety test is to action the firearm, engage the safety, and pull the trigger. The safety, thusly engaged, should prevent the action from firing. Assuming this test is passed, disengage the safety to ensure that doing this also does not fire the firearm.

This ensures that the working parts are not "hooked up" on the safety mechanism and then held by that mechanism over the trigger mechanism.

The final test is a bump test. The firearm is actioned and the safety disengaged. Then the rifle, from several inches away, is thumped or bumped down on its butt onto a solid surface. The firearm should not fire in this circumstance. This test ensures that the trigger mechanism has sufficient weight and engagement to prevent the firearm from discharging should the firearm be dropped while actioned and with the safety off.

These tests are critical to ensure the shooter's safety and the safety of those around them. Always perform these tests on unknown firearms to be satisfied that the firearm is mechanically safe.

*Polishing of surfaces and use of different weight springs can make a difference. This Remington 700 trigger sear has been polished and the spring replaced.*

## TRIGGER TUNING

Correct tuning of trigger mechanisms is a job best left to gunsmiths who have the correct tools and measuring instruments. However, in terms of a process, here's how such a job is performed.

Initially, the trigger is disassembled and the parts cleaned. The trigger mechanism is then reassembled, sometimes in a test bed (depending on the trigger mechanism), and the qualities of the trigger assessed. This information is coupled with the requests of the shooter for a lighter or less creepy trigger, for instance, and then a plan for proceeding can be made.

Of primary concerns are the working surfaces of the trigger mechanism. These surfaces are generally polished first with abrasive grit, then jeweler's rouge, to deliver mirror-finish surfaces. This polishing alone will smooth out the pull of any trigger and generally lower the pull weight, due to decreasing the friction between the surfaces. In some cases, the angles of the working surfaces need to be re-profiled. This is a more complicated task requiring a jig, so that the new angles can be set accurately.

Having set the working surfaces, the issue of springs can next be considered. Different springs of different weights can be added to achieve lighter (or heavier) trigger weights. A number of companies manufacture spring kits for most commercial trigger mechanisms. These manufacturers will claim the spring kits are simple drop in-style kits. They might be, but, to achieve the full potential of the kit, the rest of the trigger work should be completed, as well. As it is with springs, new pins can be added that secure the working parts to a higher degree and take out any slop in the fit of them. Finally, the trigger parts must be cleaned again and assembled without lubricant, then tested for performance and safety.

# CHAPTER SIX

# Rifle Scopes, Sights and Optic Accessories

A rifle's scope is the shooter's link to their target. The scope allows the shooter to spot for and acquire targets, assess the range to the target (and, in some cases, set the scope for the range and wind or hold-off and -over as necessary), engage targets, and then follow through after the shot to assess the fall of the shot and begin spotting for the next target. This is a complex set of operations, all being carried out by the one piece of fairly innocuous and generally overlooked equipment.

Most scope decisions tend towards fixed and variable magnification strength, objective lens sizes, windage and elevation adjustment knobs, bullet drop compensators (BDC), tube diameter and, of course, the all important reticle. There are many other options available on scopes, such as illuminated reticles and built-in spirit levels, but these options tend to stray from accuracy-driven decision making towards personal preference. Beyond these differences, many commercial manufacturers would have

shooters believe that all scopes are essentially the same. This simply is not true.

As in most things, with scopes you get what you pay for. A cheap scope is the quickest way to poor performance. Good quality scopes are characterized by the use of multi-coated lenses, steel internal windage and elevation mechanisms, and lenses of high light transmission. Good quality scopes also come with robust internal mountings for the lenses (to handle varying recoil levels), a strong 6061 or 7075 aluminum body, and nitrile rubber seals to prevent moisture from entering the scope. Poor scopes, on the other hand, lack many of these refinements and characteristically "grey out" at higher magnifications. This can be due to poor quality lens glass. Scopes of lesser quality can also produce varying point of impact after adjusting the elevation and windage, due to a weak adjustment mechanism that has excessive backlash and movement in the parts. Such problems prevent a scope from returning to zero when shooting a "box" of adjustments, because adjustments in different directions are not equal. Further, poor scopes suffer from lens flare, due to internal reflections of light between lenses within the scope caused by either the lack or incorrect use of lens coatings or weak internal mountings for the lenses or other parts that lead to recoil-induced changes in point of aim. Flare can also be caused by inferior seals on the scope, which allow moisture to enter and interfere with the image in

*Scopes technologies in glass manufacture, lens coatings, and reticles have changed greatly over the last 50 years.*

cold temperatures. Color shift, noticed as a fine line of purple on one side of an object within the field of view, and distortion of the image at the edge of the field of view, are also signs of a poor lens or lens coating system.

That said, it is not enough to simply purchase a good quality scope and expect it to fulfill the shooter's needs perfectly. As a case in point, the shooter may purchase the perfect scope for the job, but, due to incorrect setup or usage, will not achieve the potential the scope can provide. The shooter needs to choose the correct scope for the purpose and employ it correctly and, to do this, the shooter must have defined the purpose for the firearm that the scope will be mounted to.

## MAGNIFICATION

When it comes to magnification, most shooters will generally say that more is better. It can be. Excessive magnification can also be a shooter's worst enemy. As magnification increases, the field of view the scope provides decreases. This means that shooters will not be able to see as much around their target with a higher magnification scope. Such shrinkage can affect a hunter's ability to spot for targets and can make it extremely difficult to both track moving targets and then pick the target back up after the shot has been taken. Likewise, competition shooters with excessively high magnification may have trouble assessing the wind conditions on the range, because the flags will be outside their field of view; in severe cases, a competitor may shoot the target on either side of their own, because they can't see the lane numbers.

Increasing magnification also has the effect (in conjunction with the objective lens), of decreasing the exit pupil diameter. Exit pupil diameter is the circle of light projected from the eyepiece of the scope onto the retina within the shooter's eye, showing the image through the scope. Ideally, the diameter should be the same as the shooter's eye (four to seven millimeters), and is calculated by dividing the diameter of the objective lens by the magnification. A larger exit pupil leads to a brighter, more vibrant image through the scope, particularly useful when shooting in low light conditions at dawn or dusk. A smaller exit pupil diameter leads to a duller image, one that is also more difficult to keep centered in the eye. This leads to incorrect eye-to-scope alignment, which will have a marked, negative impact on accuracy.

Finally, the effects of mirage are more pronounced high magnification. With very high magnification scopes, even on a cool but sunny day, the image can begin to "boil," making the shooter's job difficult and frustrating.

Looking at the differences between fixed and variable magnification scopes, fixed magnification scopes offer the most reliable and robust solution, whereas variable magnification scopes offer adaptability and multi-purpose use, though with an increase in complexity and a perceived decrease in reliability. (With good quality scopes, any decrease in reliability of a variable magnification scope over a fixed magnification scope is negligible.)

So, how should the shooter choose their scope's magnification? The choice should come down to two factors, target size and the anticipated range over which the shooter will be firing.

If a shooter is shooting at medium-sized targets at short range (100 to 200 yards), then a low-power magnification may be appropriate. If the same shooter wants to use their scope for spotting from vantage points, then perhaps a low-power variable scope may be appropriate. On the other hand, a long-range hunter may need a high-power scope for those shots 500 yards and more.

As a very generalized rule of thumb, 1-4x scopes are good for large-sized targets or short ranges (100 to 200 yards). Variable scopes of 3-9x are good for medium-sized targets at short to medium ranges (300 to 600 yards), 14x and up are good for long-range (600-plus yards) medium-sized game or short- to medium-range varmint hunting, and 25x and up is good for extreme range (1,000-plus yards). These are very broad generalizations, but they do provide some guidance.

## EYEPIECE ADJUSTMENT

Eyepiece or "diopter" adjustment is very important in setting up a scope on a firearm. It should be noted that the adjustment set is not static; it will change both from shooter to shooter and over time. This adjustment allows the shooter to focus the reticle image for their eye, so that the reticle is clearly seen when superimposed over the target.

To adjust the eyepiece correctly is simple to do, but complicated to do correctly. The shooter, having ensured that the firearm is unloaded, needs to aim the firearm at a nice patch of plain cloud or a blank surface. It doesn't matter if the picture is out of focus and, in fact, it is easier to adjust the eyepiece if it is. Next, the eyepiece is twisted until the reticle is in perfect focus. The part that most shooters don't realize is that the brain is very clever and, after a couple seconds of looking at the out of focus reticle, will tell the eye to refocus itself and bring the reticle into "focus." This puts a large amount of strain on the eye, not just in the adjusting, but every time the shooter looks through the scope. Therefore, it is very important for the shooter to only *glance* through the scope when adjusting the eyepiece. The best way to do this is to simply close the eyes while adjusting. This will ensure that the eyepiece is correctly focused on the reticle, without the shooter's eye taking up the slack.

## OBJECTIVE SIZE

The size of a scope's objective lens, measured as a diameter, has a large effect on the ultimate visual capability of the scope as a whole unit. As all the light entering a scope must pass through the objective lens, any restriction of that lens will limit the performance of the rifle scope. As a rule of thumb, the larger the lens, the greater the light-gathering potential of the lens and the brighter the resulting image.

Although this holds true most of the time, scope examples with very large objective lenses can be found that deliver only mediocre performance. Likewise, there are some scopes with average to small objective lenses that provide a brighter image than some with larger objective lenses. A lot of this has to do with the quality of the glass used in the manufacture of the lens, and also the anti-reflective coatings that are applied in an effort to improve light transmission.

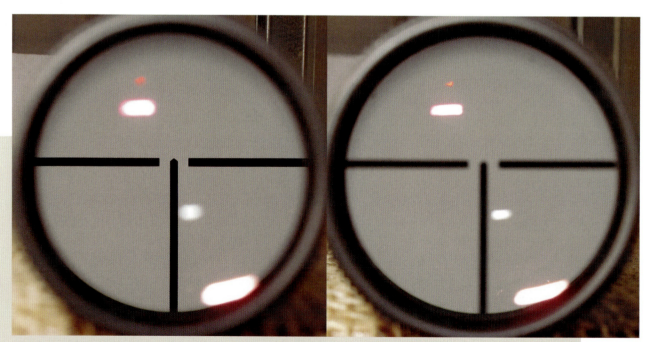

*Adjustment of the eyepiece is a simple process that most shooters overlook. The reticle and target image both need to be in focus at the same time.*

*Different objective sizes exist for different purposes. Some are designed to maximize light capture, others to keep the scope mounted as low as possible.*

Quality of the glass and lens coatings are also determining factors in the *sharpness* of the image.

Current production and marketing trends have shown that three objective lens sizes are primarily currently in use, namely the 40mm, 50mm, and 56mm sizes. These tend to coincide with the broad magnification ranges of 1-10x, 9-25x, and 14-36x, respectively. It must be noted that larger objective lenses may require the use of higher bases and ring sets with which to mount the scope, so as not to have it in contact with the receiver or barrel of the firearm. This can interfere with the shooter's shooting position and correct shouldering of the firearm,

and though this can be compensated for with a cheekpiece, adjustable stock, etc., it is an important point to consider. Further to this point, larger objective lenses tend to require longer scope tubes in order to magnify and focus the image correctly. Ultimately, this lengthens the scope and increases overall firearm weight.

Hand in hand with the greater light gathering potential of larger objective lenses is their resulting usefulness in low light conditions. Many hunters who spot for game during the half-hour before first light and after last light are acutely aware of the benefits of low magnification scopes with larger objective lenses, as they provide a brighter viewed image and greater contrast between the image and the reticle.

## TUBE DIAMETER

Many shooters are under the false impression that a larger tube diameter on a scope allows more light to pass through. In some particular cases this may be true, but, more often than not, a larger tube diameter is used for either structural integrity purposes or, in the more commonly encountered situation, to facilitate a greater range of windage and elevation adjustment.

To know how a scope tube works, an understanding of the internal parts is required. Within the scope tube is an erector and reticle assembly tube. This tube is the choke point for light transmission— all the light that reaches the shooter's eye comes from this tube, *not* the scope's body tube. The erector and reticle assembly tube is made smaller than the scope's body tube, so that is can be angled within the body tube by the windage and elevation adjustment screws. This is where the benefits of a larger body tube are found. Greater degrees of adjustment, particularly in terms of elevation, will result in a marked increase in the maximum effective range of the firearm (assuming the ammunition and shooter are up to par).

Scope tube sizes are generally in the categories of one-inch, 30mm and 34mm, although there are some less encountered sizes such as 24mm, ¾-inch and ⁷/₈-inch. Larger scope tubes are not necessarily an improvement over smaller scope tubes and will not have any effect on accuracy *per se*. However, the shooter may find a one-inch tubed scope bottoming out its elevation screw, when shooting over longer distances. The only other way this problem can be overcome is to fit a scope mounting system that is lower at the front than at the back (a mount known to have "gain"), providing an external fixed elevation adjustment of sorts and allowing the scope's internal adjustment to have a lower point of aim. Larger scope tubes, of course, require compatible mounting hardware in terms of ring sets, and these can be very expensive over the standard sizes of one-inch and 30mm.

## MOUNTING HARDWARE

Mounting hardware comprises those parts that fix the scope to the firearm, providing a platform that does not flex or move during firing and recoil, as well as one that is sufficiently stable enough to absorb the bumps and knocks associated with reasonable use. Conventionally, the mounting hardware comprises rings that are fixed around the scope and attached to bases that are fixed to the firearm. (This, of course, discounts mounting systems where the rail or base is machined into the receiver, such as the 11mm or 20mm dovetail on many smallbore firearms, the specialized mounting systems as are found on the AR platform, and others such as the Stanag system.)

There are a wide variety of ring and base combinations. The real differences between them occur in the bases. In their most basic form, bases come as either one-piece or two-piece. Two-piece bases are the easiest and cheapest to manufacture and generally are supplied with commercial firearms, but there are significant disadvantages associated with them. First, they need to be shimmed, or have thin brass plates fitted between the bases and the receiver so that the height and angles of the bases match. Second, the lengths of the bases are limited and, as such, offer limited ring and scope placement on the firearm. This can impact the eye relief or, worse, make some scopes un-mountable, due to interference and the inability to adjust the ring position on the bases.

One-piece bases offer a longer distance over which the rings can be mounted, giving far greater flexibility. One-piece bases are also manufactured from a single piece of steel or aluminum and possess a true bottom that mounts to the receiver, so they don't require shimming to correct for height and angle differences between the front and back. Most important of all is the fact that a one-piece base offers a long, rigid, external support to the action, stiffening the action above the cutout for the ejection port.

No matter which base is used, the screws holding it to the receiver should be torqued correctly, normally to 25 in-lbs, and locked using Loctite or a similar product. Zeroing problems can be caused

*Choosing the correct ring combination is critical. The incorrect choice will not only make correct eye relief and sight picture difficult to obtain, the shooter's scope may not even fit on the rifle!*

by a base incorrectly fixed to the receiver and, when this happens, the shooter will go bald pulling out their hair while looking for the innocuous problem!

Looking at rings, know that the only major differences among the many brands are the number of screws securing the ring caps and whether the ring caps are top opening or side opening. There are some other variations on this theme, such as Weaver's "catch and screw" caps intended for smallbore usage, and the European solid ring style that requires disassembly of the scope and then the silver soldering of the rings to the scope body to permit mounting.

One significant difference in rings is whether they are manufactured from steel or aluminum. This will determine whether or not the rings can be lapped, a process by which small differences between the heights and angles of the individual rings can be matched, so that the load of clamping the scope into the rings is spread over the rings evenly front and back and also within each ring separately. Also important is that the ring cap screws must be correctly torqued to normally 15 in-lbs and locked using Loctite or a similar product. Many shooters have had their scope move or rotate in the rings while firing, due to loose rings caps. Not only does this ruin the zero, it can also scratch and damage the scope.

When looking at a base and ring combination, the shooter must consider the height at which they want their scope mounted over the firearm. Ideally, the scope should be mounted as low as possible and as comfortable for the shooter, ensuring the shooter can maintain a strong cheek weld to the buttstock and allowing the shooter to correctly shoulder the firearm in such a way that correct eye position behind the scope is achieved without moving the head after the firearm has been shouldered. Not only will this make a stronger connection between the scope and the firearm, it will also limit the effects of "canting," or holding the firearm on a slight angle during firing, which will lead to a difference between point of aim and point of impact.

The most significant difference in ring and base mounting solutions is the way in which the rings and bases interface onto each other. These interfaces range from almost permanent to quick-detachable. In the simplest system, Leupold's basic setup, the front ring is held to the base by first slotting a fitting on its bottom into the base, then turning the ring 90 degrees. The rear ring is held on the base by a transverse dovetail with a screw on either end to lock in the ring.

The Leupold system is very lightweight and robust and also allows for coarse windage adjustment via the rear screws. It is particularly ideal for a dedicated hunting rifle. However, it is difficult to disassemble and it will only accept the scope that is fitted to the firearm, preventing the use of multiple scopes for different situations.

Looking at a more modern system, the Picatinny or Mil-Std (military standard) 1913 rail uses a transversely notched base with chamfered edges. The rings for this base hook over the chamfered edges, and a cross bolt built into the bottom of the ring fits into the notch on the rail. The ring is then locked on by a transverse screw and hook. This system is more complicated than the Leupold-styled system, but it does offer several advantages.

First, the Picatinny system is stronger than the Leupold system (and also heavier). Second, this system allows placement of the rings at any point on the rail, providing the shooter maximum flexibility in scope mounting. Third and most important, this system allows for the dismounting and mounting of different scopes or optical systems, such swapping taking place without losing the zero of the scope to the firearm (although, confirming zero is a good idea for piece of mind if nothing else). This is a huge advantage for hunters who wish to use different scopes, even night scopes, and also for competition shooters who wish to use scopes for some competitions and iron sights for others.

It should be noted that the screws securing the scope ring to the rail of a Picatinny system need to be correctly tightened to roughly 25 in-lbs, otherwise they may not return to zero correctly. This may require the shooter to carry in their range bag or backpack a spanner, socket wrench or, ideally, a small torque wrench (palm-sized models are available).

The final system, the quick-release type, is based on the Picatinny or Mil-Std 1913 rail system. The quick-release system uses side-mounted levers and spring steel plates to act as the locking screws, although the rest of the ring is the same as a standard Picatinny ring. This system, again, allows the shooter to remove, swap, and fit scopes to the firearm without affecting the zero of the scope and without the use of specialized tools. Even better, the swap can be carried out, in many cases, in under one minute!

Although predominantly suited to military applications, this type of system is applicable to some types of competition and dangerous-game hunting firearms, where a damaged scope can be removed quickly to enable the use of backup iron sights, . This system does come with a notable disadvantage, namely that a quick-release setup is not as robust as a standard Picatinny or Mil-Std 1913 rail. Too, the levers and spring steel plates are subject to fatigue and can change the pressures they exert on the rail over time, which will alter the return-to-zero characteristics of the system. It should be noted that the return-to-zero characteristics of both the Picatinny or Mil-Std 1913 rail and the quick-release version are not necessarily perfect, although they are very good.

As a final note, it is very important to use heavy-duty rings and bases where required. Most centerfire firearms above .30-caliber will require heavy-duty mounting hardware to absorb the recoil shock from firing. Failure to use the correct grade of hardware may result in the scope moving while firing, at minimum ruining the zero and at worst causing the mounts to crack or break, which will damage the scope and/or the shooter.

## RETICLES

Reticles are quite possibly the least understood piece of equipment the shooter has at their disposal. Most shooters see a reticle only as something to place over the image of the target in order to aim their firearm. Unbeknownst to many, the humble reticle can be used for range, target size, wind speed, and target speed estimations, as well as bullet drop compensation for long-range shots and the implementation of holdover/hold-off for elevation or windage. Although all reticles are different, they can be broken down into three major groups: simple reticles, rangefinding reticles, and bullet drop compensating reticles.

Simple reticles are exactly as the name suggests. In their most basic form, it is a fine crosshair made from thin tungsten or palladium wire or, in some notable, vintage cases, black widow spider silk. This style of reticle allows the shooter to have an excellent view of the target, although the thin vertical and horizontal wires can be difficult to pick up in low light conditions.

In Europe, the post reticle, comprised of a thick vertical aiming post just crossing a thin horizontal crosswire, is the preferred simple crosshair. This system offers the benefits of a defined aiming point the shooter can see around well and is easily picked up in low light conditions. For the shooters who wish to get the most out of their equipment, this reticle can serve as a rudimentary rangefinding or bullet drop compensating reticle, by understanding the distance between the very tip of the vertical post and where it crosses the crosswire and to what distance this subtends at particular ranges.

An example would be to fire a round at a target at a known range, 100 yards for instance, using the tip of the post to aim, and then fire another round using the intersection between the post and the crosswire. Then measure the distance between points of impact. This measurement is then a known distance in the reticle. As an example, if the measurement is 12 inches and the shooter then aims at a target that fills the distance between the tip and crosswire in the reticle at 100 yards, the shooter knows the target is 12 inches tall. Conversely, if the shooter aims at a target that is 12 inches tall and it fills the distance between the tip and crosswire, then the shooter knows the target is 100 yards away; if a 12-inch target only fills half the distance, the target is 200 yards away, and so on. Although this seems complicated, once learned, it is a very fast

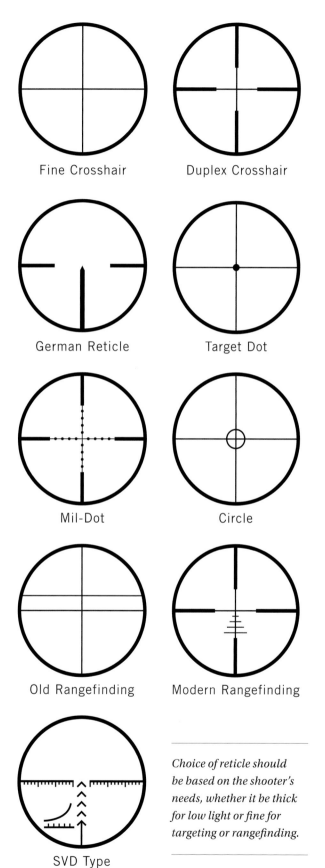

Fine Crosshair

Duplex Crosshair

German Reticle

Target Dot

Mil-Dot

Circle

Old Rangefinding

Modern Rangefinding

SVD Type

*Choice of reticle should be based on the shooter's needs, whether it be thick for low light or fine for targeting or rangefinding.*

and quick reference that can be used without the shooter leaving the shooting position. This technique can be used with any style of reticle. All the shooter needs are two reliable aiming points in the reticle.

A further development of the post and fine crosshair reticles is the standard duplex reticle. This reticle combines the features of both the post and fine reticles by having thick vertical and horizontal crosswires on the outer half of the field of view, switching to fine as the reticle comes into the center. This allows fine aiming in good light conditions and easier sight picture acquisition in low light conditions. These reticles are perfect for the recreational short- and medium-range hunter. They allow the shooter to place rounds on target accurately and quickly. For longer-range shooters, where the specific range is known, they can be zeroed to the range the shooter wants and allow a greater portion of the sight picture for wind estimation and glassing for targets.

True rangefinding reticles have been around for many years. An early example is the Redfield Accu-Range reticle, comprised of a standard fine reticle, with two extra crosswires in the top section separated by a critical distance. On the right-hand side of the reticle are a series of vertical hash marks and speci-fied ranges. To use this reticle, the shooter would then place the two extra crosswires so that they bracketed a target of known size, in this case 18 inches. The shooter would alter the magnification setting on the scope, making the field of view smaller, until the two extra crosswires bracketed the target perfectly, then the shooter could simply read off the range from where the ranged hash marks cross the now limited field of view. Of course, the shooter would then have to either hold over the required amount or adjust the elevation in the scope.

This system was later refined by other manufac-turers, so that manipulation of the magnification automatically adjusted the elevation, thus speeding up the process. Although a good idea in concept, it did require the shooter to use a particular magnification at a particular range, which becomes troublesome, if the shooter is engaging a very small target at short range.

Other rangefinding reticles, notably in the old Soviet PSO-1 fixed 4x scope, use the wedge-style rangefinder, which is comprised of two lines arranged like a wedge (although the top of the wedge is actually curved), allowing the shooter to place a target of known size (generally 1.7 meters) within the wedge until the two lines bracket the target perfectly. The shooter can then read off the range. A slight refinement in this reticle is that there are aiming points that coincide with the various ranges, allowing the shooter to immediately engage the target without having to adjust the scope.

It is important to note that rangefinding reticles are fairly rudimentary and rely on the use of an accurately known target size. Small errors in range estimation begin to have a large effect on the point of impact at longer range. For instance, a rifle chambered in .308 firing at 168-grain projectile at 2,570 fps, aimed at a target 800 yards away but with an incorrect range estimation of 775 yards, will shoot low by more than a 15 inches—enough to go between the legs of a buck or whistle clean past a target!

A more modern innovation to rangefinding reticles is the Mil-Dot reticle. Originally developed for military use, this reticle comprises a fine cross-hair separated by a series of Mil-Dots both on the vertical and horizontal crosswires. This reticle offers an excellent view of the target, while also being reasonably visible in low light conditions. Further, given that the rangefinding Mil-Dots are on both crosswires, they can also be used for estimating target speed, as well as holdovers/hold-offs for both elevation and windage.

Specifically, the distance between the centers of two Mil-Dots is exactly one milliradian (Mil). The dots themselves cover only 0.2-Mil. A Mil, or mil-liradian, is an angular unit of measurement; there are 6,400 Mils in a 360-degree circle (technically, there are 6,175 Mils in a circle, but, by convention, the number is rounded to one easier to remember). One Mil (the distance between the centers of two Mil dots) subtends exactly one meter at 1,000 meters. This formula is what is used for rangefinding. The shooter takes a target of known size in meters and multiplies

it by 1,000. Then the shooter will divide the resulting number by the number of Mils the target covers in the reticle. This leaves the shooter with a range in meters—target size (m) x 1000/Mils = range (m). But wait, that's not all! The shooter, then looking at their range data card, sees that, at this range, for instance 500 meters, the drop experienced by the projectile will be 81.2 inches. Knowing that the centers of the Mil-Dots are separated by exactly one Mil and that one Mil equals 3.6 inches at 100 meters or 18 inches at 500 meters, the shooter can divide the drop of 81.2 inches by the subtended distance of one mil at 500 meters, which is 18 inches, and then the shooter can hold over 4.5 Mil-Dots and successfully hit their target. This may all seem complicated, but, once learned, the Mil-Dot ranging and holdover system is fast, accurate, and reliable.

A further refinement of the Mil-Dot reticle is the TMR, or tactical milling reticle. This reticle is a conventional Mil-Dot reticle with hash marks separating the Mil-Dots denoting 0.5-Mil. This refinement offers a better opportunity for accurate ranging, which is the weak point of all rangefinding reticles. The downside is that many shooters find this reticle cluttered, which may be a distraction leading to bad mathematics! Many shooters who use Mil-Dots carry a small, solar-powered calculator as part of their shooting kit or with their range data card to ensure no mistakes are made.

The final style of reticle is the bullet drop compensating reticle. This reticle can take many forms, and these days it generally comprises a Mil-Dot center portion. This reticle also shows points of aim for different ranges for a specific type of ammunition. So, to shoot at 500 meters, the shooter simply holds the 500-meter aiming point onto the image of the target. This does work quite well, though it does rely on the shooter using the exact ammunition specified by the manufacturer of the scope, because, if the ballistic characteristics of the ammunition differ from the ballistics the reticle is calibrated to, error will result.

A further development of the bullet drop compensating reticle includes known hold-off points for five,

10, and 15 mph crosswinds. This requires the shooter to use the scope at a specified magnification and really can only be considered an estimate (due to the arbitrary positioning of the points), based on top of the estimate of wind strength.

Like the TMR, these bullet drop compensating reticles are cluttered, enough so that they can cover up important features of the sight picture, such as identifiers of wind conditions (grass or flags that may be in the field of view). That said, these reticles do provide a limited solution to the more involved mathematics associated with Mil-Dot reticles. It should also be noted, however, that bullet drop compensating reticles and their underpinning range data cards are also calibrated to particular *atmospheric* conditions such as temperature and air pressure, among others.

Consequently, unless those conditions are the same every day you shoot, a small error will result, one that will be compounded with distance.

Ultimately, the choice of reticle will be governed by the choice of scope and magnification. For a shooter that shoots mostly at one range or within a close band of ranges, a simple fine crosshair or duplex is adequate. For the shooter involved in timed competition shooting or tactical competition, a bullet drop compensating reticle would provide reasonable drop compensation with very fast adjustment times for firing at different ranges. And, for the shooter who wants absolute precision, such as a benchrest shooter or long-range hunter, the Mil-Dot system is the most efficient to use and, once learned and internalized, is fast to employ and faster to enjoy!

# Range Estimation

Putting aside technology in the form of laser range-finders and rangefinding reticles, there are several methods available to the shooter for range estimation. Techniques such as the known-distance comparison, bracketing, map method, and short-distance method allow the shooter to make a structured estimate of the range, which is far superior to a flat-out guess. Each of these methods results in estimations, which

*Range estimation—the buck stops with you!*

therefore are subject to inaccuracy and variance, but the strength of these methods is that they can all be used at the same time. This enables the shooter to develop a "composite range" that's averaged from the results of all the methods. With practice, this does provide a reasonably accurate representation of real range.

The known-distance method takes a distance that is visually very well known to the shooter, such as a football field or the distance between power poles, etc., and then asks how many times that known distance fits into the space the shooter is trying to measure. The known

## ADJUSTMENT KNOBS

If reticles are the least understood piece of equipment at a shooter's disposal, then correct usage of adjustment knobs or turrets comes in second! Adjustment turrets are generally provided for both windage and elevation adjustment and normally have hash lines marked on them to provide a scale for the adjustment, as well as an audible and tactile *click* for each increment. In their most basic form, turrets allow a shooter to zero their scope to their rifle so that the point of aim overlaps the point of impact at a specified range. Many shooters consider this to be a static adjustment—once set, it's best left alone.

Windage and elevation turrets divide the adjustment into increments, or clicks, of known size. Traditionally, one click equals one inch at 100 yards. This has been refined to .5-inch and even .25-inch clicks. Then the Europeans came up with minutes of angle, or MOA, which has effectively taken over as the standard. One MOA equals 1.047 inches at 100 yards (1.145 inches at 100 meters), and the turrets come in 1 MOA, ½-MOA, ¼-MOA, and even $1/8$-MOA per click adjustments.

To use windage and elevation turrets properly, the shooter requires a range data card for their chosen firearm and ammunition. This card is a table of the ballistic characteristics of the firearm/ammunition combination, either developed from field testing or from a data book or ballistic calculator, and it includes details such as bullet drop with range and wind deflection at range for a given wind strength. This information culminates in cross-referencing the distance over which the shooter is aiming, along distance can even be the viewed distance to the target at the 100 yard/meter shooting mound. The shooter may decide that there are two football fields or eight power poles that can fit between their location and the target, thus yielding an estimation of the range.

The bracketing method works on the same principle as the known-distance method, but applies it differently. Essentially, the shooter makes a best guess both on what the range could not be less than and could not be more than, then takes the middle point between these two. The result is generally fairly accurate.

The map method works with the shooter finding their position and that of their target on a map and simply measuring the range in between. This method is reliant on the shooter's ability to navigate and to locate features on the map and apply them to the ground to accurately place the target's position on the map. If the shooter is proficient in these forms of navigation, the range can be accurately measured.

Finally, the shooter can employ the short distance method. This method works by estimating the range to a secondary target on the path to the actual target, one the shooter feels they can accurately estimate the range of, and then multiplying this distance out to the actual target to achieve the estimate of range to the target. This method works particularly well, when the shooter can accurately measure a short distance, but not far enough so as to range the actual target.

Finally, as mentioned, a GPS can also allow the shooter to estimate the range to the target. This does require the shooter to pinpoint the position of the target on a map and measure the intervening range.

The key to using any of these methods properly is practice. The shooter should estimate range on all manner of targets in all manner of environments. Further, the shooter can practice by learning what common objects look like at long range or, even better, borrow a laser rangefinder and practice by estimating the range using these methods, and then measuring the range to see how close your estimate came to the actual.

*From flush-mounting adjustment dials to large, quick-adjust target knobs, the shooter's choice will depend on how often the they need to make ballistic corrections.*

with the wind strength, so as to determine the correct windage and elevation adjustments in MOA. The shooter then simply dials in the windage and elevation and proceeds to fire.

The use of turrets is pretty well foolproof, but there are two catches. First, and what should be the obvious one, the turrets need to be used with accurate data. Second, depending on the internal mechanism of the shooter's scope, there are a limited number of clicks or MOA in one rotation of the turret. If the shooter needs more adjustment, that's fine, they can keep winding, but they do need to remember that they are *plus* one full rotation—many shooters have found themselves a full rotation out with their point of impact high or low and have wondered why! More recent scopes have tried to limit this problem by making the turrets spiral or corkscrew in and out with the rotations, revealing a second scale that indicates the number of rotations.

Many shooters get bogged down counting clicks. Adjustments such as up 61 clicks are very difficult to input correctly and the shooter can waste a lot of time counting them all. A far better method is to count in whole minutes. For example, on a four-click per MOA scope, 61 clicks is 15.25 MOA—a far more sensible adjustment!

## BULLET DROP COMPENSATORS

Bullet drop compensators (BDCs) are special adjustment knobs or turrets that have specific calibration marks on them that show the adjustment required for different ranges. They are normally broken down to 50-meter increments, though smaller increments can be found. As a rule, normal turret markings are present to allow normal turret adjustments; just because a scope has a BDC doesn't mean its owner is locked into using it.

The BDCs of the past used a cam arrangement to make an elevation adjustment with which to zero the scope to a particular range via just one click. These days, the range increments are simply shown on the turret, along with the other click increments.

Today's BDCs are calibrated to operate with a particular firearm and ammunition; technically, they are not interchangeable with different setups, although they may happen to come close. Current BDCs are also calibrated to particular atmospheric conditions that affect the trajectory of the projectile, those being temperature, barometric pressure, altitude, and humidity. Deviation from the calibrated conditions will incur an error in the point of impact, an error that increases with range. For example, the

*Bullet drop compensators (BDCs) have been around for a long time. The two left and center are from the Second World War. They allow the shooter to adjust for elevation by using predetermined settings. The modern iteration on the right isn't all that different, though it perhaps offers more adjustment.*

.308 at sea level will experience 81.2 inches of drop at 500 meters. This same firearm at 5,000 feet above sea level will experience 75.5 inches of drop at the same range, due to the thinner air.

It is very important for the shooter to confirm their BDC by shooting at each range increment and noting the results, then fine-tuning their shooting for various conditions. Today's BDCs are excellent tools for shooters who need to engage targets quickly, such as in a hunting situation where the game is moving from clearing to clearing, or when in a timed or tactical competition. Modern BDCs are also appropriate for recreational shooters who wish to stretch their range without going to the full extent of data cards and full elevation calculation and adjustment.

## SUNSHADES

Sunshades are a very important piece of ancillary optics equipment. They provide two very important functions for scopes. First, they force light to only enter the scope lenses from the front (and not from the sides). Second, with particular reference to hunting, they will mostly eliminate light reflecting off the front lens and frightening the shooter's prey.

As many shooters will know, in the early or late part of the day, when the sun is low to the horizon, there can be a lot of glare in images seen through scopes, particularly when the target is silhouetted by or close to the axis of the sun. This glare occurs because the suns rays are shining through the side of the objective lens and setting up an internal reflection off the mirror-like surfaces of the internal lenses. This will look like a "whiting-out" of the image, or a loss of clarity and contrast in the image.

In the second case, an external reflection is set off the outside of the objective lens, and will provide a flickering/flash towards the prey. This will no doubt spook them, even at great range. Fortunately, for competition shooters and hunters alike, most scope manufacturers make sunshades to screw onto the objectives of their scopes.

Ideally, a longer sunshade is better. As a minimum, a sunshade the length of the scope's objective lens is required, in order for the sunshade to be truly effective. Many sunshades these days will screw into each other, allowing for customizing longer lengths.

Some shooters make their own sunshades from aluminum tube or simple cardboard. Another form of sunshade actually covers the lens, leaving only a slot for the light to enter the scope. This particular sunshade is most useful in snow conditions, where it can prevent snow blindness and tone down the otherwise dazzling brightness that can be encountered with snow in full daylight.

## TENEBRAEX FILTERS

Tenebraex filters are a relatively new solution to the old problem of glare in scopes and can be used in place of sunshades. Tenebraex filters, also known as kill-flash filters, are an item originally designed for military purposes. Today they have found application in hunting and competition, due to their size and weight advantages over sunshades.

A Tenebraex filter is a short length of honeycomb (about half-inch or 12.7mm thick), made into a disk shape that screws into the scope's objective in place of a sunshade. Instead of having one all-encompassing sunshade for the objective lens, the honeycomb cells create many small sunshades all over the surface of the lens. This provides far better shading across the lens and will almost completely prevent reflections bouncing off the scope's objective.

The benefits come at a cost. Due to the fact that there is a honeycomb covering the objective lens, resolution or sharpness of the image of the scope will be reduced, as will the apparent brightness of the scope, particularly in low light conditions.

## EYEPIECE SHADING

Eyepiece shading is a predominantly forgotten concept and technique in shooting. The purpose of eyepiece shading is to remove light sources that may enter the scope through the eyepiece lens or the eye from the side while it looks through the scope. By shading the eyepiece, not only is the light directed solely at the shooter's pupil and coming from the

*Optical shading from the simple to the supreme. Correctly shaded optics allow the shooter to see the best image possible.*

scope, but also the shooter's pupil will dilate with shading, allowing more light from the scope in to the shooter's eye. This will improve the contrast of the seen image and will cause an apparent increase in resolution—I say apparent, because the scope isn't really transmitting a sharper image, it's just that the shooter's eye is able to see the transmitted image more sharply.

Eyepiece shades generally take the form of a collapsible rubber eyecup or, in some cases, a sliding tube similar to an objective lens sunshade. This system allows the primary eye to be shaded to get the best image through the scope possible, while leaving the secondary eye still able to scan the wider environment for safety and target tracking purposes. That said, something so simple as a dark cloth placed over the shooter's head and eyepiece, even the peak of a baseball cap, can make a difference. It should be noted that, if a shooter installs an eyepiece shade of the rubber or tube types, the shooter must be cautious as to the recoil of the rifle making the eyepiece shade contact the eye. At the least, the cut to the eyebrow will be embarrassing; at worst, it could damage or destroy the eye.

## IRON SIGHTS

Iron sights these days are generally thought of as something for the old timers, nostalgia shooters, and as second-rate to a scope. This is not the case. Iron sights are just as useful and can be just as accurate as a scope. In fact, this system can be difficult to use by older shooters, because it requires the eye to change focus from the target to the front sight blade quite quickly, and the lenses in older eyes are less inclined to flex far and fast enough.

The largest advantage of iron sights is the extended length between the front sight and rear, this span known as the "sight radius." They allow for very fine aiming. Most shooters are familiar with the old military "V"-notch rear sight and front blade, and this is the most basic form of the iron sight. Adjustable for elevation on a long leaf that denotes range (and sometimes for windage, albeit this latter is a coarse

adjustment), this system is extremely robust and fairly accurate, provided the correct ammunition is used.

An enhancement of the basic iron sights is the ghost ring. This particular sight has the same front blade of the traditional military iron sight, but, instead of a "V"-notch rear sight, it has a round ring. This style of sight is also adjustable, but uses a micrometer screw to achieve elevation adjustment. It is a far more accurate solution.

The advantage of this sight is that it allows a much greater view of the target and also allows the shooter to look through the ghost ring (which more easily permits it to go out of focus), while concentrating on the front blade and the target. The ring simply forms an even concentric circle around the aiming point. This style of aiming can take a little bit of getting used to, but is very efficient and easy to use once one gets the hang of it. Indeed, shooters are generally surprised at how good the sight picture looks using these sights.

A further development of the ghost ring is the aperture sight. Similar in many ways, this sight instead has a disk with a small hole, or aperture, in it that allows the shooter to achieve a sight picture. The bigger difference between an aperture and a ghost ring is that, with an aperture, the hole size is usually adjustable. This permits varying of the light levels coming through to the shooter's eye. It's a good way to respond to cloud cover or bright sunlight, which can make the sight picture uncomfortably dark or very bright.

Parker Hale has a particularly good range of aperture sights. Some models have up to seven different apertures in one disk. All the shooter has to do is rotate the disk to change the aperture size. It should be noted that, as a rule, this type of sight also has micrometer adjustments for both windage and elevation, and they may be in increments as small as ¼-MOA.

Modern iron sights are not much different these days from their "V"-notch design of yesteryear, though there have been some upgrades. One advance is to have an adjustable front sight that also contains an aperture suited to a particular target in completion. These sights are really only suited to competition. Another great advance has been that fiber-optic

*Fixed leaf and micrometer-adjustable sights come in a variety of forms. The illuminated sights shown at the bottom might look gimmicky, but the effect is striking!*

PHOTO COURTESY BARRETT FIREARMS

elements have been incorporated both into the front blade and also the "V"-notch itself. Usually appearing as a colored piece, the fiber-optic elements channel surrounding natural light and direct it to the shooter's eye. With both front and rear sights employing this element, the shooter has three glowing points they can line up, even in very low light conditions.

Shooters should not discredit the virtues of iron sights. Dangerous-game hunters should *always* have iron sights fitted to their rifles, should their scope fail at an inopportune moment. Even long-range or competition shooters can be very effective with iron sights, but short-range hunters, in particular and in many cases, are best served with iron sights. They provide very fast target acquisition, a their ability to assist in and the ability to track with or lead a target via iron sights is almost unsurpassed.

## SPECIALTY RIFLE SCOPES

Specialty rifle scopes offer the shooter a specific shooting advantage that other optics cannot offer. Night vision scopes, for instance, offer the shooter the ability to engage targets in and at varying low light conditions and ranges. Then there are the scopes with a built-in laser rangefinder and ballistic computer, which allow the shooter to carry out ballistic calculations with the press of a button.

Looking first at night vision scopes, these are identical to a normal scope with the exception of a piece of equipment called an "image intensifier" that's fitted inside the scope. An image intensifier takes photons of light coming through the objective lens, then converts and multiplies them into electrons that then hit the back of a tiny television screen. This creates an image for the eyepiece to

PHOTO COURTESY BURRIS COMPANY, INC.

magnify and display to the shooter. Night vision scopes come in varying generations through to the current third generation. Newer generations amplify the light better and create a sharper and brighter image.

Night vision scopes tend to be heavier than day optics and do use batteries. They are quite robust in their construction and are perfectly suited to hunters conducting crop protection, for instance. There are inherent dangers associated with the use of night vision scopes, and the shooter must be very careful to ensure their targets are clearly identified and safe to shoot at.

Rifle scopes with a built-in laser rangefinder are a fairly new addition to the market. With these, the shooter selects a cartridge or data setting from the user's manual that would mimic the load the shooter

is using. Then, when in the field or at the range, the shooter presses a button on the scope to find the range to the target. The target range is displayed in the eyepiece and an aiming point is illuminated on the vertical post of the reticle that shows the required holdover for striking that target at that range.

This system is an excellent option for the shooter who does not wish to explore the ballistics of their firearm and develop ballistic tables or data (though the shooter may wish to utilize "close fit" ballistic solutions). These scopes tend to be heavier than normal scopes. Also, the range capability on the laser rangefinder tends to be shorter than that of handheld models. It's worth noting, too, that the ballistic solutions provided by the computer on these scopes will get the shooter into the ballpark, but will rarely be perfect.

# CHAPTER SEVEN

# Firearm Accessories

Fortunately for shooters, there is a huge commercial manufacturing base for firearm accessories. Many can make a big difference in the performance of a shooter and their firearm. Although these accessories will not make the firearm more accurate, they will make the shooter more accurate *with* the firearm, and they can assist the shooter in learning critical components of accurate shooting, such as proper eye relief, trigger control, and shooting positions.

## CHEEKPIECES

A cheekpiece is a riser or comb added to the stock that increases the height at which the stock contacts the shooter's cheek. A solid and consistent cheek weld or positioning of the cheek on the stock, as I'll discuss in the chapter on the shooter, is critical to correct eye alignment and eye relief behind a scope.

A cheekpiece or comb that is too low will distort the sight picture with a black crescent visible through the scope. The shooter will experience a loose weld of the cheek against the stock, with their head moving independently of the firearm. A cheekpiece or comb

that is too high will result in the same distortion of the sight picture through the scope, but now the shooter will have their head tipped over at a severe angle in an attempt to achieve the correct sight picture.

Improper cheek weld is easy to spot in shooters who shoulder their firearm, only to move their head back and forth, up and down, until they are finally happy with their eye position—and then discover they have nearly broken their neck to achieve it! A cheekpiece will alleviate this problem and enhance the accuracy potential of the shooter and their firearm by forcing the shooter the assume the same cheek weld every time the firearm is shouldered.

Cheekpieces come in a variety of shapes and materials, including adjustable, non-adjustable, and temporary. Traditionally, the correct height for the shooter would be established, and then a stockmaker would manufacture a cheekpiece from wood and permanently attach it to the stock. More recently, and particularly in the modern sporting rifle market, cheekpieces are manufactured from high-density plastic or composite material and cross-bolted to the

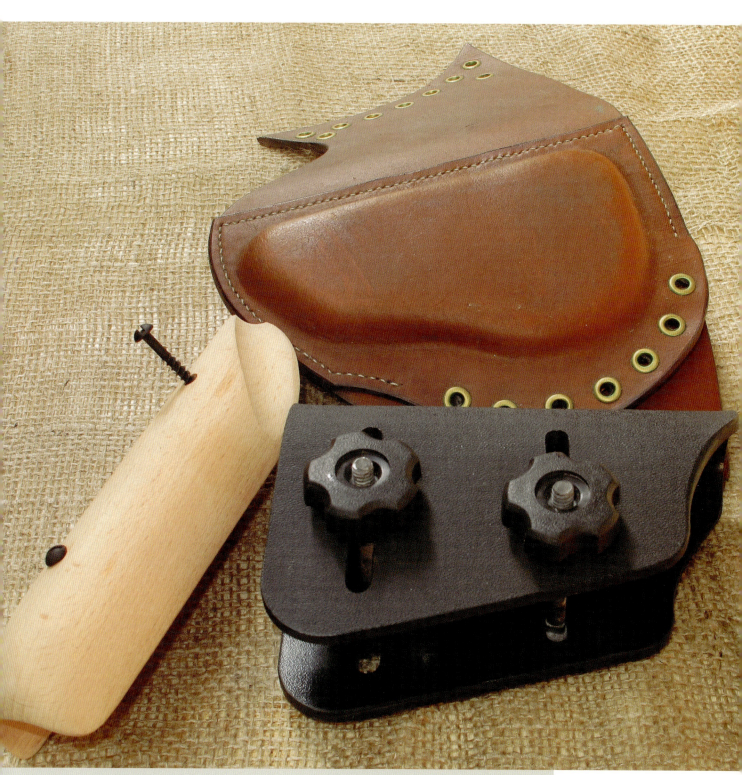

*Screw-on, lace-on, and bolt-on. There's a cheekpiece to suit every firearm and shooter style.*

stock, if not already incorporated into the stock. This may sound as though the cheekpiece may be very hard against the cheek during firing, but a firm surface is desirable to establish and hold a consistence cheek weld; when established correctly, they are surprisingly comfortable. These cheekpieces are generally adjustable for height, but, as they tend to be quite long, rarely for longitudinal position, as such is generally unrequired. Karsten makes an excellent cheekpiece that is simple, lightweight, and effective.

The final cheekpieces that need discussing are the lace-ons and clip-ons. The first style was pioneered for military purposes and consisted of a lace-on leather pad that helped to raise the shooter's head and offset it to the left to coincide with a side-mounted scope. A more recent innovation is a relatively soft cheekpiece, generally made from 1,000-denier nylon, that has several straps and quick release clasps, or an elastic sock that secures the cheekpiece to the rifle. These cheekpieces tend to come equipped with a small, loop-style ammunition carrier or zippered pocket in which to store range data cards or other material. While these cheekpieces do raise the shooter's head, there is the capacity for the cheekpiece to come loose over time or begin to collapse—and not necessarily with the shooter's knowledge.

It is very important to note that, before installing any cheekpiece, the shooter must establish the correct eye relief from the scope using the method detailed in the section called "Shouldering Arms" in Chapter 15. This will allow the shooter to know exactly where the cheekpiece needs to be fitted.

Ultimately, a cheekpiece can be made of anything, right down to a few layers of leather held on with duct tape to form a pad to raise the shooter's head by half and inch. The benefits of having a correctly adjusted cheekpiece, of any type, will be reflected on the trophy wall or in range scores.

## BIPODS

Bipods are indispensable tools. The bipod fulfills the role of supporting the fore-end of the firearm in the prone positions or whenever a bench is used.

They create two points of stability for the firearm, leaving the shooter to form the third point. Bipods come in all shapes, sizes, and styles. The current line of Harris bipods have set a standard in reliability, simplicity, and adaptability and have produced a style of bipod that many other manufacturers have copied.

A bipod is comprised of two legs and a center section that the legs extend and pivot from. Most bipods have pivoting legs that collapse and position out of the way, when the bipod is not in use. The legs on most bipods are also spring loaded for extension and have a locking detent so that the legs can be extended and set at varying heights independently of each other. This is an important feature that allows the shooter to deal more effectively with uneven shooting surfaces.

The center section on the basic bipod is usually static so that once the bipod legs are extended, the point of aim of the firearm is more or less fixed. Other bipods allow for some degree of lateral movement, which assist in small changes in point of aim without having to relocate the bipod. Of course, in partner with allowing a small degree of movement when the shooter wants it, the same may be experienced when the shooter doesn't.

A further development allows the bipod center section to cant left and right. The center section is then locked with the use of a lever. This is another benefit when the ground isn't completely level, and it allows the shooter to make adjustments with far less disruption to the shooting position. A downside, if it can be called that, is that the bipod *should* be re-centered before folding the legs up. In the normal system of extended legs, the detent button is pressed and the legs are withdrawn by spring pressure no matter their length, and then the bipod is folded up.

Bipods are exceptionally good at holding the elevation for shots, but nearly all bipods experience some lateral swing in the point of aim. The shooter will see this as the reticle wandering left and right ever so slightly. This is an issue the can really only be solved by the use of a sandbag under the butt of the firearm

*Bipods are detachable, adjustable, and mobile. They are built to aid stability and designed for flexibility.*

or a monopod fitted to the rear of the stock, either of which provides a third point of stability.

Another useful trick when using a bipod is to place a sandbag against the front of the bipod, and then press the firearm forward onto the sandbag as part of assuming the firing position. This tends to stabilize the bipod and firearm and reduce the lateral swing, while not tying down the rear of the firearm with other paraphernalia.

Correct fitting of the bipod is critical to ensuring that full advantage is taken from the bipod without interfering with the firearm. Ideally, the bipod should be fitted as far forward on the fore-end as possible. By extending this distance forward where the bipod is placed, the triangle of stability between the bipod legs and the shooter is greater. Most firearms have a sling swivel stud in a forward location on the fore-end. Most bipods are capable of attaching to this point.

Having installed the bipod, the shooter must ensure that, when in the prone position, the upward pressure created by the bipod does not cause the fore-end to flex and touch the barrel. If this occurs, it will detrimentally affect accuracy. Finally, the shooter should ensure that the location of the bipod does not interfere with any other shooting position, for instance, it should not prevent the secondary hand from grasping the fore-end properly, nor should it interfere with the use of a sling.

## MONOPODS

A monopod is a relatively new addition to the shooter's resources. It effectively does the job of a bipod for the rear of the rifle for use in the sitting benchrest or prone positions. The monopod allows for an additional point of stability for the firearm, thereby not only creating a very solid shooting platform, but also one that is less affected by small, involuntary movements on the part of the shooter.

There are several different types of monopod, from the most basic "pin"-type, where a rod is unlocked and comes straight down from a recess in the butt, to the more elaborate folding varieties that allow for

*Monopods are a third point of stability, where and when you need one!*

height adjustment of the monopod while in the shooting position, and also for fine elevation adjustments to the point of aim.

Although a useful piece of equipment, the pin type requires setup before the shooter enters into the shooting position. This feature limits its usefulness for being at the perfect height for the shot. Pin monopods are best used with a sandbag to rest the pin on, not only because this allow the shooter to use the monopod to get the point of aim into the ballpark, but also to then use the sand bag to set the elevation and correct the point of aim as necessary. Using a sandbag also helps to prevent the monopod from digging into the ground with each successive shot.

Pin monopods, to their credit, are incredibly lightweight, and because they retract inside the butt of the firearm, they have less of an impact on the lines of the stock. Their design also limits the opportunity of having it get caught up on branches and other obstructions while moving in the field.

Folding monopods offer the same flexibilities as the modern Harris bipods. They fold down from the stock, where they are locked when not in use. Once extended, they can be used to make fine adjustments to the point of aim.

Folding monopods tend to have a wider base and shaft than the pin designs and, therefore, don't tend to dig in to the ground. Further, the monopod itself provides an excellent grip for the secondary hand in both the prone or sitting benchrest positions, again allowing the shooter to make fine adjustments to the elevation of the monopod and point of aim by moving only their fingers. They are an excellent solution to aiding consistency and accuracy.

## MUZZLE BRAKES

Muzzle brakes are a contentious issue amongst shooters and, interestingly, are banned at many ranges. A muzzle brake reduces the felt recoil of firing, by directing the chamber and bore gases produced to the sides of the barrel at the muzzle as the projectile leaves the muzzle. In so doing, the gases exert a forward push on the muzzle brake as they are forced

to turn the corners of the brake. This has the effect of pulling the firearm forward and reducing transmitted recoil. Felt recoil is a function of the firearm's weight, the weight of the projectile, and the amount of powder used as the charge. In essence, muzzle brakes redirect the residual energy of the powder charge into reducing the recoil.

There are a huge number of muzzle brake styles available, all claiming "massive" reductions in recoil. The reality is somewhat different. In fact, many styles have little effect on the felt recoil.

Traditionally, muzzle brakes were designed for self-propelled artillery and field guns. These brakes directed the gas left and right at 90 degrees to the axis of the bore, and sometimes up. This style was adapted to rifles, and it certainly works for them. Later enhancements to this design direct the gas rearward at 45 degrees and include ports in the top to direct gas straight up. Notably, no gas is directed downward. The ports on the sides are angled at 45 degrees to the rear and increase the recoil reducing effects of the muzzle brake by making the gas move around the tighter corner. The ports on the top of the muzzle brake directing gas up help to suppress muzzle rise and keep the point of aim on the target. This allows the shooter to spot the fall of shot and maintain their aim on the target.

Some muzzle brakes have a central beam running longitudinally along the top of the brake and separating the top ports into left and right vents angled 45 degrees to the vertical. This is important, because, in low light conditions, the blast coming up vertically can interfere with the shooter's sight picture, and the bright flash can ruin the shooter's vision for a short period.

Another common style of muzzle brake is the radial, wherein a cylindrical extension with a large number of spirally arranged holes drilled in, in either a circular or spiral pattern, is fitted to the muzzle. Unfortunately, while visually appealing and trim in profile, this style has only a small effect, if any, on reducing felt recoil. As a rule, the ports are too small to allow a bulk flow of gas to pass through. Further, as the ports are arranged in a spiral fashion, gas is directed down, causing dust,

*Various muzzle brakes: thread-on, clamp-on, and fitted. Be careful with your selection. Some muzzle brakes look great but perform poorly.*

dirt, and grit to be kicked up around the shooter. At the same time, the ports on top of the brake direct blast into the shooter's field of vision, interfering with the sight picture and overall vision quality. Finally, as the ports are drilled into the brake on a 90-degree angle, what gas that does pass through the ports exerts a lesser force on the brake, thereby limiting the recoil reducing potential.

It seems as though this brake has become common, due to the low cost of production, the visual effect of the brake, and ease of installation (it does not have to be indexed to the barrel to ensure it is the correct side up when tightened). However, these factors do not improve accuracy or reduce felt recoil.

Selecting the correct brake for the specific firearm is also very important. Port size is the key issue. A large cartridge with a large powder charge, such as

a .300 Winchester Magnum, will require large ports to allow an adequate volume of gas to escape. If a muzzle brake with small ports is used, the pressure inside the brake will continue to increase until the projectile exits the brake, then the gas will simply follow the projectile out the front, rather than flow through the ports. Conversely, if a muzzle brake with overly large ports is paired with a small cartridge such as .223, the muzzle brake will not work correctly, because there is an insufficient volume of gas to generate the required recoil reducing force before exiting the ports. Although there is a range of mathematical calculations that can be used to determine the perfect brake for a particular firearm, an easier rule of thumb is to avoid the extremes in both cases. For large cartridges, use a large (but not ridiculously so) muzzle brake, the opposite for small cartridges.

Application of muzzle brakes is an important issue when considering their usage. Many shooters don't know when a muzzle brake would be an advantage on their firearm. That said, deciding whether or *not* a muzzle brake is required on the shooter's firearm is a matter principally of personal preference. If the shooter is having trouble holding a sight picture or reacquiring the target directly after the shot, then they may benefit from a brake. For the shooter who has recently begun shooting a larger caliber and has begun to experience a flinch, then a brake may be used as a training tool to eliminate that. Likewise, if the recoil with a particular firearm is simply uncomfortable for the shooter, then the shooter may choose to add a brake.

These choices do need to be measured against the possible degradation of accuracy that adding a brake can produce. This can happen due to changing the way gas exits the bore, and because adding a weight to the end of the barrel affects the natural harmonics that the barrel exhibits during firing.

Another type of muzzle brake can be had by porting the end of the barrel. This method involves drilling or EDM-machining ports through the barrel. While this may be an effective way of braking and one that doesn't require parts to be fitted that may interfere with harmonics of the barrel, it does lead one to question the effects of having a projectile running across the ports and, perhaps, removing metal from that projectile. The effectiveness of porting itself has been questioned by many, as there is only so much metal that can be removed before the integrity of the barrel becomes an issue.

An alternative to the installation of a muzzle brake is to weight the rifle by adding some lead shot embedded in epoxy resin into the butt cavity underneath the buttplate. This will lessen the felt recoil, though at the expense of making the firearm heavier.

Correct cleaning of muzzle brakes is necessary after use. Ideally, the brake should be removed each time the rifle is cleaned. This allows the shooter not only to clean the brake, but also the face of the muzzle. If this is not done properly, it is not uncommon to see a buildup of carbon akin to tar, which will interfere with accuracy. The brake itself is best cleaned by spraying it with a solvent and brushing it out with a toothbrush.

As a final note, muzzle brakes do tend to increase the report from firing. They also direct an uncomfortable shock wave of blast to the sides and rear that can quite happily take the hat off the head of a passerby, hence the banning of muzzle brakes at some ranges.

## SLINGS

A sling is an indispensable part of a shooter's equipment. Traditionally, the sling was intended to be used as a glorified carry handle for a firearm, when traveling. A rifle, for instance could be slung over the shoulder or back, leaving the hands free for other tasks and generally making carriage of the rifle easier. For the shooter who shows ingenuity, however, the humble sling offers methods of stabilizing the shooter and the firearm in almost any shooting position.

There is an almost limitless variety slings, regarding their width, length, and style. Many slings come fitted with a soft pad that is wider than the sling strap. These should be avoided for the purpose of using a sling to steady a shooting position, as the pad interferes with the sling's proper usage. Slings are generally made of leather or nylon. Ideally, they should be at least 1.25 inches wide, be 2.5 times the length between the sling swivels on the firearm and, of course, be adjustable either by a buckle and hooks or by slider. Surplus military web slings make a great general sling and, unlike leather slings, are pretty much care-free, can be machine washed, if necessary, and tend not to stretch.

The most basic sling is the loop sling. These slings are generally 1.5 to two times the length between the sling swivels and serve jointly as a carrying sling and a useful stabilizing sling. These slings are not really long enough to use as a full stabilizing sling, though a hasty sling position (which will be discussed later), is easily employed, generally without adjusting the sling from its carrying position.

Looking beyond the basic sling, we have the target sling. Originally designed for the military and heavily

*Slings have evolved alongside rifle technology, from basic straps of material to adjustable quick-release varieties.*

adopted by hunters and competition shooters, these slings are multi-loop in design, sometimes with sections made up from different sling material, and are highly adjustable. They are intended to be used both from a hasty position and from the target position (again, to be discussed later). In use, they are released from the rear sling swivel and reconnected to either the front swivel or a middle swivel, thus forming a shorter loop that the shooter passes their arm through and, so, achieves stability. There are several methods for doing this, and the target slings are generally accommodating of all of them. Interestingly, they have no application in carrying the rifle, except in an improvised sense.

The final type of sling is known as a cuff sling. This sling is similar to the target sling, with the exception that the loop the shooter uses to stabilize the rifle is permanently attached to one end of the sling and detachable from the other. This allows the shooter to use the sling for carriage and the hasty sling position, and then, very quickly, unclip the rear of the cuff or arm loop for immediate use as a target sling. These slings can also be used in the prone supported position or when benchrest shooting, when the secondary hand is used underneath the butt. Some cuff slings have a loop attached to the shooter's arm or wrist with Velcro and which is separate from the sling. Then, when the shooter wishes to use the sling for stabilizing purposes, they simply connect a quick-release buckle on the arm loop to the sling itself. This provides a fast and simple solution to getting into and out of a sling position.

Looking at sling positions, the shooter can employ the hasty position, the target position, and the loop or cuff position. It should be noted that any sling position can be used in any shooting position and will most definitely improve the stability of that shooting position. It must also be noted that the sling can be used in conjunction with a bipod and monopod and should be so done whenever possible.

The hasty position has the benefit of being able to be used with essentially any sling and, for snap shooting deployment and for hunters, is probably the position of choice. The shooter on a hunt, for instance, can even move around with the sling already in this position.

To adopt the hasty position, the shooter, while gripping the wrist or pistol grip with the trigger hand, slips the secondary hand through the loop of the sling and underneath the forearm, allowing the elbow or just above it to come in contact with the sling. The secondary hand then slides down the forearm towards the primary hand, tightening the sling. If the sling is too long for the slack to be taken up, then passing the secondary hand through the loop a second time can be done, in effect creating a second loop wrapped around that arm.

In the target sling position, the shooter releases the rear of the sling and reconnects it to the middle or front swivel. From there, while gripping the wrist or pistol grip with the trigger hand, the shooter slips the secondary hand through the loop of the sling and underneath the forearm, then brings the secondary hand down and around and passes it through the loop of the sling again. After having shouldered the rifle, the shooter then tightens the sling through a combination of moving the elbow out and the secondary hand back and forth. The shooter should be applying positive pressure onto the forearm of the stock, while at the same time applying positive pressure to the sling through the secondary arm and elbow, which in turn pulls on the forearm of the stock. These balancing forces are what assist in stabilization.

The loop sling is employed in a similar fashion, but there is no tightening through movement of the secondary arm. The length of the loop or position of the cuff is set as part of a pre-shoot or pre-hunt setup. This allows the shooter, in the case of a loop sling, to simply detach the rear end of the loop and pass the secondary arm through it to just past the elbow. It doesn't matter which way the loop is oriented, so long as it's not twisted. The secondary arm is then rotated towards the rifle and placed against the forearm of the stock.

The cuff sling is even easier. With this one, the shooter simply detaches the loop or strap from the

*The sling helps to brace the rifle by creating two more points of stability to the shooter. The shooter can tighten and loosen the sling brace, just by moving their hand on the fore-end.*

rear of the sling and attaches it to the cuff on the shooter's arm. Presto!

There is one slight difference in the application of the loop or cuff sling in the prone positions. Because, as a rule, the secondary hand will be placed underneath the butt of the rifle when shooting prone, the shooter needs to utilize these slings differently. Where otherwise the sling would be placed so that it contacted the shooter's secondary hand above the elbow, in the prone positions, the sling needs to contact the shooter's secondary arm just *below* the elbow. The elbow is then bent to the rear, and the shooter's secondary hand is placed underneath the gun's butt. This gives the sling a very steady anchor point in the crook of the elbow, and it also allows the shooter to use their secondary hand underneath the butt to make changes in elevation or manipulate a sandbag or monopod. A further benefit is that, when the sling is set correctly, the length of the loop will not need to be adjusted between the two different methods, making it just as easy to use in either and switch between them!

Two final types of specialized slings should be mentioned. They are the three-point and single-point slings.

Another creation intended for military usage, the three-point sling is comprised of a conventional sling, but with two points roughly at one-third the distance from each end of the sling and having quick-release buckles. These buckles attach to another large loop that passes around the torso, over the shoulder of the secondary arm, and under the primary arm of the shooter. The three points of contact are one at each end of the simple sling attached to the rifle, plus a third at the point of contact of the butt with the shooter's shoulder. This sling does offer excellent stability when shooting offhand in the standing, kneeling, or sitting positions, particularly in rapid-fire sequences. However its usefulness is limited when already supported, and it is not usable when prone. It also allows for very good carriage, promoting fast shouldering and stabilization for a snap shot on a hunt, while also leaving the hands free for using a GPS or, heaven forbid, a map and compass, if anyone still knows how to use them (and you should)!

The single-point sling is exactly as the name suggests and is a simplification of the three-point sling. It is comprised of a strap that attaches to the rifle at a midpoint on it, generally on one of the sides, with a quick-release buckle that attaches to a large loop that

*Shooting sticks can be purchased or simply created in the field.*

is the same as the large loop used on the three-point sling. This sling really only provides convenience and is not as stable as a three-point sling, but a single-point sling can be used more easily in supported positions, and it can be used in the prone position, with adjustment.

It should be noted that slings have wide-ranging applications. For instance, slings can be detached and strung between two points in a blind in order to provide a shooting rest. They can be hung from a point on a tree or from a tree hook, and then attached to the forearm, or the rifle can be slipped through a small loop at the end and provide a mobile shooting rest. A sling can also be looped around a tree limb when in a treestand, to achieve greater stability. The options really are limitless, and if the shooter can only afford one shooting accessory, that shooter is best served with a sling.

## SHOOTING STICKS

Shooting sticks and their use were originally pioneered by skiers who used their ski poles, held near the top together in the secondary hand and with the bottoms of the poles splayed out, to create a small "V" at the top into which the forearm of a rifle was placed. This technique has since been adopted by hunters, particularly backpack hunters and turkey hunters, who value light weight in their travels and whom often shoot from standing or sitting positions.

Today, shooting sticks can be made to virtually any length, some incorporating a leather thong at the top that can be wound around where the sticks cross to provide extra support. Traditionally made from wood, they are now also made from carbon fiber in the same way that hiking sticks are made, with built-in hand grips, wrist loops, and shock absorbers. Shooting sticks can also be made into sections that connect to form a single walking stick, or be made telescoping so that the one set of shooting sticks can be set at different heights to compensate for uneven terrain much in the same way a bipod performs.

Some shooters have incorporated a third stick attached to the other two at the cross point, creating a tripod that, although highly effective, does detract from the adaptability of shooting sticks generally. It should also be noted that shooting sticks can be used in conjunction with a sling, which is important, given that shooting sticks need to be used in sitting, kneeling, or standing positions. Finally, shooting sticks are a valuable shooting accessory that can be made at home (or even in the field, with a good knife), are very light weight, and can provide a standing, kneeling, or sitting shooting rest with which to clear shooting lane obstructions.

## SAND SOCKS

A sand sock is another invaluable piece of shooting equipment that can be used in any of the supported positions. A sand sock is exactly as the name suggests, that being a large, thick sock filled with fine sand. (When possible, the sand should first be placed in a plastic bag, otherwise the sand will work its way out.) Although sand is specified, any material will do, provided it is dense and will allow the weight to be applied to it without collapsing. Too, although a sock is specified, any sturdy and flexible material can be used.

The sand sock basically has two uses. First is under the fore-end of the rifle, perhaps to provide a soft interface against some environmental support. Second is when a bipod or other support is used in the prone position and the sand sock is placed under the butt to provide a third point of stability and prevent lateral swing.

Looking at using a sand sock underneath the fore-end, it is critically important *not* to use hard support against the hard material of the fore-end, as this will amplify any movements on the part of the shooter and transfer them to the point of aim. A sand sock can be used to act as a shock absorber, simply by laying it on the base support and then working the fore-end back and forth to create a "V" in the sand sock. This will allow the rifle to be properly supported, resisting canting, and can also be used to compensate for base support that isn't flat by simply manipulating the sock until it forms a

*Squeeze the sand sock to lower elevation (raise the buttstock and tilt the muzzle down), relax to raise it.*

wedge shape against the support. A further advantage is that, as the firearm recoils during firing, the rifle will slide backwards in the sock's "V" and then can be run forward into almost exactly the same position, thereby increasing consistency.

Using a sand sock under the butt of the stock when shooting from the prone supported position fulfills the same shock-absorbing role as a sand sock under the fore-end, but, when used with a bipod at the fore-end, the sand sock allows the butt to be supported by the ground as well as the shooter's shoulder. This creates a third point of contact with the ground in much the same way as a monopod, greatly increasing stability and serving to eliminate the lateral swing in the point of aim experienced with bipods. Further, with a sand sock in this position, small changes in elevation of the point of aim can be set by simply squeezing or releasing the sand sock.

A final use for a sand sock (or, preferably, a sandbag), is to place one hard against the front or rear of a bipod. This will improve stability over a bipod alone and also serves to anchor the bipod to the ground to resist movement through recoil.

The only real disadvantage of a sand sock can be its weight. This is exacerbated with a bigger sandbag. This is a serious consideration to hunters, as they're generally impractical to tote in the field. There are custom-made sand socks available that have belt clips, but these aren't particularly practical, either, in having a weight swinging from the shooter's hips and catching on things while trying to hunt. A better solution is a sand sock with a zipper, which allows the shooter to fill the sock using sand or dirt found at a particular shooting position.

## COSINE INDICATORS

When shooting uphill or downhill, shooters will notice that the projectile always strikes high, a confusing proposition for most shooters. This is a simple matter of physics and gravity. A projectile fired at a target on level ground 1,000 meters away travels across 1,000 meters of the Earth's surface. More correctly, it travels 1,000 meters horizontally (broadly) through the earth's gravity field. The same projectile fired at the same target but one on a 30-degree incline (uphill or downhill) travels only 866 meters across the earth's surface and, therefore, is exposed to 866 meter's "worth" of gravity, even though the projectile still travels 1,000 actual meters to the target.

This solution and compensation is calculable by multiplying the range to the target by the cosine of the uphill/downhill angle. The shooter then calculates the drop for the shot based on this figure, rather than the actual range to the target. It is important to note that, as the angle increases, the effect increases exponentially, leading to a relatively small affect on ballistics at a shallow angle of five degrees (0.004-percent ballistic correction), to a large effect at 15 degrees (3.4-percent ballistic correction). This is the crux of the cosine rule to uphill/downhill shooting. The greater the angle, the greater the compensation required.

There are several tools to assist shooters in shooting correctly in such situations, not only in assessing the angle, but also in calculating the required compensation. The simplest tool is a laser rangefinder that incorporates a true ballistic range readout. These rangefinders will show the actual distance to target and provide a second range reading incorporating

*Shooting uphill and downhill can drastically affect the elevation of a shot. Incorrect calculations here will make all shots go high! Cosine indicators take the guesswork out of determining this effect.*

the compensation for any uphill/downhill angle (the true ballistic range), which the shooter would use to calculate the drop for the shot.

Another very simple tool to use is the cosine indicator. This is a small dial gauge that attaches to the scope or the scope mount and is comprised of a needle and ladder scale. The left-hand side shows the uphill/downhill angle the firearm rests on. The right-hand side displays the number the shooter must multiply by the range in order to obtain the true ballistic range, or cosine, of that angle. Noting that the effects of cosine shooting only become noticeable at longer ranges and/or steeper angles,

the shooter should consider their own shooting needs before employing these tools.

## LEVEL INDICATORS

A level indicator is a small spirit level that attaches to either the scope or the scope mount. It will show if the rifle is being canted when shouldered. Many shooters are unaware that, if the rifle is held on an angle, the scope becomes offset vertically from the bore of the rifle and is lowered to the bore. This will most definitely affect the point of impact, displacing it left or right and lowering it. Some sources state that the formula for calculating the error is the

*Spirit levels come in many forms—rail-mounted, scope tube-mounted, and even built into some scopes' reticles. For reliability in fitting, however, the shooter cannot do better than the basic rail-mounted models.*

bullet drop for the particular range multiplied by the tangent (abbreviated as "tan") of the cant angle. The error at long range (1,000 meters) for a fine canting (five degrees or so) will be measured in feet.

Although this will get you into the ballpark, it does not consider the vertical error canting introduces into the ballistic equation by effectively lowering the scope tube to the bore. Suffice it to say, although calculating the error accurately is one thing, it is far better not to have the error at all.

A spirit level preferably attached to the scope mount will help the shooter monitor the canting and correct any such deviation before firing. There are spirit levels that attach to the scope tube, but they require the scope tube to be mounted perfectly level (which should be the case in anyway), and that the spirit level is mounted level to the tube and to the rifle as a whole. This can lead to the multiplication of small mounting errors. A spirit level that attaches to the scope mount can really only go on one way and, provided the scope base is level, the spirit level will be accurate.

The other benefit of scope base-mounted spirit levels is that they help train shooters to keep both eyes open. In fact, the shooter can aim through the scope with one eye, while the other eye focuses on the spirit level.

## SCOPE DOPES AND RETRACTABLE BALLISTIC CHARTS

It is very important for the shooter to have their ballistics information at their fingertips. Scope dopes and retractable ballistic charts allow the shooter to record their ballistics information and attach it to the firearm in such a manner than it can be accessed and read while in a shooting position.

The scope dope is a small disk of plastic that can be written on and then placed inside the eyepiece lens

cover. When the lens cover is flipped up, the information can be read; in the case of detachable scope covers, the data are nearby or attached to the scope.

Retractable ballistics charts are a spring-loaded strip of light-gauge steel that rolls up and is fitted to a scope ring. When the shooter needs the information, the shooter need only use their secondary hand to pull out the chart from its rolled-up position. Once the information has been read, the chart will automatically retract itself. The retractable ballistics charts offer an advantage over the scope dope disk, in that far more information can be recorded. Either way, by having the information available to the shooter while they are in the shooting position, the shooter can engage targets far more quickly and with less movement to upset position, breathing, and trigger control—not to mention that big buck standing on the next hill over!

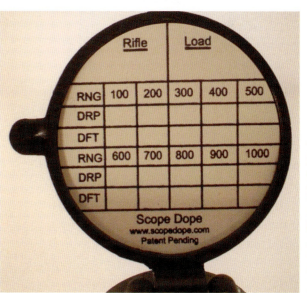

PHOTO COURTESY SCOPE DOPE

*It's one thing to have ballistics data, it's another to have it at your fingertips. Both items here allow the shooter to use their hard-earned data without leaving their shooting position.*

*Field and range accessories make the job of hitting the bull or buck that little bit easier!*

## FIELD AND RANGE ACCESSORIES

These are items that, although not directly related to the firearms, can assist the shooter in improving accuracy. These accessories allow the shooter to improve accuracy by being able to better gauge and assess weather conditions, develop better ballistic solutions for long-range shots, or simply make the shooter more comfortable in the shooting position. Although these accessories won't make up for poor technique, they will allow the shooter to get the most out of the shooting equipment they have.

## BINOCULARS

A binocular is an excellent observational tool and fulfills a completely different role to that of a rifle scope. The strength of a binocular is not in its magnification, but in the width of its field of view and the stereoscopic nature of the image produced when looking through it. A binocular, in particular, allows the shooter to view a target area with a very wide field of view.

The wide field of view allows the shooter to visually cover a lot of ground quickly, and this is of particular importance to hunters. A wide field of view also allows the shooter too "see" the wind. For example, scanning over a grassy field or past a multitude of range flags, gusts and wind strength can be better identified. Also, both tasks generally require the shooter to look through the binocular for a longer period of time. Most shooters would agree that looking through a rifle scope for any real length of time is exceptionally tiring and results in eye strain. A binocular, on the other hand, because of its dual eye system, is far less straining to the eyes, thus observation can be carried out  longer.

A binocular allows the shooter to scan their shooting area, either for targets in the field or to determine the conditions on the range, all without the eye strain experienced with extended use of a rifle scope.

There are many types of binoculars available on the market, with differing magnifications. For hunting and competition, 8x30 models tend to offer the best compromise between magnification, exit pupil diameter, field of view, and weight. That said, many shooters will opt for 7x50 binoculars for their extra-large exit pupil diameter, which leads to a brighter image.

There are specialist binoculars available, such as stabilized units, that contain a gyroscope that dampens the shaky image that is sometimes characterized by larger magnification powers. There are also binoculars that contain a laser rangefinder. Although both advances assist the shooter, their cost and weight can be prohibitive.

## SPOTTING SCOPES

The spotting scope serves a different purpose than that of a rifle scope. In fact, the spotting scope is generally not even used by the shooter, but rather by their spotter. Spotting scopes are characterized by high magnification and a large objective lens, and they are usually mounted on a small camera tripod.

The purpose of the spotting scope is exactly as its name suggests—it is well known that the spotting scope enables the spotter to call or spot the fall of shot and so provide feedback to the shooter as to the point of impact and any corrections needed for the next shot. The spotting scope also enables the shooter to determine the distance to the target (in most cases), as well as assess the wind conditions and speed both at the target and *en route* by looking for environmental indicators and mirage. Such an optic also permits the spotter to track the projectile in the air by seeing the "vortice," or spiral of condensed water vapor that follows a spinning projectile in flight.

## LASER RANGEFINDERS

A laser rangefinder is a tool that combines optical magnification and a laser, so that the shooter can focus on a distant target and then, using the laser,

Simple spotting scopes allow the shooter's spotting partner to see the fall of the shot and assist in creating a ballistics solution.

PHOTO COURTESY BURRIS COMPANY, INC.

determine the range to the target. Laser rangefinders come in all shapes and sizes and are generally priced on the maximum distance they are capable of measuring. Laser rangefinders work by firing an invisible laser beam to the target and then measuring the amount of time it takes for the reflection of the laser beam to return to the unit.

Laser rangefinders have a number of other functions. For instance, by taking two range readings on a target that is moving, target speed can be determined. Likewise, some laser rangefinders have a built-in level, so that, if the range to an uphill or downhill target is measured, the true range to target can be displayed alongside the ballistic range.

Rangefinders do have certain limitations. Strong sunlight can reduce the maximum range that can be measured. Further, some targets are difficult to range, because they do not reflect the laser beam sufficiently well for the rangefinder to receive it. Good examples of this are game animals and pine trees.

When using a laser rangefinder, the shooter should seek to range flat, shiny targets. This contrasts severely with the natural environment in which a hunter would normally find themselves. A good alternative is to range objects that are near to or at a similar viewed distance to the actual target, then apply that range measurement to the actual target. In any event, it is always advisable to take several ranges to the same target. This ensures that the reading is consistent and correct.

Another form of rangefinder is the lenstatic type. This type is an older, handheld rangefinder that works not with laser beams, but by aligning two different images on top of each other and then reading the range off a scale. These rangefinders are excellent out to medium ranges and are very convenient and cheap.

*Small size, but a big punch. Laser rangefinders are essential for making long shots connect.*

While they do require regular calibration with a known distance, they do serve as an excellent backup or the perfect tool for a backpack hunter on a budget.

## COMPASSES

The humble compass, normally used in navigation, can be used to better assess the conditions for a long-range shot. By taking a bearing to the target and to the wind, the shooter can define a more accurate windage solution for their shot. Further, the use of a compass and more correctly knowing the magnetic direction of the shot will assist the shooter in calculating any error introduced by the Coriolis effect, or rotation of the Earth, which will be discussed later.

## GPS UNITS

The GPS, or global positioning system, is a series of satellites orbiting the Earth that can pinpoint the latitude, longitude, and elevation of a GPS receiver. A GPS not only allows the shooter to navigate and assist in calculation of the error created by the Coriolis effect, it allows the shooter to calculate more accurate ballistic solutions by knowing the altitude of the firing position and the target. Finally, a GPS used in conjunction with a map can allow a shooter to estimate the range to the target, by plotting the position of the target and measuring the distance between it and the shooter.

## PDA UNITS

A PDA, or personal data assistant, is basically a lightweight, palm-sized computer not much bigger than a wallet. Although sounding like an incredibly gimmicky item, when correctly used with ballistics software, it is a valuable and important shooting tool, particularly for long-range shooting. The PDA allows the shooter to do three very important things. First, it stores information. Second, it calculates data. And third, it assesses and compares data.

The PDA allows the shooter to store all the ballistically important information about their firearms and ammunition, such as muzzle velocity, projectile weight, and ballistic coefficient, sight height above the bore line, and the original atmospheric

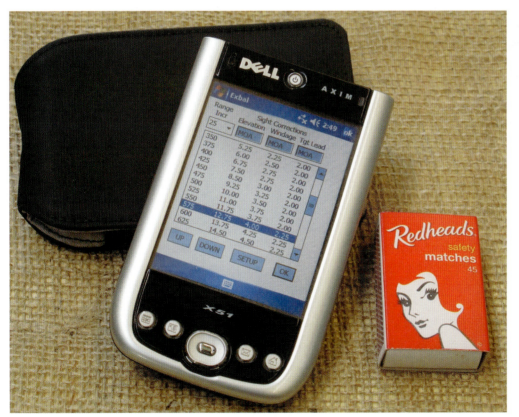

*Not much bigger than a box of matches, a PDA with ballistics software is perfect for on-the-spot shot solutions!*

conditions under which the firearm was zeroed. All this information is used to calculate real-time ballistic solutions for medium- to long-range shots. This brings us to the second use of PDAs, which is to calculate ballistic solutions.

Most shooters rely on range data cards containing a table of ranges and drop values for their firearm and ammunition, or at least an average based on their ammunition. The shooter looks up the range, cross-references the associated drop value, and adjusts their scope. While this is an okay method and can work accurately, the PDA offers the shooter a computerized, real-time range data card corrected for the exact atmospheric conditions of the day and for the exact ballistics of the firearm and ammunition. Further, this information can be fine-tuned again, by inputting real-world results over the computer-generated solution, combining the two to form a adjusted and near-perfect ballistic equation for the firearm and ammunition. When used correctly, the shooter ends up with a perfect data card for the day, every time they go into the field on a hunt or onto the range for a competition. Further, the shooter can calculate values such as the point-blank range for a given target size (the zero range at which the rise and drop of the projectile trajectory will fall within a particular target size), spin-drift effect (the effect of a spinning projectile moving in the direction of spin), and Coriolis effect (projectile drift caused by the rotation of the Earth).

Finally, the PDA allows the shooter to compare data and assess data. Here the shooter looks at similarities and differences in the ballistic qualities of different cartridges and loadings, assesses changes in zero with the use of different ammunition, and sees the effect of change in altitude on the zero for a particular firearm and ammunition.

## HANDHELD WEATHER STATIONS

Handheld weather stations are a relatively modern, lightweight and convenient, pocket-sized device that provides crucial environmental data for calculating long-range ballistic solutions. Although there are several brands available and different models to choose from, most will provide the minimum, maximum, and average wind speed, barometric pressure, relative humidity, air temperature, and altitude. This data, when combined with a PDA and ballistics software, is capable of providing extremely accurate solutions. That said, for the shooter who doesn't use a PDA, being able to measure the wind speed at the firing point exactly will provide a much better opportunity for calculating windage. For the shooter who uses a manual range data card, the data provided by the handheld weather station can be compared against the conditions in effect when the range data card was developed, to correct for the current conditions in the field.

## DRAG MATS

A drag mat combines the benefits of a shoulder-carried rifle soft case with a shooting mat. Drag mats are generally made from heavy canvas or 1,000-denier nylon for durability, and are heavily padded to protect the shooter and the firearm. Internally, drag mats are made up of three large panels that fold and zip to form the bag and contain pockets for notebooks, PDAs, and other equipment, as well as ammunition loops and straps for securing the firearm within the drag mat. When the shooter has reached their firing point, the mat, which has been shouldered like a back pack or dragged behind the shooter, is unzipped and opened, exposing the rifle and a large (generally four-foot by three-foot) padded mat with a two-foot by three-foot sheet extension for the shooter's feet.

The benefit of a drag mat is that it allows the shooter to move into a position quickly and easily after hiking, knowing that the rifle is protected in case of a fall and keeping the hands free if the terrain is difficult during the hike. Once in position, the shooter is able to adopt their shooting position comfortably on virtually any terrain—a rarity in the field! This is equally important at a range, where the shooter takes up a position either on a grassy mound or on a concrete slab. The absence of twigs jabbing the shooter in the hips and sharp stones getting under

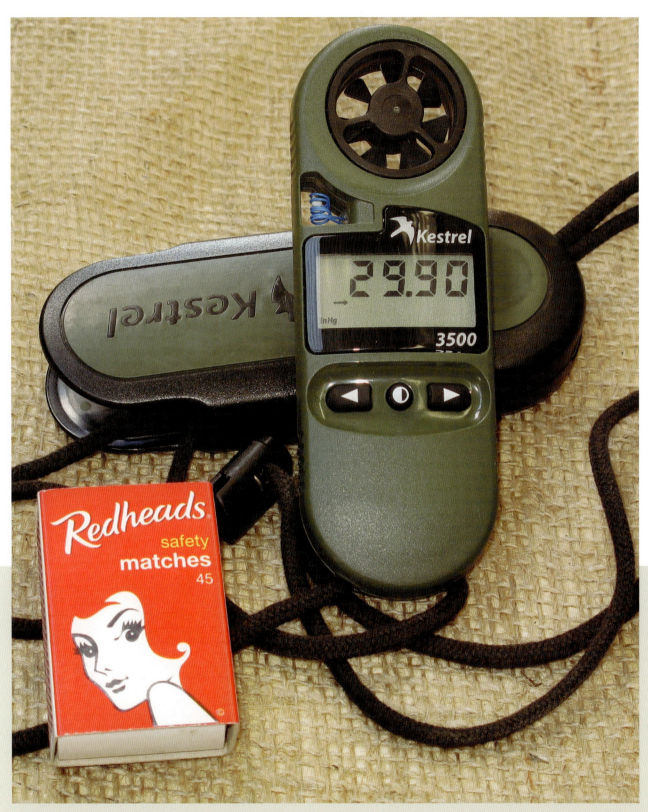

*No more guessing and Kentucky windage. Live weather data is available in this simple, handheld weather station.*

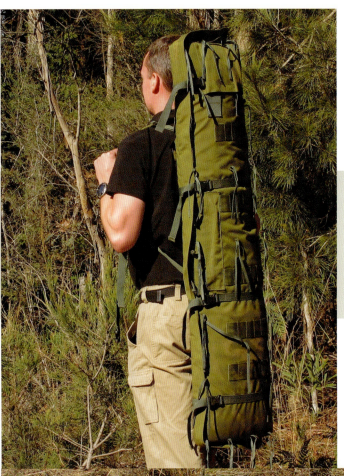

*Designed for comfort and adaptability, modern drag mats make transport and shooting more comfortable—not to mention that, with all the pockets available, the shooter can store all their essentials in the one bag.*

the elbows assists the shooter in their concentration, and also assists the shooter in not moving between shots, due to discomfort after recoil. Finally, the use of the padded drag mat will enable the shooter to remain in the shooting position for much longer. This is especially important for long competition serials or a long wait during a hunting ambush.

## DATA BOOKS

A data book is far more useful than most shooters believe. It is a place for the shooter to record performance information, not just on the rifle and ammunition, but also on themselves. Each time the shooter attends the range or goes into the field, they should record the atmospheric conditions, such as wind speed and direction, altitude, barometric pressure, relative humidity, and the angle and range to the target. The shooter should also record the ammunition type or handload recipe used, along with the lot or batch number of that ammunition. Finally, the shooter records the actual points of impact, either as a group size and deviation from the point of aim, or graphically, where the rounds hit the target.

This information sounds long-winded and annoying to record. It is. However, over time, the shooter will build a performance profile of their rifle, their ammunition, and themselves. The shooter will know, for instance, that there is a 1 MOA change-up in the point of impact when switching from the prone to the kneeling position, due to changes in the way the rifle is held, that the accuracy of their rifle drops off after 20 rounds due to fouling, and that the first shot, being cold, will impact 2 MOA left. This type of information, which can only be collected, not calculated, allows the shooter to fine-tune their shooting to suit the firearm and ammunition.

The data book provides an excellent opportunity for the shooter to analyze their shooting, with the results

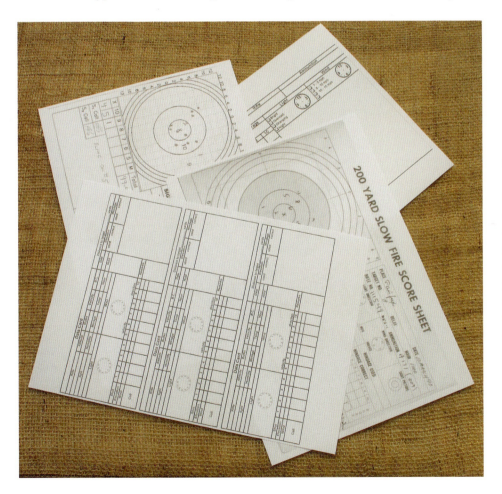

*Data books exist for the shooter to keep track of the performance of their rifle and ammunition. Reading back over them, the shooter can match up past experiences with present conditions and make corrections for odd situations that would otherwise result in a miss.*

of their performance in black and white highlighting areas of deficiency where improvements can be made and areas that the shooter is clearly competent in.

## CHRONOGRAPHS

A chrony, or chronograph, is a device that measures the velocity of projectiles by detecting the projectile's movement between two points. This is very simple, but the use of the information the shooter gains is quite complex.

At its simplest, the shooter knows the speed of their projectiles, an essential figure in even the most rudimentary ballistic equations. With this information, the shooter can make accurate predictions on the trajectory and drop of the projectiles. The shooter can also use the chronograph to work out the extreme spread of velocities, noting that it is very rare for all the fired projectiles in a group to leave the muzzle at exactly the same speed. The extreme spread will give the shooter a minimum and maximum velocity for

their chosen ammunition in their rifle and will then allow the shooter to calculate the vertical spread for points of impact at medium to long ranges, given that a large proportion of a group's vertical size is due to inconsistencies in the ammunition used and the muzzle velocity achieved.

The shooter can also calculate the standard deviation across their ammunition. This will allow the shooter to gauge the average amount of dispersion from the average muzzle velocity for each round. This figure can be used for the tuning of handloads, finding that sweet spot in terms of powder charge with a given case, projectile, and primer that offers the minimum standard deviation of velocity and dispersion of group size and, therefore, the greatest accuracy. Without a chronograph, the shooter will be hard-pressed to assess the ballistic qualities and calculate trajectories of their ammunition, whether they be handloads or commercial loads, and, so, will essentially be barred from fine-tuning their handloads.

*Chronographs are a fantastic tool for ballistics analysis, but be careful. When testing for velocity, it is not a hard thing to accidentally shoot your own chronograph, as the author has done here!*

# Part II: The Ammunition

# CHAPTER EIGHT

# Overview

Ammunition and its correct selection, storage, or handloading is the second primary component of accurate shooting. There is an old adage that states "you are what you eat," and the same applies to shooting. Many shooters believe that any old stuff that goes bang is good enough. Unfortunately it is not. A firearm will produce groups only as good as the ammunition the shooter feeds it.

There are many types of ammunition available to the shooter, ranging from surplus military ammunition to budget hunting ammunition, premium hunting ammunition, and premium match or target ammunition. All these types are based on averages, coupled with particular specifications, for instance, in the case of hunting ammunition, a soft-point or ballistic tip bullet backed by enough powder to get it up to speed in a standard barrel, with a primer to suit and in the ammunition manufacturer's own case. The shooter with a sharp eye will see that this is an ammunition recipe suited to no rifle in particular, but one that should be fine in most.

As a rule, regular commercial ammunition is capable of producing 1 MOA to 3 MOA accuracy, which is perfectly fine for regular hunting. Surplus ammunition, on the other hand, is very much a mixed bag, when it comes to accuracy. In fact, the quality of surplus ammunition is generally less reliant on the style and load than it is on how the ammunition has been stored for the last 40 or so years! Surplus ammunition that has been stored correctly and then returned to service should deliver accuracy commensurate with regular commercial ammunition. Surplus ammunition that has sweated on the docks in Pakistan for a couple of decades and is corroded, dented, and discolored may not even fire!

Match ammunition tends to be more finely tuned or an adaptation of a tuned military specification. As such, it is capable of producing better accuracy, generally in the region of 1 MOA or less.

For the shooter who wants the optimum from their equipment and themselves, handloading is the way to go. Handloading is the science and art of taking separate ammunition components and assembling them into loaded ammunition, individually and with great care and accuracy. Handloading, however, does not end with a completed round of ammunition. The ammunition is then tested in the firearm

*With the myriad choices available between factory-loaded ammunition and handloading, it's a real game of chess for the shooter looking for the perfect load!*

for which it is intended, and the recipe is adjusted until the greatest level of accuracy is achieved. In essence, the shooter creates specific ammunition suited specifically for a single firearm. Regardless the precision one takes in reloading, realize that the act alone is not the "silver bullet" for accuracy, when it comes to either a poorly maintained firearm or a shooter who lacks good technique.

## CONDITION

Most shooters don't recognize that ammunition should be cared for in the same way a firearm is cared for. Ammunition should be inspected and checked before usage, must be stored correctly and, for ammunition that has been in storage for some time, a procedure for readying the ammunition for usage should be carried out. By carrying out these tasks, the shooter is ensuring that their ammunition is not only safe, but also reliable and consistent. This puts the ammunition in the best shooting condition possible.

When inspecting the condition of ammunition, the shooter must consider the exterior condition of the case, primer, and projectile, and also the internal condition of the components, including the powder charge. Let's start with the exterior.

Beginning at the case, the shooter looks for dings, dents, cracks, and scratches in the brass, indicating possible mechanical damage. Dings and dents if small and not deep are acceptable in the case of surplus ammunition. Modern commercial ammunition should not have these defects, although, if found this way, most are acceptable for shooting. Scratches, if not deep, can be acceptable, but cracks in any part of the case are not. Cracks are generally found in the case neck, particularly in surplus ammunition, where the case has been reloaded, perhaps several times, without annealing or softening of the case neck. Fitting of a new projectile will eventually cause the work-hardened neck of such a case to expand and crack.

A close inspection of the web that runs from the base of the case should be done. Bright bands of color or other distortion could indicate a thinning of the case wall. Such a situation may cause a case head separation, which can be very serious, when fired.

When looking at the primer, the shooter needs to ensure it is level in the primer pocket, tight, and not deformed. Any sign of corrosion in the area of the primer is cause for concern and could indicate that the cartridge may fail to fire.

When inspecting the projectile, the shooter needs to ensure that the projectile is firmly fitted into the case neck, without any gaps; if there is a crimp at the case neck, that crimp must be tight and uniform. A loose projectile will allow moisture to get to the powder and may cause a misfire, or at least lead to poor ignition and burn rate of the powder charge.

The projectile should not show any deep scratches or scoring. The tip of the projectile should also be straight and not hammered, or flattened, at the very tip. Projectiles that have this structural damage are essentially safe to fire, but accuracy will be diminished.

Having completed the exterior examination, the shooter needs to assess the interior of the cartridge. Although the shooter can invest in a kinetic bullet puller and pull the projectiles from a couple cartridges to examine the powder and interior of the case and the primer, it's not really necessary. Given that powder and primers are really only affected by moisture (and this is relatively undetectable by visual examination), the shooter is best served by examining the packaging for evidence of moisture. For instance, if the ammunition is stored in a rusty old ammunition can in the back garden shed, it's far more likely that moisture will be a problem, as opposed to the same ammunition that has been stored in a dry, heated basement.

## AMMUNITION STORAGE

Correct storage of ammunition is not only a matter of safety, but a matter of preserving the accuracy characteristics of the ammunition. Ammunition is best stored at a constant temperature, in a moisture-free environment, and out of the light.

An example of good ammunition storage, putting aside any legal requirements, would be in a closed metal container with a desiccant satchel, that container placed on top of a water heater. The combined effects of constant, near room temperature from the water heater coupled with the desiccant pack will keep the ammunition dry and free of water vapor, and the closed box will keep it out of the light. Ammunition stored in this way will retain its accuracy characteristics for decades, and the powder and primer will not deteriorate at an accelerated rate.

Examples of poor storage would be having loose ammunition in the pouch of a hunting backpack or in a damp garage. Too, exposure to the summer sun as ammo sits on a windowsill would be bad choice. That said, ammunition stored in this way will still take some time to deteriorate.

## RETURNING STORED AMMUNITION TO SERVICE

Using ammunition that has been in storage for more than a year should be specially treated to return the ammunition to service. This is particularly important for military surplus ammunition that may have sat undisturbed for many years.

The first thing to do with stored ammunition is to bring it out of its storage receptacle and expose it to constant room temperature, preferably for at least 24 hours. This will begin the process of driving moisture off the ammunition. The shooter can also carry out their initial external ammunition inspection at this stage, discarding rounds that appear to be unsafe.

The next step is to lightly agitate the ammunition. This is done because, over time, powder tends to clump together, forming clusters. This has the affect of altering the burn rate of the powder. By lightly agitating the ammunition, the clusters can be broken back down into their individual grains.

The best way to agitate the ammunition is to tumble it for about five minutes—no longer. If the ammunition is agitated for longer, the shooter runs the risk of breaking up individual grains. This will

*Ammunition needs to be stored correctly and inspected before firing. Poorly stored or manufactured ammunition can range from unreliable to downright dangerous.*

decrease the grain size, which, in turn, increases the burn rate, leading to higher chamber pressures and danger.

Having inspected the ammunition, driven off the moisture, and broken down any grain clusters in the powder charge, the ammunition is ready to fire. That said, it is a good idea to preheat the ammunition directly before firing, so as to equalize the burn rates between cartridges. The best way of doing this is to simply keep the ammunition in a pocket close to the body. The shooter should only use body heat for preheating ammunition, as the heat delivered is mild and even. Placing ammunition in front of a mechanical heater is never a good idea!

# CHAPTER NINE

# Projectiles

The current array of projectiles both in weight and style can be bewildering to most shooters, when choosing loaded commercial ammunition or bullets for use in handloads. Projectiles generally take the form of a lead (or similar metal) core, surrounded by a copper jacket, with their ballistic characteristics defined by their shape and weight. That shape and weight are simplified into a "ballistic coefficient" (how well they fly) and their terminal ballistics (how they perform on impact, important to hunters).

Before discussing styles and ballistic coefficients, it should be noted that different projectiles are made to different standards. As such, there can be great variance in the weights and balance of the same projectiles from some manufacturers, while other manufacturers go to great lengths to ensure their projectiles weigh and balance the same. That said, it is the individual features of projectiles that really distinguish them from each other. These features generally relate to the style of tip and the style of base.

Looking at the styles of tip available, soft-point, round-nose, pointed soft-point, hollow-point, open tip, full metal jacket, and ballistic tip are the styles most in use. Let's look more closely at each.

## PROJECTILE TIPS

The round-nose profile is a very old style of projectile, one generally reserved for large-caliber firearms and low-velocity cartridges. These projectiles tend to be fairly dirty, in terms of their ballistic coefficient (they are low in this number), but their terminal ballistics tend to be devastating on large game, where the projectile has time to slow down without breaking up, thus delivering the maximum amount of energy to the target.

Soft-point projectiles tend to use a spitzer (pointed) projectile with the very tip of the jacket removed and the lead core extended to the flat tip. This style of tip is designed to mushroom quickly upon impact with a target, though at the expense of ballistic coefficiency. These tips tend to be used by budget ammunition manufacturers.

Pointed soft-points are a development of the soft-point tip, with the lead core allowed to flow out of the jacket to form a pointed lead tip. This does have the effect of improving the ballistic coefficient, though the soft lead tips are extremely susceptible to damage and can be deformed before firing, ruining both the ballistic coefficient and the consistency between projectiles.

A particular problem with pointed soft-points occurs in firearms that have a magazine. In the magazine, the cartridges will "surge," i.e., the cartridges push forward during firing, impacting the forward face of the magazine. This tends to flatten, twist, and damage the pointed soft-points before firing.

Looking at full metal jacket (FMJ) tips, these projectiles are generally a hangover from military production. They are characterized by a spitzer shape and pointed tip and by having a complete jacket that is not open to the core at any point. This can lead to extreme penetration and, in many game animals, over-penetration, with the projectile exiting the animal without delivering all its energy into it. For this reason, FMJ projectiles are generally unsuitable for hunting.

Full metal jacket projectiles are generally used in military service competition, where duplicate military loads can be constructed and used to level the playing field. By having a continuous jacket, the ballistic coefficient can be improved over that of pointed soft-point tips. Many full metal jacket projectiles are of the military surplus variety and, as a result, their quality varies.

Hollow-point projectiles are similar to soft-points, but here the lead core is depressed inside the tip of the projectile, producing a crater shape in the tip. The purpose of the hollow-point is to maximize mushrooming of the projectile upon impact with a target. In fact, some hollow-points are almost explosive in their expansion. This expansion tends to begin immediately upon impact, often leading to little penetration on larger game.

Because the lead core is depressed, hollow-point projectiles tend not to have balance or ballistic coefficient as good as other hunting-oriented projectiles. They are also of extremely limited use in competition. However, in terms of delivering energy to a target without over-penetration, there is no better projectile than a hollow-point.

Ballistic tip projectiles are an advancement of the humble hollow-point. In an effort to obtain a better ballistic coefficient and balance, while still preserving the terminal ballistic properties of the hollow-point, ammunition manufacturers have developed a polymer or plastic pointed tip, which is bonded into the hollow-point. This provides the classical spitzer shape to enhance flight, but, upon impact, the ballistic tip disintegrates, leaving the hollow-point underneath for expansion. Ballistic tips generally tend to have slightly better penetration, due to the fact that the polymer insert retards expansion at the initial point of impact.

Open-tip projectiles were designed purely for competition target shooting. As such, they are manufactured to a very high standard, where not only is there little variation between projectiles, but also little variation in the thickness of their jackets. Of particular note are MatchKing projectiles manufactured by Sierra, and VLD (very low drag) projectiles manufactured by Berger.

The opening in the tip is a small, shallow dimple in the tip of the jacket, and it is actually a result of the manufacturing process. It is important to note that the jacket itself remains continuous underneath the dimple; the lead core is not exposed. The purpose of the dimple is to create a high-pressure air zone inside the dimple. This, in turn, forces the air the projectile is moving through to be pushed out of the way by the "cushion" of air in the dimple, rather than by the projectile itself.

*The choice of projectiles can be bewildering. The shooter needs to rely on their purpose and needs, as well as the manufacturer's information to make an appropriate selection. Anecdotal comments from fellow shooters of "This works good in my gun" can cause a lot of frustration and cost a lot of money!*

Shooters who have the affliction of playing golf will immediately recognize the similarity with the dimples on golf balls, and their purpose is the same.

Open-tip projectiles are capable of producing very high ballistic coefficients and very high levels of accuracy. The caveat comes for use in hunting, where they should only be reserved for those shooters capable of precision shot placement. The terminal ballistics demonstrate that these projectiles tend to pass straight through targets without delivering much energy to them, unless they deform on a solid structure, such as bone.

## PROJECTILE BASES

When considering the style of base for projectiles, either as loaded ammunition or as a component to handload with, there are really only two choices, flat-based and boat-tailed.

Flat-based projectiles are as the name suggests, that simply being a 90-degree base that is the same diameter as the widest part of the projectile.

Flat-based projectiles were the original base style, one utilized for its simplicity of construction. Flat-based projectiles tend to shoot well in any type of firearm, particularly so in worn, dirty, or poorly manufactured bores. This is because, under firing pressures, the base tends to flatten further and the jacket at the base of the projectile tends to upset or be squeezed into the rifling more, allowing the rifling to "grip" the projectile better and provide a more complete gas seal between the bore and the projectile. The results are more consistent rotation and velocity.

Flat-based projectiles do tend to have inferior balance, due to the weight displacement to the rear of the projectile. They also tend to have an inferior ballistic coefficient, due to the poor aerodynamic flow of having a flat base.

Boat-tailed projectiles possess generally either a nine- or 13-degree cone-shaped base that terminates in a flat-base after a short length. The purpose of the boat-tail is to blend the aerodynamic shape of the projectile and smooth the airflow. This leads to a higher

ballistic coefficient. Also, by centralizing the main mass of the projectile, a boat-tail offers better balance.

It was thought that boat-tailed projectiles tended to put the rifling and throat under greater stress by directing hot gas and powder around the sides of the base into the boat-tailed zone of the projectile. This has been quantitatively shown not to be the case and, in fact, boat-tailed projectiles wear out barrels no faster than flat-based projectiles. Boat-tailed projectiles can create problems in worn bores, however, and can even keyhole in a bore that shoots flat-based projectiles well. On the plus side, boat-tailed projectiles are far easier to handload and are pressed into cases with far less chance of any misalignment between the axis of the cartridge and the axis of the projectile. This, of course, leads to higher quality handloaded ammunition.

## WHAT IS THE BALLISTIC COEFFICIENT?

Having considered the different projectile tips and bases, it can be easily seen how the different features contribute to the mass of the projectile to define the aerodynamic efficiency of that projectile. This efficiency, known as the "ballistic coefficient," is calculated by the sectional density of the projectile (the projectile weight divided by the diameter at the widest point), divided by the projectile's shape (defined by a "form factor"), which itself is a standard and based on shape. The only other way to determine the ballistic coefficient is by firing at a known velocity in a standard atmosphere, over a known range, and measuring the velocity loss between two points.

Fortunately, nearly all manufacturers publish the ballistic coefficients of their projectiles, allowing the shooter to compare different projectiles at different velocities to determine the best projectile for their needs. It should be stated that the projectile with the highest ballistic coefficient *isn't* necessarily the best choice. When choosing a projectile, the shooter needs to consider the range over which they are shooting, as the advantage of a high ballistic coefficient is greater at greater ranges (of particular importance to competition or long-range shooters), versus the terminal ballistics or expansion qualities required (important to hunters), as well as the cartridge and possible velocities that will be driving the projectile.

The ballistic capabilities of a projectile to lessen drop and windage and retain energy over range are a function of the ballistic coefficient and the muzzle velocity at which the projectile is fired. As ballistic coefficients tend to increase with raw projectile weight as well as the aerodynamic features, it can be seen that, as a rule, a projectile with a high ballistic coefficient may be limited in terms of velocity by the safe loading capacity of the cartridge from which it is being fired. Conversely, a projectile with a lower ballistic coefficient may be fired with a higher velocity from the same cartridge. In many cases, given that ballistic performance is a function of muzzle velocity as well as the ballistic coefficient of the projectile, better ballistic performance, in terms of drop, windage, and energy retention, can be obtained from a projectile that has a lesser ballistic coefficient, but is fired at a higher velocity.

Ultimately, there is a crossover point, where a higher ballistic coefficient of a projectile offers a ballistic *disadvantage*, due to the reduced velocity it must be fired (inherent to the limitations of the cartridge). The shooter can easily plot the velocities each projectile is capable of with a given cartridge to assess the correct projectile to use in their own individual case.

A recent development in projectile technology has resulted in special coatings being applied to projectiles to achieve various advantages. Most of these coatings utilize molybdenum disulfide, a high-pressure dry lubricant. Many shooters believe this coating, known as "moly," increases muzzle velocities and improves ballistic performance. This is erroneous. A projectile with this coating has its *friction* reduced—and that is all. The flow of effects from this include a reduced chamber pressure, due to the projectile moving along the bore with less friction—but this also results in a lower muzzle velocity. Further, due to the lowered friction, in theory, the rifling experiences less stress during firing and less copper fouling is deposited in the bore. Extending from that, ease of cleaning is enhanced, as such coatings provide a surface that copper and powder fouling is less inclined to adhere to. This increases the number of rounds that can be fired before accuracy deteriorates due to fouling.

All this sounds fantastic, but it comes with a very big "but." In order to experience the benefits of moly-coated projectiles, the shooter must care for the projectiles and bore in a very particular way. First, the bore must be absolutely clean before using moly projectiles, otherwise the coating will be laid over existing fouling, causing constrictions in the bore. Second, the bore must be cleaned using a moly-safe solvent and a nylon brush. Third, moly is hydroscopic, meaning that it attracts moisture, thus, it can cause a bore to rust quickly if left fired and uncleaned. Last, once a shooter has started using moly, the shooter should *not* shoot normal projectiles through the bore. If these guidelines are not followed explicitly, the moly coating can quite happily ruin a bore, by leaving random and extremely hard deposits behind—which are almost impossible to remove.

# CHAPTER 10

# Propellants

Propellants, otherwise known as gunpowder, provide the explosive energy required to accelerate the projectile out of the cartridge and along the bore to reach the desired muzzle velocity. The original propellant, blackpowder, has long been superseded by cordite and, then, today's nitrocellulose-based powders. These powders come as flake, ball, or extruded cylinder grains.

There are many different types of propellants available to the shooter these days, and they are broken down and defined by their burn rate. Interestingly and unbeknownst to most shooters is the fact that, in most cases, propellants of different burn rates are chemically the same, it is simply the size of grain that changes the burn rate, with finer grained propellants burning faster than those larger grained.

Different propellants are used to achieve desired muzzle velocities in different cartridges. For instance, a pistol or rifle with a short barrel or employing a light projectile would use a faster burning propellant to achieve greater acceleration over a short time span and without creating excessive chamber pressure. Likewise, a large magnum rifle with a heavy projectile would use a slower burning propellant to accelerate the larger projectile more slowly. Interestingly, in

a converse manner, a smaller projectile requires more propellant for the same cartridge, while larger projectiles require less propellant for the same cartridge. This is due to the fact that a smaller projectile will move and accelerate faster down the bore than a larger one. Also, as the propellant burns behind a smaller projectile, a larger space for the propellant gas to expand into is created more quickly, thus requiring a greater amount of propellant to be burnt before the projectile can leave the bore.

Propellants are affected by a number of environmental factors and can be degraded through inappropriate storage. All of these factors affect the burn rate and can be a source of accuracy problems.

Propellants should be stored in an airtight container, in a dry place, out of the sun. Propellants are hydroscopic and will absorb moisture from the air, so it's a good idea to store them in a box with silica gel crystals or another moisture absorbing product (even dry white rice in a bowl will work for a little while), to keep the moisture levels down and consistent.

When in the field, either at the range or on a hunt, propellant contained inside loaded ammunition is susceptible to temperature. Lower temperatures will decrease the burn rate and make it irregular. It

will also retard ignition from the primer. This lowers muzzle velocities and can lead to excessive pressures, because the projectile leaves the bore too slowly. In extreme cases, the propellant may even fail to ignite at all. In higher temperatures, the propellant will burn at a faster rate, leading to higher muzzle velocities. Too, in a firearm left in the sun and heated up too much, its heat can be transferred to the cartridge, eventually causing the primer to ignite and fire the cartridge. This is known as a "cook off" and is an extremely dangerous

occurrence. A good technique for stabilizing the propellant temperature prior to firing is to simply carry the loaded ammunition in a pocket that is close to the body, allowing the body to warm the ammunition ever so slightly. This works just as well with commercially loaded ammunition as handloaded.

Propellants can be affected by compressed loads, when handloading. In a compressed load, the propellant column inside the case is pushed down, usually in an uneven manner. This has the

*Propellants come in various forms, such as flake, extruded, and ball. The shape and size of the individual grains help determine the burn rate.*

effect of creating bands of propellant that are tightly compressed along with bands that are still free and loose. This can interfere with ignition from the primer by shielding some areas of the case from the primer jet. It also causes the heavily compressed sections to burn more slowly.

Finally, propellants are affected by continued vibration, causing the grains to fracture. This changes the burn rate by changing the grain size. While some vibrations to the propellant can be helpful in breaking up grain clusters in ammunition that has been in long-term storage, leaving a box of ammunition in the back of the SUV or four-wheeler for a month or two is not advisable.

As always, if stored properly, propellants can be quite stable for many years and, when used appropriately, will yield stable and consistent burn rates, pressures, and muzzle velocities. That said, at the end of the day, a propellant is an explosive and must be treated with the respect it deserves.

# CHAPTER 11

# Cases and Primers

The ammunition case is comprised of the neck at the top, the base at the bottom, and the case walls joining the two. In most modern cases, there is also a shoulder reducing the diameter of the case wall at the base down to the diameter of the case wall at the projectile or neck.

The case serves to contain the propellant inside the correct volume of space. It also supports the primer at the base of the case and the projectile at the neck. Additionally, the case serves to guide the completed round from the magazine or loading platform, by virtue of its shape, and it provides a rim to facilitate extraction and ejection after firing.

Cases are generally made from brass, though some manufacturers also use nickel, and some military suppliers even use steel. The case is manufactured usually from a tube or cup of the base material that is then formed using heat and pressure, interspersed with stages of annealing or softening of the base material, to create the correct shape.

Although the case seems to be a fairly innocuous part of the completed round, in terms of accuracy,

the case does, in fact, play a large role, particularly in the production of consistent velocities across a batch of ammunition. The internal volume of the case will, to a great degree, determine the pressure curve during firing as the propellant burns, and will have a significant impact on the muzzle velocity of the projectile.

The diameter of the flash hole and the depth of the primer pocket will determine the speed of ignition of the propellant, particularly in cold weather. It will also affect how evenly the propellant burns within the case. Both factors will impact the stability of the muzzle velocities and the standard deviation of velocities across groups.

Finally, the neck tension or the amount of force exerted by the case neck gripping the projectile will also have an impact on the final muzzle velocity, and different case neck tensions or an uneven tension within the case neck will affect the outcome. Although shooters who use loaded commercial ammunition are pretty well stuck with the make of case used by that manufacturer, handloaders are offered

*Different cases offer the shooter many options for handloading. Carefully consider your needs before making a decision.*

a good opportunity for the fine tuning of loads by the use of different cases, as well as by case modification.

Many shooters believe that purchasing premium brand cases is the best way to achieve high-quality handloads. Although this may be true to an extent, better results can be achieved with the minimal efforts of case culling and uniforming, processes that can be carried out on any case.

Case culling involves weighing the cases and placing them in groups of similar weights, then using those discreet groups of ammunition for their group shooting. The theory behind this is that cases with the same weight are likely to possess the same internal volume.

Uniforming of cases takes this to the next level, and although the cases are not weighed (they can be, if the shooter wishes), their vital characteristics such as case length, primer pocket depth, flash hole diameter, case neck squareness, and case neck wall thickness are made uniform. All of this will be discussed later.

Handloading of cases also allows the shooter to fire-form cases and, then, when resizing the case for reloading, only size the neck, as opposed to returning the entire case to its original specifications (something most handloaders tend to do). Performing neck sizing only on cases has the effect of allowing the case to swell during firing to a perfect fit for the firearm it's being used in, maximizing and evening out the internal case volume between cases. Neck sizing allows the shooter to set the case neck tension, and it also removes any excess headspace, by allowing the case to fill the chamber back to the bolt face.

Fire-forming *does* require the case metal to be soft enough for reforming, and this is probably the greatest difference between case manufacturers. A softer case metal is desirable, because all cases over repeated firings will "work harden" and, eventually, crack at the neck during reloading or separate at the junction between the base and the case wall during firing (the last a very dangerous condition). A softer case will enhance the case life or the number of times it can be reloaded. (The plus sides to harder cases is that they are more resistant to structural damage and are better suited for use in autoloaders or firearms with a scored or damaged chamber.) Although cases can be annealed to soften the metal, this really only staves off the inevitable. At some point, the case will wear out and have to be discarded.

As it is with all aspects of shooting, the shooter is offered the easy way by commercialism and the not so easy way, which, though it brings more work, also brings greater knowledge, understanding, and accuracy. For the shooter who takes the time to cull or uniform suitable cases instead of buying premium (and so called "perfect") cases, excellent accuracy results await. Take the time, reap the rewards!

## PRIMERS

Primers are that part of loaded ammunition that transmits and converts the kinetic energy from the firing pin to release the chemical energy of the propellant. In essence, the primer is a small amount of impact-sensitive explosive contained in a brass (or sometimes steel) cup, otherwise known as the "primer cup." It has a part over the open end of the cup called the "anvil," which the explosive mixture gets compressed against to cause it to fire. The primer is pressed into the base of the case when the ammunition is manufactured. When the primer is impacted by the firing pin, the hot fiery gasses, known as a "primer jet," travel past the anvil and through the flash hole in the bottom of the case to ignite the propellant within the case.

It is a common misconception that the primer causes the propellant to burn from the base of the cartridge up to the top. Correctly, the primer jet should travel the full length of the case and burn the propellant from the inside of the case to the outside. This prevents the propellant from being blasted forward before being burnt, which would cause the development of unstable pressures, and increase throat erosion in the barrel due to abrasive propellant grains being blasted through the throat under high temperatures and pressures.

Primers come in many sizes, depending on the cartridge being used. For instance, there are Small Rifle, Large Rifle and Magnum primers. It is

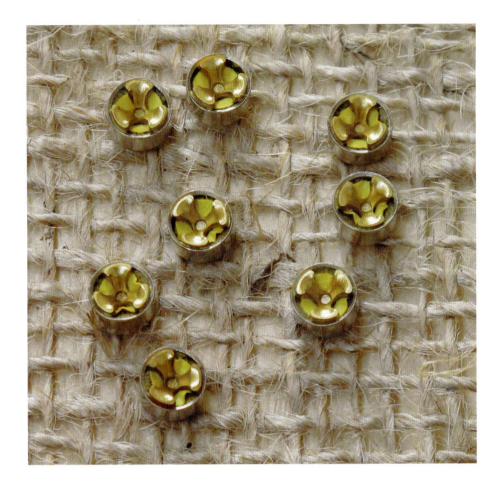

*Primers are an integral part of the handloading equation and their importance should not be overlooked. Primer choice will influence the accuracy of the shooter's handloads. Indeed, careful experimentation with primers can offer the shooter significant benefits.*

very important to use the primer specified for the cartridge, though there are some exceptions. In very cold conditions, Magnum primers can be used by experienced handloaders in substitution for most Large Rifle primer applications, to ensure correct, even, and stable ignition of the propellant. Further, in particularly long cartridges like the .303 British and .30-06, a Magnum primer can be used by experienced handloaders to ensure that the longer than normal powder column is burnt correctly from the inside out.

When handloading, primers come in small trays of 100-count. They must be treated very carefully. Not only are they volatile, they are also susceptible to damage, which can lead to primer failures when struck by the firing pin. The most common form of primer failure is due to case lubricant finding its way into the explosive mixture contained within

the primer cup; the primer mix becomes inert. For handloaders experiencing mild signs of excessive pressure, particularly primer cratering, wherein the pressure causes the base of the primer cup to be pressed into the firing pin hole around the sides of the firing pin, the use of a primer with a steel cup, such as CCI's primers, can be used to alleviate these problems. Not only will it improve the quality of the handloaded ammunition, it will extend the life of the firing pin and prevent the size of the firing pin hole in the bolt face from being expanded.

As a final note, some primers are mildly corrosive. This type of primer is generally found in military surplus ammunition, with the corrosive action being caused by the use of stabilizing salts that increase the stable storage life of the projectile. This problem will be discussed in more detail later.

# CHAPTER 12

# Handloaded Ammunition

Handloading offers the shooter the pinnacle in accuracy, consistency, and reliability from their ammunition. The practice is very much a science, one that complements the art of marksmanship and riflemanship. Handloading allows the shooter to alter all the variables that go into ammunition production, not just manipulation of the components, but also how they are assembled to achieve varying pressure effects and create ammunition to suit a specific firearm.

Before any handloading can be done, a sensible course of action is to consult a loading manual. This will supply the shooter with all the safety precautions required to safely load ammunition. The shooter should remember that, at their core, propellant and primers are explosives and must be treated accordingly.

Having learned how to handload properly, the shooter will require a number of (preferably) once-fired cases derived from the firearm for which the shooter will be handloading. The benefits of once-fired cases will be discussed later. The shooter then must consult recognized load data. This information

is usually provided free of charge by most propellant manufacturers and will supply information such as minimum and maximum charge weights of different powders in conjunction with different projectiles. The load data will also normally provide an average velocity from a standard barrel (the barrel length is usually provided in the data), so that the shooter can estimate the resulting velocity of the handloaded ammunition without firing a shot. The shooter can then set about culling or uniforming and accurizing their cases, followed by priming, charging, and then the seating of projectiles. It is important to note that, when handloading for a firearm for the first time, the shooter will more likely than not produce a number of different handloads with different propellant (or charge) weights. This will allow the shooter to later assess which specific charge weight provides the best accuracy with their firearm.

With a batch of freshly loaded rounds in hand, the handloader should select a number of handloaded cartridges (if not all), and inspect them. First, the shooter must ensure they are safe to fire, the primers

*From basic to advanced, the handloader can choose the level of complexity and involvement.*

are properly seated, and the overall length of the completed round is correct according to the load data or chamber dimensions. Second, the shooter should inspect the completed handloaded cartridges for concentricity between the projectile and the case. This can be done simply by rolling the cases on a flat surface and watching the tip of the projectile to see if it rotates around its axis or moves in an arc. There are concentricity gauges available, but, as a rule of thumb, the human eye is adept at spotting an inconsistency or a projectile that is not seated properly or is seated at an angle or otherwise improperly.

Once the handloaded ammunition is made, it's time to head to the range and conduct some specific range tests. These tests will identify which propellant weight and resulting velocity provides the best

*The handloader must consult the loading data provided by propellant manufacturers before attempting to handload.*

accuracy, in terms of group size and standard deviation of velocity. The shooter can then choose whether to carry out a second group of tests, further refining the propellant weight and velocity, or they can simply select the best propellant or charge weight so far and use that combination for all subsequent loadings.

Another aspect of handloading is known as "wild-catting" and revolves around shooters developing their own unique cartridges from existing cases through the use of specialized forming dies. An example would be adding smaller projectiles to larger cases by making the neck tighter and, so, producing higher velocities. Conversely, one could go about adding larger projectiles to smaller cases. Many conventional cases these days started life as wildcats, such as .300 Winchester Magnum and .22-250. The most common style of wildcat in use today relates to those from P.O. Ackley, who pioneered increasing the case capacity of standard cases such as the .22-250 and .243 to create Ackley Improved variants. These sport slightly higher muzzle velocities, yet don't require expensive forming dies; Improved brass is formed by firing a standard case in an Improved chamber, allowing it to swell to the Improved size.

Handloading can be a rewarding experience and knowledge-building activity. Done properly, handloaded ammunition will provide the shooter with a large accuracy advantage over commercial ammunition and force the shooter to improve their technique, as deficiencies in either the shooter or the firearm will be highlighted by the superior quality ammunition. Proper handloading does require the shooter to put in a lot of effort to achieve the results—but there really isn't any reason this shouldn't be done. Lazy handloading will provide the shooter with some gains, but they will be marginal. Too, done improperly, handloading can be frustrating and flat-out dangerous. A wise shooter will consult known data and loading manuals.

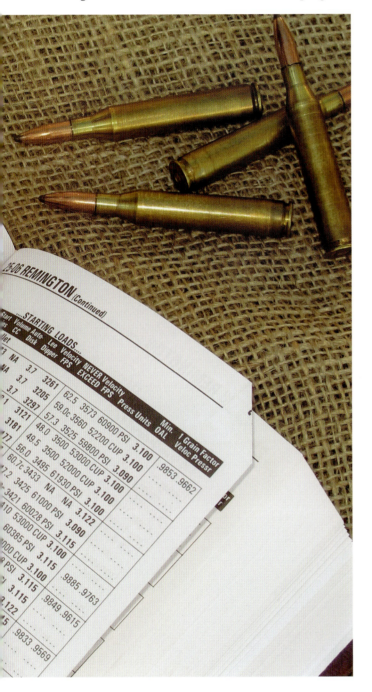

## RECOGNIZED DATA

The use of recognized data is mandatory for the first time handloader. Not only will this ensure that safe cartridges are produced, but also that the charge weights given as a range will include the loadings that provide the best accuracy and most stable velocities.

When utilizing this data, the shooter should never simply start by using the highest recommended charge weight. First-time handloaders and any handloader working up a new load should always begin loading at least 10-percent below the maximum charge weight and then work upward. Conventionally, the shooter should, in fact, begin at the minimum load and work upwards at 0.5-grain increments, perhaps making three to five rounds in each charge weight. This will allow the shooter to test the different charge weights against each other objectively, using the tests discussed later. Following this, the shooter can look at the charge weights that produced the highest accuracy or most stable velocity and then load in 0.1-grain increments between the best 0.5-grain loadings to determine their "perfect" charge weight

It is quite common for there to be two major accuracy "nodes" in the minimum to maximum charge weight band. Generally speaking, the first accuracy node will occur early on and provide a "soft" but accurate loading. The second accuracy node will nearly always occur one to 1.5 grains beneath the maximum load and provide the same level of accuracy and a higher muzzle velocity, but with slightly inferior stability in terms of the velocity yield.

Recognized loading data should include an analysis of projectile performance with different muzzle velocities. For the shooter who chooses not to use ballistics software or calculations, this tabulated data can provide accurate estimations of drop and windage over distance. The shooter simply looks up the exact type of projectile they intend to use and correlate that with the estimated muzzle velocity for the propellant charge they are using. The tabulated data will then show, for instance, drop in range increments of 100 meters or 100 yards, the windage for five, 10, and 15 mph 90-degree crosswinds, and energy and velocity remaining at each range increment. Many shooters would correctly say that this is an estimation on an estimation. Still, when done properly, carefully, and objectively, tabulated data can provide a reasonable level of accuracy in the short to medium range.

## UNIFORMING CASES

When handloading ammunition for accuracy, the shooter should start with the cases. As previously discussed, the ammunition case carries out a variety of tasks that go beyond just containing the propellant. Although an individual case may carry out its role perfectly, the chance of the next standard case carrying out its role in exactly the same way is limited. Due to manufacturing techniques, virtually no two cases are the same, in terms of lengths, wall thickness, primer hole size, and so on. These differences affect chamber pressures, ignition rates, and muzzle velocities. Even the highest quality commercial match cases are a fair ways off of being identical and, so, will still benefit from being uniformed.

*Perfectly uniformed cases take effort, but the dedication will show up in tight group sizes.*

*Primer pocket reaming before and after.*

The process of uniforming cases takes cases that have been fire-formed and uses various cutters and tools, not to make the cases similar, but to make identical various aspects of the cases as they relate to the guides on the tools, case to case. In the world of advanced handloading presses and powder throwers that enable many handloaded cartridges to be made quickly, uniforming is a time consuming process. Many shooters don't have the patience to sit down with a bag of cases and go through them. This is unfortunate, as this process has the capacity to drastically improve the quality of the handloaded ammunition. Bearing in mind that this process is only done once for the life of the case, the shooter should find time to do the job properly. So, pull up a comfy chair, turn on the NASCAR, and make some chips—brass chips, that is!

## PRIMER POCKETS

The primer pocket of an ammunition case is a stamped recess in the base. It is designed to support the primer in front of the flash hole. Unfortunately, due to commercial manufacturing standards, the stamping tends to differ between cases. Normally, the recesses are stamped at different depths, maintain different tensions and, in some cases, are not concentric about the flash hole. All this leads to inconsistency.

Several problems can occur. First, new primers can become seated at different distances from the flash hole. This changes the shape of the primer jet flame front as it moves through the case during firing, causing a different ignition rate and, ultimately, a different muzzle velocity. Second, the primers may not seat evenly in the recess, leading to gas leakage or blowback during firing. Finally, soft-strike misfires may occur, due to the primer actually moving forward as it is struck by the firing pin.

Uniforming of the primer pocket recess is a simple process using a specially made hand tool known as a "primer pocket reamer." The reamer cuts into the stamped primer pocket, opening it up to the correct diameter and ensuring that the primer pocket is concentric. Next, the reamer removes the rounded stamped corner at the bottom of the pocket and replaces it with a sharp, square-cut corner. After that, the base of the primer pocket is cut square to the base of the case and, finally, the depth of the primer pocket is slightly increased, ensuring that all primer pockets are of exactly the same depth. All these points add up to primer pockets that are the same depth, square to the base of the case, and support the primer with the correct amount of tension.

Aside from the initial reaming of the primer pocket and removing excess brass, the reamer can also be used to clean the primer pockets after firing. As the pocket has been cut exactly by the reamer, primer ash and carbon is removed almost instantly through reapplication of the reamer. This prevents the ash from interfering with the seating of the next primer and also prevents accumulated ash from being blown into the case by the primer jet when it is next fired. Cleaning the primer pocket in this way leaves the base of the pocket perfectly clean and matched, ready for the next primer to be pressed into it.

Primer pocket reamers come in different sizes to suit pistol, rifle, and magnum sizes and are relatively inexpensive. The benefit of carrying out this once in a case lifetime operation is consistency—and, as we all know, consistency is accuracy.

## FLASH HOLE

The flash hole in the bottom of the primer pocket allows the primer jet to advance through the case and ignite the propellant. Contrary to popular belief, the flash holes are stamped at the factory, not drilled or cut. Consequently, the hole itself is generally not very even. Further, there are "burrs" of brass on the inside of the case, where the flash hole was stamped. These inconsistencies lead to variations in ignition of the

*Flash hole reaming before and after.*

*Case neck turning before and after.*

propellant, as the shape of the flame front is altered as it passes through the uneven flash hole, much liked a partly blocked nozzle on an aerosol can. As a consequence, the propellant isn't ignited evenly and, as such, muzzle velocity varies from case to case. Further, the burrs themselves burn off eventually and pass down the bore—not an ideal thing to have happen!

The flash hole deburring tool is designed not just to remove the burrs on the inside of the flash hole, but also to make the flash hole a uniform diameter and shape. It also chamfers the edges of the flash hole on the inside of the case to 60 degrees. This assists the primer jet flame front to expand into the case. Flash hole deburring needs only to be done once, and a side benefit is that the same tool can also be used to clean

the flash hole after firing. Flash hole de-burring may seem like an insignificant task, one not worth the effort, but, for the shooter who wants the most from themselves and their equipment, flash hole deburring does offer gains.

## CASE NECK TURNING

Case necks, when manufactured, tend to be fairly inconsistent, in terms of their concentricity and wall thickness. These variations will create an error in the alignment of the projectile to the axis of the case and change the amount of tension that holds the projectile in place, ultimately leading to inconsistent muzzle velocities. Neck turning or uniforming of the case necks is the solution to this.

The process works by placing a projectile-diameter mandrel inside the case neck, then turning a small cutter around the neck's outside radius to remove a small amount of brass. The combined effect of the tight-fitting mandrel and the cutter evens out the wall thickness of the neck and the neck tension from case to case, and it ensures that the case neck is square.

When carrying out this uniforming operation, the shooter must ensure that only the bare minimum brass is removed. If too much is removed, the neck will not apply any tension to the projectile. Ideally, only 80 percent of the neck needs to have been cut to ensure the correct amount of brass has been removed. The case neck turner, again, is a simple and inexpensive hand tool. Like some other processes, this is one that needs only to be done once in a case's lifetime.

Sometimes, after repeated firings, cases can develop a thickening of brass, pushed forward under firing pressures, that forms a "doughnut" at the neck's base. This thickening can interfere with reloading and, in some cases, chambering of the affected brass. A case neck turning tool can be used to remove this thickening. A further use for a neck turning tool is to produce ammunition for use in a tightly throated firearm.

The shooter should start with measuring the diameter of their rifle's throat, then measure the wall thickness of the brass they're using. Ideally, with tightly throated firearms, there should be about 0.003-inch clearance between the outside of the case walls and the wall of the throat. Therefore, the shooter can subtract 0.003-inch from the diameter

of the throat, the result being the target diameter of the necks of those cases to be used. The shooter then turns the neck as normal to achieve that dimension. Having done this, the shooter will have matched their cases to the chamber and have a perfect fit.

## CASE LENGTH

Case length is an important basic specification. Not only are case lengths inconsistent when new from the manufacturer, cases will "grow" with the number of times they are reused. This is caused by brass being pushed forward from the shoulder of the case and being deposited around the neck. The case then extends with repeated resizing. Further to the length, the squareness of the case neck opening is inconsistent from the factory, and the depositing of brass at the neck with firing is an uneven process that leads to different lengths around the radius at the case neck opening. A case that has grown too long will not only be inconsistent when fired, it will eventually no longer chamber and will resist being resized.

A case length gauge and cutter will return a case to its specification length by removing excess brass from the case neck opening. This process also squares the opening to the base of the case, ensuing that, as the projectile leaves the case, it isn't tipped in any direction by a case neck opening that is uneven around its circumference. Cases should be cut when new and after having been sized. Many shooters only trim their cases once in a while, but it's a good idea, for the purpose of keeping the cases uniform to each other to carry out this quick operation at every firing.

*Trimming cases for length before and after.*

*Neck chamfering before and after.*

## NECK CHAMFER

Having trimmed and squared the case neck opening with a case length gauge and cutter, it is important for the shooter to put a mild chamfer on the case neck opening, both on the inside and the outside. An inside-chamfered case neck will assist in pressing the new projectile into the case, and the chamfer on the outside will ensure smooth feeding from the magazine to the chamber (as opposed to the hard square cut edge left by the case length gauge and cutter). Further, small burrs can form on the case mouth and, if these are pushed into a case when a projectile is seated, it will knock the projectile off axis, leading to poor accuracy.

## INSIDE NECK CLEANING

Most shooters believe that tumbling cases after firing in a tumbler with something like corn cob media is the best way to clean fired cases prior to reloading them. Unfortunately most shooters are unaware that the purpose of tumbling is to clean the *outside* of cases so that grit doesn't score or damage the reloading dies. Although cleaning the inside of cases isn't really necessary, cleaning of the inside of the case *necks* is. A dirty case neck will not only score a new projectile as it is pressed into position, it will also create a great amount of friction and lead to much higher neck tensions supporting the projectile. This will lead to inconsistencies in pressure and muzzle velocities.

Cleaning the inside of the case neck will allow the tension to be provided by the case neck only; the amount of tension is easily controlled by the reloading dies used. The best way of cleaning the case neck is to simply use an old bronze phosphor brush of the same caliber as the firearm, placing the brush in a drill press. Then simply turn it on and run the cases up and down the brush twice. This will remove the grit and leave a smooth surface for the projectile to slide upon.

## FULL-LENGTH SIZING

Full-length sizing of cases is exactly as the name suggests. It uses a set of full-length dies to return the fired case to its original unfired or SAAMI specification. Most shooters use full-length sizing dies with a lubricant on the case, and it is a simple matter of setting the dies to position the shoulder of the case and press away.

Full-length sizing is the most basic sizing system and allows a handloaded round to be used in any chamber of the same caliber. Full-length sizing is also a good idea for rounds used in auto-loading firearms, as it will reduce the chance of misfires due to failures to feed and extract/eject caused by using cases that are slightly smaller than the chamber.

## NECK SIZING

Neck sizing is an advancement over full-length sizing. In neck sizing, the case is left at its expanded sized, except for the neck, which is returned to its specification size. The purpose of the process is to restore neck tension.

Neck sizing has several advantages and disadvantages. On the plus side, neck sizing leaves the rest of the case as a perfect, fire-formed match for the chamber it was and will be fired in again (a large accuracy improvement over a specification-sized case). Second, it marginally increases the interior capacity of the case, leading to greater propellant charge capacity or a reduction in chamber pressure. Third, neck sizing increases the life of the case, because it does not expose the case to the work-hardening stressors of being constantly reformed. Fourth, neck sizing can be used to take up minor cases of excessive headspace in that, when the case is fired, it will expand to fill the chamber. Without being full-length sized down to specification again, the case will again fill the chamber when chambered again, removing any excess head-space between the case and the chamber.

Neck sizing does not work so well in auto-loading firearms that benefit from a slightly looser fit between the case and the chamber. Also, neck-sized rounds rarely chamber easily in firearms other than that which they were intended for, the problem manifesting in a binding of the bolt or working parts and then a jam.

Neck sizing does require the use of a special neck sizing die, but it does offer the shooter a large advance over standard full-length size handloading and, once implemented, is no more difficult to do.

## FIRE-FORMING

Fire-forming of cases is a process by which standard specification cases are made into a perfect

*Inside neck cleaning before and after.*

match for a particular firearm. The process of fire-forming is very simple. The shooter takes a standard handloaded or commercial round of ammunition, chambers it, and fires it. That's it! The resulting case will be a perfect match for the chamber.

There is another method that uses a light charge of propellant and a case filler without a projectile, to achieve enough chamber pressure to fire-form the case. However, when regular fire-forming can be done while also, perhaps, broadly zeroing in a new

*Fire-forming before and after.*

firearm, firing live ammunition on hand is probably a better idea.

Use of fire-formed brass must be done in conjunction with neck sizing, but, as previously discussed, the advantages of greater internal volume and lower chamber pressures, taking up excessive headspace, and being a perfect match for the chamber are worth their weight in gold!

## PRIMING

Priming is the process by which primers are pressed into cases prior to these cases being charged with propellant. Priming, aside from a few matters, is more an issue of safety than accuracy. Primers are highly explosive and sensitive items. Primers should always be stored in a cool, dry, and dark place and should only ever be removed from their packaging when their use is imminent. Primers should never be handled by the shooter. They should always be transferred from their tray to the priming device without touching them. The actual process of priming is generally done on the reloading press or with a hand primer such as a Lee Auto Prime. Either tool allows the shooter to transfer the primers from their packaging to the tool without touching them. Primers should also never be exposed to microwaves, high-powered radios or high-tension power lines.

Having loaded the priming device with primers, the cases are cleaned, dried, and fitted to the tool, and the primers are then pressed into the primer pockets one by one. The only real trick is that the primers must be pressed flush to the base of the primer pocket recess. This permits the primer to interact with the flash hole correctly and develop the correct primer jet shape when fired, allowing the propellant to be ignited in the correct way. When the primer has seated correctly into the primer pocket recess, the shooter will experience sudden and firm resistance from the priming device.

The only pitfalls the shooter can really run into when priming, aside from accidental ignition of a primer due to mishandling, is to allow lubricant from the case sizing process to find its way into the primer

*Priming of cases must be done gently and with care. Done incorrectly, a misfire may result due to a damaged primer. Far worse than that, the primer could ignite as it is pressed into the case.*

pocket recess. This wax or lubricant will then happily migrate into the primer itself, causing damage to the explosive compound within and an improper ignition or misfire.

## CHARGING

Charging is the process of weighing out the correct charge of propellant and putting it into cases. While this may seem a fairly pedestrian process, there are some tricks. Looking first at safety, propellants should always be stored in a cool dry place and out of the light, as moisture, temperature, and light degrade propellants. Propellants should never be handled by the shooter, as this will also contaminate the propellant with oils, salts, and moisture from the skin (and that assumes the shooter has clean hands!). Propellants should never be mixed, even if they are from the same batch or type, as this may alter the burn rate and chamber pressures developed when fired.

The process of weighing out the correct charge weight can be done in three separate ways, by using powder dippers, powder throwers, or powder scales.

Powder dippers are small buckets on a spoon handle, those buckets calibrated to certain weights when filled to a certain point with a particular propellant. While acceptable in theory, powder dippers generally give wide-ranging results, in terms of the actual charge applied. Accuracy in charge weight down to the grain can be achieved with practice, but this is the limit for powder dippers. Most important, the shooter will not know (without scales) how accurate they are with a dipper, and powder dippers can only be used with the powder they have been calibrated to. Use of other powders will lead to an error in charge weight that may be dangerous. For accurate handloading, the shooter can rule out the use of powder dippers.

The second method of weighing out the correct charge of propellant is with the use of a powder thrower. A powder thrower is a device that has a hopper to hold the powder, a measuring and calibration mechanism, and a trigger. The shooter simply calibrates the thrower to give the desired charge weight, tests several of the delivered charges using a set of powder scales, and then the shooter is ready to charge cases. While all of this sounds great, powder throwers do have limitations. Much like powder dippers, powder throwers work on averages. While the thrower may be set for a specific weight, the actual charges delivered will oscillate higher and lower than the specified charge. Powder throwers also tend to wander further out of calibration with each charge delivered, forcing the shooter to recalibrate or at least test the delivered charges every five to 10 deliveries. Powder throwers do speed up the charging process and are capable of sub-grain accuracy, but they don't deliver absolute consistency, so the shooter who uses a one should expect their muzzle velocities to vary.

The final method of weighing out the correct charge of propellant is with the use of a powder scale. Powder scales are simplicity defined and the traditional way of weighing charges. The scales are a simple balance beam and weight style, with the scale in grains and a fine section scaled to one-tenth of a grain. To use the scales, the shooter simply sets the weight to zero, testing to make sure it measures zero with no charge on the weighing plate. The shooter then sets the desired charge and places propellant on the weighing plate, adding more, perhaps with a powder trickler, until the exact charge is weighed out. The shooter then puts the charge in the case by pouring it off the weighing plate, which normally has a pouring spout. For the modern shooter, there are now powder scales available with a digital readout. These scales are just as good as the balance beam scales, though digital readouts have to be read, while a balance beam can simply be looked at to see if it is at its level. That said, digital scales can offer a greater degree of accuracy.

The main difference between powder dippers, powder throwers, and powder scales is that the scales will deliver the exact charge and, as we know, this will assist in providing consistency in muzzle velocities.

For the shooter who uses maximum volume or compressed loads, the method of pouring the propellant into the case can also make a difference to any inconsistencies developed. If a shooter uses these loads,

*Powder charging must be a slow, methodical, and accurate process. Many handloaders over the years have over- and undercharged cases—and many have missed the charge on some cases completely!*

it is advisable to use a drop tube to pour the propellant into the case. A drop tube is a simple tube of any length greater than one millimeter that has a funnel on one end and attaches to the neck of the case. The propellant is simply poured into the funnel; gravity packs the propellant into the case uniformly, rather than the crushing effect from pressing a projectile in on top of the propellant column. At worst, using this method will allow for a uniform propellant distribution through the case. At best, it will take a normally compressed load down to a maximum volume or less load, stabilizing burn rates from round to round and improving consistency.

## PRESSING PROJECTILES

Pressing projectiles into charged and primed cases is a simple process using a press to seat the projectile into the neck is such a way that the axis of the projectile follows the same axis of the case. This is a fairly self-contained procedure and, due to the dies and press involved, difficult to do improperly.

The important aspect of pressing projectiles is that the handloader can define how far the projectiles are pressed into the cases. This is important for several reasons. First, the shooter can determine the maximum completed round length possible for their chamber and then press the projectiles so that they have a minimum distance to "jump" from the throat to the rifling of the barrel. This limits the opportunity for the projectile to go off axis. Second, by changing the seating depth of the projectile, the shooter can increase or decrease the internal volume of the case, allowing for more or less propellant. Finally, the shooter can adjust the seating depth with the same charge of propellant to achieve higher and lower chamber pressures.

Looking first at seating depth with regard to the rifling, many shooters have shown that limiting the amount of jump the projectile has to be exposed to when traveling from the case neck, along the throat, and then to the rifling can improve accuracy. The first step in this process is to measure the chamber length with the projectile the shooter intends to use. It is important to use the actual projectile that will be loaded, because the curvature of the projectile towards the tip (ogive) will affect the measurement. There are many off-the-shelf tools that can take a very accurate measurement, though the shooter can also use a dowel of wood slightly smaller than the caliber.

To use the dowel method, having ensured that the firearm is unloaded, the shooter closes the action and places the dowel down the bore until it bottoms out on the bolt face. A mark is then scribed on the dowel precisely where it leaves the muzzle. The dowel and bolt are then removed and the chosen style of projectile is then placed into the chamber and moved forwards until it contacts the rifling. The projectile is then held in place with another piece of dowel, while the first piece of dowel is inserted back down the bore from the muzzle end. The projectile will now be touching the rifling and sandwiched in place by the two pieces of dowel. A second mark is now scribed on the first dowel and the distance between the two marks is measured. This is the overall maximum length of a completed round that will fit into this particular chamber.

It is very important that the shooter not simply set his or her dies to this maximum measurement. Loading to the maximum length or beyond tends to drastically increase the chamber pressure, resulting in a pressure spike, because the projectile isn't able to get a run up before being squeezed onto the rifling. The shooter should start about 0.020-inch beneath the maximum (or "off the lands," as it's called), and work forwards from there. Accuracy peaks can generally be found at about 0.005-inch beneath maximum, although this varies from chamber to chamber. The shooter may choose to load "touching the lands," where the loaded round will contact the rifling when the bolt is closed, or the shooter may choose to load to a "press fit," where the projectile may go as far as 0.005-inch onto the lands when the bolt is closed. Both these options should be worked up to very carefully.

Looking at the second issue of internal volume and projectile seating depth, the shooter will be aware that, as the projectile is backed out of the neck, a greater internal volume of the case is achieved. Take, for instance, a .30-06 with a SAAMI internal volume of 61.1 grains when loaded with a Sierra 175-grain Matchking projectile pressed to the SAAMI overall length of 3.340 inches. If that projectile is seated out by only 0.010-inch (this would be a very conservative amount in most chambers), internal volume is increased by 0.2 grains. This could easily take a load from compressed and velocity unstable to a maximum volume load and velocity stable. As a further example, although the standard load length in .30-06 is 3.340 inches, it is not uncommon to see maximum lengths, due to elongated throats, out as long as 3.380 to 3.400 inches. At 3.380 inches, the internal volume is increased by nearly one grain and is capable of providing a significant ballistic advantage!

Looking at the third issue of projectile seating depth and chamber pressure differences with the same charge weight of propellant, the shooter can vary the seating depth to achieve small changes in chamber pressure and resulting velocity. Taking the example of .30-06 again, the shooter has a load at the standard length that develops 50,849 psi (well below maximum). The shooter may want to take advantage of backing the projectile out to 0.010-inch off the lands, requiring seating the projectile out by 0.020-inch from the standard 3.340 inches, making the completed round length 3.360 inches. The effects of this are that not only does the shooter obtain the benefits of shortening the projectile jump from the throat to the rifling, they have also lowered the chamber pressure by 560 psi, yet the velocity drop is only seven fps! The shooter now has an accurate load with less recoil, and it only cost seven fps in muzzle velocity! Bargain!

A final consideration when looking at the projectile seating depth is that of magazine limitations. Most rifles these days have a magazine, whether it be external and detachable or internal and permanently fitted. The magazine will only function correctly with rounds within a certain range of lengths. If the rounds are too short, they will misfeed. Too long and they won't fit in the magazine in the first place. It is a good idea for the shooter to measure the maximum size their magazine will accept and couple this information with the maximum complete round length their chamber can accept. (That said, there is no reason why the shooter cannot load their rounds longer than the magazine and simply hand feed each round. As always, this is a matter to be determined by the purpose of the firearm and the shooter's needs.)

Many shooters finish their projectile pressing by adding a "crimp" to the neck. Crimping is a process by which the tip of the neck of the case is compressed about the projectile to increase the tension on the projectile and hold it more firmly in place. Crimping was initially developed for lever-action rifles that had a tubular magazine, where the rounds sit end to end and are compressed with a magazine spring. In some cases, this pressure could push projectiles back into their cases. Crimping has also been used by the military to ensure the same thing didn't happen to loose rounds or rounds in a magazine in the rough and tumble of a military environment.

Unfortunately, crimping is not a precision process, and this lack of precision leads to differing neck tension on projectiles and, therefore, variance in muzzle velocities. The shooter should only use crimping in specific circumstances. First, ammunition for a firearm with a tubular magazine should be crimped. Second, any auto-loading firearm should use crimping on its ammunition. Finally, any firearm with a magazine that tends to surge when fired or where the ammunition is capable of running back and forth under firing pressures should have a crimp applied to the case neck. Bolt-action, single-shot, and light-recoiling firearms, as a basic rule, should not have a crimp applied.

## INSPECTION

Inspection of handloaded ammunition is a critical process, to ensure safety and improve accuracy. The inspection is carried out in two ways. First, the exterior of the loaded ammunition is visually inspected for various faults. Second, the loaded ammunition is weighed and this figure checked with the accumulated data and against other individual rounds of ammunition within the handloaded batch.

Looking first at the exterior visual inspection, the shooter initially measures the overall length of the loaded rounds, ensuring they are the correct length. This is done with a simple dial caliper taking a measurement from the base of the case to the tip of the projectile. Be aware that the measurement may change when using some hollow-point match projectiles, as the tip of the hollow-point, or "meplat," is generally uneven. In cases such as these, a tool called a "bullet comparator" can be used, which simply allows the measurement to be taken from the ogive of the projectile. Having ensured that the rounds are the same length and, within limitations, the same as the specified length, the shooter can move onto the inspection proper.

First, the shooter must look at the neck to ensure that the neck has not distorted while having the projectile pressed into position. Bent, dented, and cracked necks and necks that have been pushed back into the case are all cause for alarm. A neck that shows signs of dents has generally been sized with an excess of lube.

*Good and bad handloads. The cases here range from ideal to frightening! If any handload fails the inspection, no matter how small the failure, it should be safely discarded.*

*Simple roll testing will tell the shooter if their projectiles have been seated true and on axis to the case.*

Aside from shortening the life of the case through work hardening, loaded rounds with small dents the size of a pinhead should be usable. Cracking, on the other hand, is a far more severe condition: rounds exhibiting this damage should be discarded. Rounds showing a bent neck will probably fail to chamber and, if they do, will be quite erratic (and possibly unsafe). Best to discard these rounds, as well.

Second, the shooter can inspect the case walls, again for dents and cracks and also for a bright circle near the base of the case, on the case wall. Dents and cracks should be treated in the same way as if they had occurred in the neck. The bright circle or band about the circumference of the case near the base is a sign of the case wall becoming thin through usage and work hardening. When a bright circle or band has been detected, the shooter should sacrifice one case and cut it in half longitudinally to see if and how much the case wall has eroded. The real danger here is that if a weakened case is fired, the base may separate from the case wall and allow the highly pressurized bore gas to move backwards through the firing pin hole towards the shooter, showering the shooter with gas, propellant, and brass fragments. At worst, it may cause a structural failure of the action, leading to serious injury.

Third, the bases of the cases are inspected, paying particular attention to the primers and primer pockets. Although the base of the case itself is fairly impervious to problems, the rim should be inspected to ensure there are no burs or damage that may interfere with extraction and ejection of the round once it has been fired.

When inspecting the primers and primer pockets, the shooter should first put the loaded rounds on their bases on a flat surface and ensure that the primers are not the first point of contact with the surface; the rounds will wobble around if the primers sit out from the bases. This is important because, if the primer is the first point of contact with the bolt face, the pressure when closing the bolt may cause a slam-fire to occur, which is dangerous not just to the shooter, but to bystanders, as well. Second the shooter should inspect the primers to ensure they are sitting flat inside the primer pocket, with no gaps around the primer and the wall of the pocket, and, finally, that they are firmly pressed in and not loose.

As one of two last tests, the shooter can also roll the rounds on a flat surface and observe the tip of the projectile. A projectile that is on axis will rotate about its longitudinal axis, while a projectile that is off axis will scribe a circle about its tip.

The last test that can be carried out is the testing of concentricity between the projectile and the case. Ideally, this is done with a concentricity gauge, though it can also be done in a metal lathe with a dial gauge. Essentially, the case is rolled around its long axis, while the measuring needle is placed on the projectile just forward of the case mouth. The gauge will register any run out or difference in axis between the projectile and the case. Any change greater than about 0.007-inch will lead to inferior accuracy, while a run-out of 0.003-inch or less is considered very good. Measurements below this figure will have no noticeable further benefit on accuracy.

The shooter, knowing the individual weights of the powder charge, projectile, and case can now add up those weights, along with that of the primer, and compare this completed weight with the weights of the actual loaded ammunition. This is a handy test that will show any problems, for instance, accidental over- or under-charging with propellant. The loaded rounds can then also be compared with each other to assess the consistency in weights and charges. If the shooter wishes, the rounds can be separated out into groups of similar weights. As a rule, weights between completed rounds of ammunition, consistently loaded, will not exceed one grain of difference.

The loaded rounds, having passed their inspections, can be considered safe to fire and should be stored appropriately until required.

## TESTING

Live-fire testing offers the shooter the opportunity to quantitatively assess their ammunition and improve their loading recipe to achieve greater accuracy, or

assists the shooter in choosing the most accurate commercial ammunition for their firearm. In its most basic form, testing of ammunition is as simple as firing a group of three to five rounds at a known distance and measuring the group size. This can be compared against, in the case of handloaded ammunition, other group sizes using different charge weights, or, in the case of commercial ammunition, different brands, projectile weights, or styles.

A part of your testing should be a chronograph, or "chrony," a valuable tool that measures velocity and one that can assist in improving the shooter's handloads. The most effective method for testing in this manner is to use the ladder test, which incorporates both group size analysis and measured velocity analysis.

To conduct a ladder test, the shooter takes either single rounds or three-round groups of charge

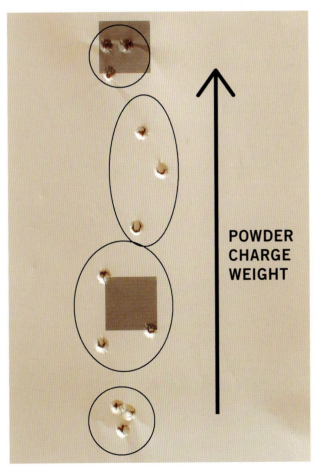

**POWDER CHARGE WEIGHT**

*Ladder testing can help the shooter identify accuracy "nodes" and help fine-tune loading recipes.*

weights that increase in perhaps half-grain increments. The shooter then fires these at the same target and aiming point at 200 meters. The result will be climbing bullet impacts that will congregate in groups. With the help of a spotter, the shooter will know which bullet impacts are which and will quickly see that, as a charge weight approaches optimum, a tight group, or "node," will be seen, with a minimum of vertical dispersion. This group will be accompanied by velocities for the individual rounds, as measured by the chronograph, that are very close. This is an "accuracy node," and there are generally two for any given cartridge in any given firearm, one occurring in the early to middle of the available charge loadings and the other roughly 1.5 grains below maximum.

Looking more closely at the velocity data, the shooter can quickly calculate the average velocity, perfect for use in ballistic calculations and drop and windage estimations. The shooter can also easily see the extreme spread of velocities their ammunition has achieved (though extreme spread only tells the shooter the maximum the velocity may vary). A more useful purpose for the data is to calculate the standard deviation of the velocities or, on average, what the average variation is the shooter can expect.

To calculate the standard deviation of velocities, the shooter simply calculates the average velocity and then deducts the average from the measured velocity for each round in a group of the same charge weight. Then the shooter squares the result for each round, adds the results together, divides by the number of rounds in the group and, finally, takes the square root of the result. The final number is the standard deviation for that group of rounds. While this sounds laborious, it allows the shooter to optimize their loadings and really gives them an insight into what they can expect from their ammunition in the field or at the range.

## STANDARD DEVIATION FORMULA

Round 1 .... 2789 fps

Round 2 .... 2796 fps

Round 3 .... 2792 fps

Round 4 .... 2760 fps

Round 5 .... 2787 fps

*Standard deviation is a simple formula for determining the average change in velocity the shooter can expect from their ammunition. This can make a big difference at long range, where most of the vertical component of the group size is due to velocity.*

$$\text{Standard Deviation} = \frac{2789 + 2796 + 2792 + 2760 + 2787}{5}$$

**= 2785 fps Average**

$$2798 - 2785 = 13 \times 13$$
$$2796 - 2785 = 11 \times 11$$
$$2792 - 2785 = 7 \times 7$$
$$2760 - 2785 = 25X - 25$$
$$2787 - 2785 = 2 \times 2$$
$$= 169 + 121 + 49 + 625 + 4$$
$$= 968$$
$$\overline{\quad 5 \quad}$$
$$= \sqrt{193.6}$$

**= 14 fps Standard Deviation**

# CHAPTER 13

# External Effects on Ammunition

External effects are those environmental forces that produce changes on the trajectory of a projectile in flight. While ballistic coefficients and velocities determine the trajectory data of a projectile in a laboratory setting, this data must be adjusted with regard to the environmental forces between the shooter and the target to obtain a real-world solution. The environmental forces in question consist of wind direction and strength, air temperature and density, humidity, barometric pressure, and altitude. Together, they are more commonly known as weather effects. Of them all, wind direction and strength are the most influential. The remainder should be used with all ballistic calculations at least on a "daily" basis, rather than measuring for each shot.

For the precision or long- to extreme-range shooter, there are other environmental forces to be considered. These forces consist of the Coriolis effect, or the rotation of the earth's surface; gyroscopic,

*External effects are all those factors outside the control of the shooter, but for which fall within the shooter's capacity to compensate.*

or spin-drift, the effect of a projectile pulling in the direction of rotation, thereby creating windage where there is no wind; the Magnus effect, or the effect of a crosswind "twisting" a projectile in flight; and Poisson's effect of high air pressure on the underside

*Weather effects are strange beasts. Here, a cloud sits almost permanently on top of this mountain, due to wind, humidity, and temperature changes about the summit.*

PHOTO COURTESY ALLY ROLLS PHOTOGRAPHY

of the projectile, which causes the projectile to roll away from the axis of flight in the direction of rotation.

While the calculation of all of these effects benefit from the use of ballistics software, basic windage can be calculated from a data table. More importantly, in order to achieve an accurate calculation, the shooter needs to estimate or measure the weather conditions accurately. The shooter's estimation of wind strength and direction with any inaccuracies will have a far greater impact on the ballistic solution than the use of standard atmospheric pressure and temperature in their calculations.

## WEATHER

Weather and the forces it creates form the major component of any ballistics calculation. When most shooters consider the weather, they really only think of wind direction and speed. But relative humidity, barometric pressure, temperature, and altitude also play significant roles. Further, correct estimation or measurement of these forces directly prior to calculating a ballistic solution can greatly enhance the accuracy of the solution. While many shooters

may consider this unnecessary (or perhaps are more accustomed to the thumb and squint of Kentucky windage they've learned through hit and miss), it never hurts to back up the art with some science—and get the hit every time!.

## WIND

The estimation of and compensation for wind is the most challenging aspect of long-range shooting. Wind direction and strength change from moment to moment and are different at every point between the shooter and the target. Wind direction and strength also change with the topography between the shooter and the target, causing dead spots over hollows and bowls in the ground, and wind can double in strength as it comes around spurs and through valleys. Even complete reversals of direction are possible, not to mention all the eddies, updrafts, and downdrafts. Wind is very much the invisible enemy of the shooter and accurate shooting. Or is it?

Accurate estimation of wind direction and strength relies on the shooter's use of environmental clues and can be supported by the use of technology. A shooter who uses their eyes and ears can generate a fairly accurate picture of the conditions between the firing point and the target and can then accurately compensate for the conditions.

## DIRECTION

Wind direction is the easiest component of windage to estimate, but estimation of the wind direction at the firing point is only part of the equation. The shooter must also assess the wind direction at the target and *en route*. This requires the shooter not only to "feel" the wind, but also to look for the environmental clues that permit assessment of the effects of the wind—in effect, *see* the wind!

Putting aside the use of ground-level range flags, at the firing point, the shooter can stand facing towards the wind and use their ears to hear the rush of air as the wind passes. When the sound is even across left ear and right, the shooter is facing into wind. While this is fairly rudimentary, it is also accurate. The shooter can also pick up a pile of leaves or sand and drop it, looking to see which way it moves with the wind.

When assessing the wind direction *en route* to and at the target, many shooters look to the leaves in trees or large bushes moving with the wind. Even respected literature cites the movement of swaying trees as being a useful environmental clue. Unfortunately, this is wrong. As height is gained over the earth's surface, wind speed increases and direction changes several times. This is because grass, boulders, and trees are all a source of friction for the air moving over and around them, slowing down the air. Of course, these obstructions can change the direction of the wind, too. So, the wind direction at treetop height may be a perfect three o'clock to nine o'clock crosswind, but because of a spur or low ridge, the actual direction across the path of the bullet near to ground level may be a seven o'clock semi-tailwind.

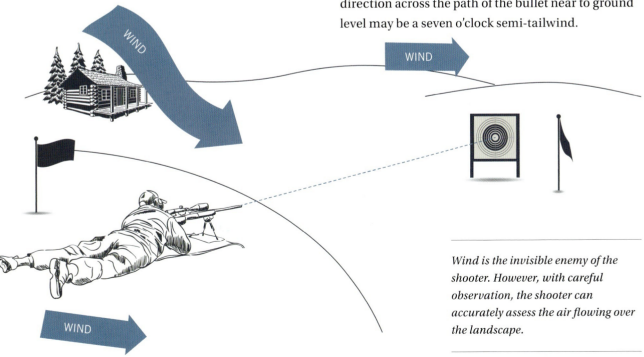

*Wind is the invisible enemy of the shooter. However, with careful observation, the shooter can accurately assess the air flowing over the landscape.*

Short and sweet, the shooter must only look at the environmental clues at bullet height or on the path of the bullet. For instance, if the shooter is taking a shot from the prone position across a flat grassy field lined by pines on either side, the grass will show the wind direction and ripples of wind can be seen like waves. Meanwhile, the clouds might be going a different direction and the tops of the pines another still.

Most shooters will assess the wind direction, as a *prevailing* condition and use that single direction for their calculations. Calculating a composite wind direction, taking into account the different wind directions between the shooter and the target, is very difficult and really only necessary for exceptionally long shots; doing so requires the shooter to consider the direction and the period of time the projectile is exposed to that particular direction before entering an area on the path where the direction is different. If a composite direction is needed, the most logical method is to break up the range to the target into thirds and consider the wind at the firing point, the target, and the path in between. The shooter can then average out the wind direction and make one calculation, rather than several.

Having assessed the wind direction, the shooter needs to consider how wind from that direction will affect the shot. To help determine this, the shooter needs to assign a direction in terms of a clock face, with 12 o'clock straight ahead, six o'clock behind, and nine and three o'clock left and right, respectively. As nearly all shooters know, with a pure three o'clock or nine o'clock

*The effect of the wind can be mitigated by its direction. Here, percentages of the whole wind value are assigned to various directions, for calculating windage adjustments.*

blow, the full force of the wind acts on the projectile to create windage. For these winds, the shooter needs to calculate the effect of the wind at 100 percent. With a headwind or tailwind, from 12 or six o'clock, there is no crosswind component, therefore the shooter calculates the effect of the wind at zero percent. In the case of a quartering crosswind, perhaps from seven to eight o'clock or one to two o'clock, there is a windage force that will push the projectile left or right in flight, but it won't be as strong as the full strength of the estimated or measured wind speed because it's not a direct crosswind. In cases such as that, the shooter applies a value to the wind of 50 percent; in some circumstances, a value of 75 percent can be used, purely for the reason that the effect of windage increases as a projectile slows down, typically over longer ranges. These percentage values are simply multiplied against the measured or estimated wind strength, and this final figure is what the shooter uses as the crosswind for their calculations.

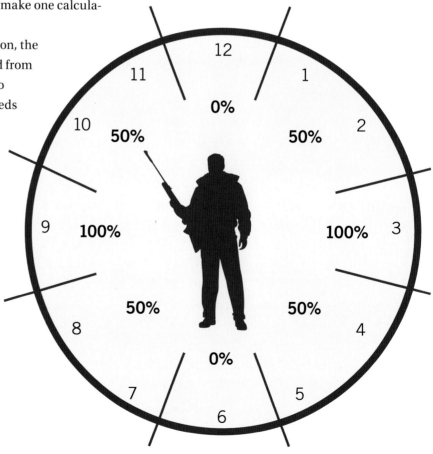

*Even over a relatively flat piece of ground,
the wind can do strange things!*

## STRENGTH

Where wind direction is the easiest part of calculating windage, estimating the wind *strength* is definitely the most challenging. That said, there are a number of methods for estimating wind strength and, with practice, the shooter can become very accurate with their wind strength estimations.

Putting aside the estimations for a moment, the best way to measure wind strength is with the use of an anemometer, of which there are many handheld, off-the-shelf varieties that will provide the shooter with not just the wind speed at any particular moment, but also the maximum, minimum, and a useful average. When employed correctly, this tool will very accurately gauge the wind strength from where it is measured.

As it is with gauging wind direction, the measurement of wind speed should be taken on the projectile's path (unless the shooter is, perhaps, firing from the precipice of a cliff where the wind strength at the muzzle is completely out of context with the rest of the projectile's path over the cliff). When estimating wind speed at the firing point or at other points along the projectile's path, there are several methods available to the shooter.

First, the shooter can employ the age-old military method for wind strength estimation. Where there is wind at one to three miles per hour, tall dry grass will move. Two to four mile per hour winds can be just felt on the face, while those at four to eight will sway standing crops, six to 10 will sway tall bushes, and 10-plus mile per hour winds will sway trees. This method can be accurate if the shooter is familiar with their environment and has practiced and calibrated their senses with known wind strengths or has made an estimation and then checked it on an anemometer.

The second method uses a rifle scope or spotting scope to observe mirage (if any). This method is best used with a scope having a magnification of 10x or greater. When observing the mirage, if it is boiling or moving upwards, there is no wind. If the mirage is moving across the field of view at about 60 degrees, the wind speed is between one and three miles per hour. If the mirage is moving at 45 degrees, the wind speed is between four and seven and, if the mirage is moving at 90 degrees across the field of view, the wind speed is in excess of 10 miles per hour.

The third method uses angles on visual clues to estimate wind speed. For instance, if a flag can be seen, the shooter takes the angle of the flag to the flagpole and divides the angle by four. This will yield the wind speed in miles per hour, remembering, of course, that this is the wind speed at the top of a flagpole, not the path of the projectile. Likewise, if the shooter picks up a handful of leaves or a handkerchief and drops it from shoulder height and then points at the spot where the leaves lands, the shooter can take the angle between the their arm and body and divide this angle by four to yield the wind speed. In a third example, the shooter can observe a column of smoke and take the angle between the dead vertical and the column and divide this angle by four to yield the wind speed.

As you can see, there are many methods available for measuring and estimating wind speed. You must remember, though, that your measurement, although accurate, only measures the wind speed *at the measuring point*. To determine the wind speed on the projectile's path, that must be combined with estimation techniques to determine the overall "air picture." Estimation techniques, while not as accurate, can provide good solutions with practice, and, of course, the shooter can use more than one estimation technique for the same wind.

## IMPLEMENTATION

Having determined the wind direction and estimated the wind speed, the shooter now needs to convert that information into a windage value that can be input into a scope via the windage turret, or held over for using the scope's reticle. Accepting that the shooter has moved beyond thumb-and-squint Kentucky windage, the shooter first consults their data table.

Produced by commercial ammunition producers or, in the case of handloads, either the projectile manufacturer or via the use of good quality ballistics software, this table will show the windage adjustment required at given wind speeds at particular ranges. As a rule, commercial producers of ammunition and projectiles generally show the ranges in increments of 100 yards or meters, and the windage values in increments of five, 10, and 15 miles per hour. In this case, the shooter simply looks up the range at which they are shooting and cross references that with the wind speed value.

Ideally, if the shooter is constructing their own data tables using velocities, ballistic coefficients, and suitable ballistics software, the shooter should calculate their data table in range increments of 25 yards/meters, and the windage should always show the deflection for a one mile per hour wind. Not only

will this allow a high degree of accuracy in terms of the elevation adjustment, the windage adjustment can be quickly and easily multiplied out against the actual wind speed for an exact windage adjustment.

Having cross-referenced the range and wind speed, the shooter can then read off the windage adjustment. This adjustment will either be expressed as a distance of deflection in inches or centimeters or as an angular adjustment in minutes of angle (MOA). The shooter then inputs this adjustment into their scope using the manufacturer's instructions, although most scopes use systems such as "one click equals one inch at 100 meters." In such cases, an adjustment value expressed in minutes of angle (MOA), noting that one MOA equals 1.145 inches at 100 meters and 1.047 inches at 100 yards, is close enough to one inch for a scope turret set in whole inches to work adequately.

An adjustment value expressed as a distance of deflection can be converted to MOA by dividing the range by 10, next dividing the adjustment value by the resulting number, then dividing the result again by either 1.145 for distance in meters or 1.047 for distance in yards. The final result is the adjustment value in minutes of angle (MOA). Although this sounds complicated, it can really be quickly and accurately calculated. Alternately, the shooter can pre-calculate a list of specified wind speeds and, instead of calculating the adjustment for each shot, can simply refer to the list and choose the adjustment value calculated on the conditions that best match the actual conditions.

Where the shooter has access to a PDA or smartphone loaded with ballistics software, the shooter need only input the exact range, the wind direction, and the wind speed. The ballistics software will then calculate the exact windage adjustment required for that particular shot.

There is another, relatively fast method for windage solutions, and it's accurate to whole minutes of angle. The shooter simply divides the range by 10 and multiplies that number by the wind speed in miles per hour. Then, for ranges up to 500 yards/meters, divide by 15. The result is the windage adjustment in minutes of angle (MOA). For ranges in excess of 500 yards/meters, the shooter simply divides by 14 for 600 meters, 13 for 700 meters, and so on.

## TEMPERATURE

Temperature and changes in temperature can affect both how a projectile flies and how propellant and primers perform. Looking first at the effect of temperature on ballistics, many shooters know that, when the temperature increases, air becomes less dense. Air that is less dense causes less friction against the projectile in flight, therefore allowing the projectile to retain its velocity better. In essence, less dense air increases the ballistic coefficient of the projectile.

Projectiles exposed to less dense air in a warmer environment will impact higher. Conversely, projectiles exposed to colder/denser air will impact lower. To calculate the actual change in ballistic coefficient caused by the warmer/cooler temperatures, the shooter should really reach for some good quality ballistics software. Of course, that's not always possible, so, to calculate this by hand, the shooter takes the temperature of the day (in degrees Fahrenheit), minus the temperature of a standard day (or the day the rifle was zeroed), and divide this number by the temperature of the day plus a constant of 459.6. Finally, the shooter adds one (1) to this number. The result is a factor that should be multiplied against the original ballistic coefficient. The new ballistic coefficient is now compensated for temperature and can be used for ballistic calculations.

Temperature will affect the burn rate of powders and primers. As many shooters know, the chance of having a misfire in very cold weather seems to be greatly increased. This is because the explosive filler in the primer is made more stable by colder temperatures. Also, primers and their fillers are designed to be unstable, impact-triggered explosives, so it is easy to see that, if the primer is made more stable, it is less likely to fire and, if it does, it may release its energy over a longer period, leading to weak or uneven ignition of the propellant. This will lead to greater variances of muzzle velocities between shots.

### SAMPLE WINDAGE CALCULATION

.308 Winchester 175-grain (.495 C) 2635 fps

Range: 450m

Wind Direction: 8 o'clock (100% value wind)

Wind Strength: 6 mph

Windage Drift per 1 mph of crosswind: 1.8 inches

**Drift x Wind Strength**

Range in Hundreds x Conversion Factor inches to MOA

$$\frac{1.8" \times 6 \text{ mph}}{4.5 \times 1.145}$$

$$\frac{10.8}{5.155}$$

**= 2.1 MOA**

*It looks like lots mathematics, but, once learned, windage calculations are simple and fast to calculate.*

| FAST WINDAGE TABLE | | | |
|---|---|---|---|
| Range (m) | Factor | Wind Speed (mph) | MOA Windage |
| 100 | 15 | 5 | 0.33 |
| 200 | 15 | 5 | 0.66 |
| 300 | 15 | 5 | 1 |
| 400 | 15 | 5 | 1.33 |
| 500 | 15 | 5 | 1.66 |
| 600 | 14 | 5 | 2.14 |
| 700 | 13 | 5 | 2.69 |
| 800 | 12 | 5 | 3.33 |
| 900 | 11 | 5 | 4.09 |
| 1000 | 10 | 5 | 5 |

*Depending on the target size, good accuracy can be achieved through the use of the fast windage table. As always, the shooter needs to test the accuracy of the table with their own firearm and ammunition combination.*

The same problems also occur with propellants. If it is cold, the propellant will burn more slowly, leading to lower pressures and lower muzzle velocities. Low temperatures can also create an erratic and uneven burn, leading to a much greater variance in muzzle velocities between shots.

In colder temperatures, many shooters suggest that Magnum primers be used to enhance the primer jet and normalize the ignition of the propellant. This is a perfectly feasible path to take, though the shooter must ensure that their handloads have been appropriately worked up with Magnum primers and are safe to fire.

## HUMIDITY

As much as changes in temperature affect changes in air density, so can humidity. Humidity describes the amount of moisture suspended in the air at any given time. For instance, the humidity in a desert may only be five percent, while the humidity in a steamy jungle may be 90 percent. In a rain cloud, humidity is 100 percent. Humidity, as a rule, cannot be estimated.

The best source for a correct humidity figure is obtained through the use of a Kestrel weather station or other similar tool. Alternately, anticipated humidity figures can be obtained from the local weather station or bureau of meteorology. As the shooter can see, if there is more matter in the air than just air (in this case, water), the density of the air is *decreased*, because a molecule of water weighs less than a molecule of air. As the shooter knows, the less dense the air, the less friction acts against the projectile and the higher the projectile will impact. Likewise, if the current humidity is reduced from when the rifle was zeroed, the projectile will impact lower.

Again, to calculate the effect of humidity, the shooter should utilize good quality ballistics software. Still, as a rule, calculations involving humidity are not really necessary, as the change in ballistic coefficient from completely dry air to completely saturated air is only about two percent. However, it is still a variable, and for very long-range or precision shooting, humidity should be accounted for.

## BAROMETRIC PRESSURE

Barometric pressure, the natural air pressure of the atmosphere, affects air density directly. The barometric pressure changes with natural weather cycles of high and low pressure systems on a daily basis, and it also changes with altitude. During a high pressure weather event, the air density increases and, as such, the friction against a projectile increases. This, in turn, effectively decreases the ballistic coefficient of the projectile and, therefore, increases projectile drop with distance. Changes in barometric pressure have a far more pronounced effect on ballistic coefficients than humidity or temperature and should be taken into account with medium- to long-range shooting.

Ideally, the absolute barometric pressure should be measured at the time of zeroing the firearm. The barometric pressure can be easily measured with a Kestrel or other handheld weather station. Alternately, the shooter can also look at the current weather report and get a figure for the average barometric pressure on that day. On successive days when the shooter intends to shoot in the medium to long ranges, the shooter can either measure the barometric pressure again or look up the barometric pressure for that particular day.

To calculate the effect of any change in barometric pressure between the day the firearm was zeroed and the current shooting day, the shooter simply takes the barometric pressure on the day afield and deducts the barometric pressure taken the day the firearm was zeroed. This number is then divided by the barometric pressure on the day the firearm was zeroed, and then one (1) is subtracted from the resulting number. This figure is then multiplied against the ballistic coefficient of the projectile. After this, the ballistic calculations or tables are calculated as normal, compensated for the change in barometric pressure.

## ALTITUDE

Where changes in temperature, humidity, and barometric pressure can all occur independently, changes in altitude affect all three parameters. As altitude increases, temperature, barometric pressure,

# TABLE OF STANDARD ATMOSPHERES

| ALTITUDE | | TEMP. | PRESSURE | | PRESSURE RATIO | DENSITY | SPEED OF SOUND |
| (Feet) | (Meters) | (°C) | (hPa) | (in. Hg.) | | | (kt) |
|---|---|---|---|---|---|---|---|
| 40,000 | 12,182 | -56.5 | 188 | 5.54 | 0.1851 | 0.2462 | 573 |
| 39,000 | 11,887 | -56.5 | 197 | 5.81 | 0.1942 | 0.2583 | 573 |
| 38,000 | 11,582 | -56.5 | 206 | 6.10 | 0.2038 | 0.2710 | 573 |
| 37,000 | 11,278 | -56.5 | 217 | 6.40 | 0.2138 | 0.2844 | 573 |
| 36,000 | 10,973 | -56.3 | 227 | 6.71 | 0.2243 | 0.2981 | 573 |
| 35,000 | 10,668 | -54.3 | 238 | 7.04 | 0.2353 | 0.3099 | 576 |
| 34,000 | 10,363 | -52.4 | 250 | 7.38 | 0.2467 | 0.3220 | 579 |
| 33,000 | 10,058 | -50.4 | 262 | 7.74 | 0.2586 | 0.3345 | 581 |
| 32,000 | 9,754 | -48.4 | 274 | 8.11 | 0.2709 | 0.3473 | 584 |
| 31,000 | 9,449 | -46.4 | 287 | 8.49 | 0.2837 | 0.3605 | 586 |
| 30,000 | 9,144 | -44.4 | 301 | 8.89 | 0.2970 | 0.3741 | 589 |
| 29,000 | 8,839 | -42.5 | 315 | 9.30 | 0.3107 | 0.3881 | 591 |
| 28,000 | 8,534 | -40.5 | 329 | 9.73 | 0.3250 | 0.4025 | 594 |
| 27,000 | 8,230 | -38.5 | 344 | 10.17 | 0.3398 | 0.4173 | 597 |
| 26,000 | 7,925 | -36.5 | 360 | 10.63 | 0.3552 | 0.4325 | 599 |
| 25,000 | 7,620 | -34.5 | 376 | 11.10 | 0.3711 | 0.4481 | 602 |
| 24,000 | 7,315 | -32.5 | 393 | 11.60 | 0.3876 | 0.4642 | 604 |
| 23,000 | 7,010 | -30.6 | 410 | 12.11 | 0.4046 | 0.4806 | 607 |
| 22,000 | 6,706 | -28.6 | 428 | 12.64 | 0.4223 | 0.4976 | 609 |
| 21,000 | 6,401 | -26.6 | 446 | 13.18 | 0.4406 | 0.5150 | 611 |
| 20,000 | 6,096 | -24.6 | 466 | 13.75 | 0.4595 | 0.5328 | 614 |
| 19,000 | 5,791 | -22.6 | 485 | 14.34 | 0.4791 | 0.5511 | 616 |
| 18,000 | 5,486 | -20.7 | 506 | 14.94 | 0.4994 | 0.5699 | 619 |
| 17,000 | 5,182 | -18.7 | 527 | 15.57 | 0.5203 | 0.5892 | 621 |
| 16,000 | 4,877 | -16.7 | 549 | 16.22 | 0.5420 | 0.6090 | 624 |
| 15,000 | 4,572 | -14.7 | 572 | 16.89 | 0.5643 | 0.6292 | 626 |
| 14,000 | 4,267 | -12.7 | 595 | 17.58 | 0.5875 | 0.6500 | 628 |
| 13,000 | 3,962 | -10.8 | 619 | 18.29 | 0.6113 | 0.6713 | 631 |
| 12,000 | 3,658 | -8.8 | 644 | 19.03 | 0.6360 | 0.6932 | 633 |
| 11,000 | 3,353 | -6.8 | 670 | 19.79 | 0.6614 | 0.7156 | 636 |
| 10,000 | 3,048 | -4.8 | 697 | 20.58 | 0.6877 | 0.7385 | 638 |
| 9,000 | 2,743 | -2.8 | 724 | 21.39 | 0.7148 | 0.7620 | 640 |
| 8,000 | 2,438 | -0.8 | 753 | 22.22 | 0.7428 | 0.7860 | 643 |
| 7,000 | 2,134 | 1.1 | 782 | 23.09 | 0.7716 | 0.8106 | 645 |
| 6,000 | 1,829 | 3.1 | 812 | 23.98 | 0.8014 | 0.8359 | 647 |
| 5,000 | 1,524 | 5.1 | 843 | 24.90 | 0.8320 | 0.8617 | 650 |
| 4,000 | 1,219 | 7.1 | 875 | 25.84 | 0.8637 | 0.8881 | 652 |
| 3,000 | 914 | 9.1 | 908 | 26.82 | 0.8962 | 0.9151 | 654 |
| 2,000 | 610 | 11.0 | 942 | 27.82 | 0.9298 | 0.9428 | 656 |
| 1,000 | 305 | 13.0 | 977 | 28.86 | 0.9644 | 0.9711 | 659 |
| 0 | 0 | 15.0 | 1013 | 29.92 | 1.0000 | 1.0000 | 661 |
| -1,000 | -305 | 17.0 | 1050 | 31.02 | 1.0366 | 1.0295 | 664 |

*As altitude increases, temperature, pressure, and relative humidity decrease. This table of standard atmospheres can be used for calculating ballistic corrections. (To clarify some of the lesser-known measurements above: hPa = barometric pressure as measued in the number of hecto-Pascal units; in. Hg. = inches of mercury; kt = knots.)*

and humidity all change at different rates, but the important point here is that they all *will* change.

The shooter can compensate for altitude changes in three ways. First and ideally, the shooter can input the absolute measurements of temperature, humidity, and barometric pressure into their PDA or ballistics software and compare them against the temperature, humidity, and barometric pressure on the day the firearm was zeroed. The ballistics software, in most cases, will automatically make the calculation and adjustment to the shooter's elevation.

Second, the shooter can take absolute measurements of temperature, humidity, and barometric pressure and compare them against the temperature, humidity, and barometric pressure taken on the day the firearm was zeroed. This will yield a highly accurate compensation for these environmental forces by adjusting the ballistic coefficient for the calculation of data tables or adjustments. Changes in temperature, humidity, and barometric pressure are calculated in the normal way already discussed, then multiplied against each other and the standard ballistic coefficient of the projectile being used. This will lead to an altitude-compensated ballistic coefficient.

The final method for calculating compensation for changes in altitude is to compare the temperature, humidity, and barometric pressure on the day the firearm was zeroed with standard atmospheric data. Standard atmospheric data appears in a table that shows standard temperature, humidity, and barometric pressure with rising altitude, normally in increments of 500 feet.

Although this last method sounds rudimentary, it does have benefits. For one, it will deliver a useful rounds-on-target compensation of the projectile's ballistic coefficient. Some further adjustment may be necessary, but it will, in most cases, be minor. Second, this method does not require the shooter to use a Kestrel or other weather station to collect data on the day afield, useful if the shooter is backpack hunting in the mountains (or has simply forgotten it!). Third and most importantly, this method is the perfect one to use in pre-hunt or pre-competition planning, if the shooter wants to determine if any altitude compensation will be necessary on a future hunt or competition at a different altitude.

As previously discussed, error through a lack of altitude compensation, temperature, humidity, and

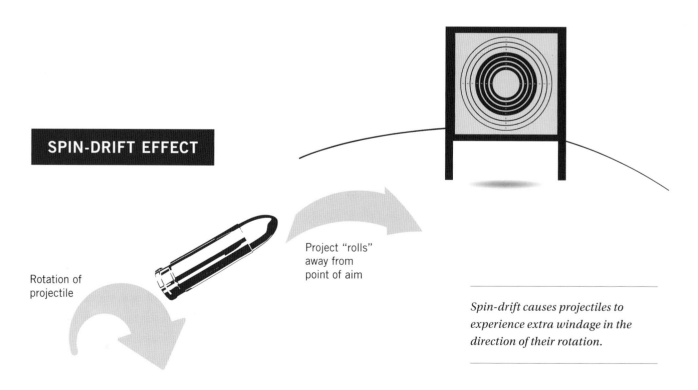

**SPIN-DRIFT EFFECT**

Rotation of projectile

Project "rolls" away from point of aim

*Spin-drift causes projectiles to experience extra windage in the direction of their rotation.*

barometric pressure independently will tend to show up from medium to long ranges onward, but be disguised at closer ranges. Though in most hunting situations and a large component of competition situations, compensation for these environmental forces are very much icing on the cake, it is not only a good practice to get into to make every shot the best it can be, but also, in the situations when a shooter wants to get out of their comfort zone, they have the correct tools to make a longer shot successfully.

## THE SPIN-DRIFT EFFECT

The spin-drift effect, also known as gyroscopic drift, is a force that acts, without any wind, on a rotating projectile in flight to effect drift. Spin drift is a function of the twist rate of the barrel the projectile has been fired from, the length of the projectile, and the range, flight time, and trajectory of the projectile in flight. Spin drift is caused by the rotational axis of the projectile deviating from the direction of the projectile's flight. Projectiles rotating to the right will tend to move to the right, projectiles rotating to the left will move to the left. The effect is similar to an unbalanced washing machine walking noisily in a particular direction.

Compensation for spin drift is only achievable by measuring the amount of drift at set ranges in perfectly calm conditions; there is no trend to allow for guestimation of spin drift. The data on actual experienced spin drift is fed into ballistics software and an algorithm is formulated to account for spin drift in that particular firearm with that particular load. Spin drift can cause significant error in shot placement, as much as 12 inches at long and extreme ranges.

## THE MAGNUS EFFECT

The Magnus effect relates to the relationship between a projectile's center of gravity along its length and the center of pressure or sideways force from a crosswind. The Magnus effect works by twisting the projectile, when the center of pressure and center of gravity are not in the same position on the longitudinal axis of the projectile; effectively, the

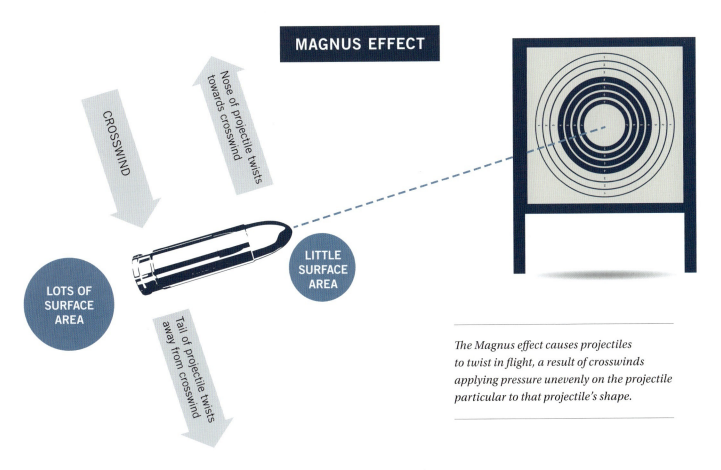

**MAGNUS EFFECT**

CROSSWIND

Nose of projectile twists towards crosswind

Tail of projectile twists away from crosswind

LOTS OF SURFACE AREA

LITTLE SURFACE AREA

*The Magnus effect causes projectiles to twist in flight, a result of crosswinds applying pressure unevenly on the projectile particular to that projectile's shape.*

crosswind pushes the tip of the projectile out of the axis of rotation. This effect is exacerbated on longer projectiles, particularly very low drag (VLD) projectiles, and with increasing crosswind strengths.

The resulting gyroscopic force pushes the projectile vertically. Projectiles with a right-hand rotation in a crosswind from the right will drift down; the same projectile with a crosswind from the left will drift up.

Although the results of the Magnus effect are not as severe as those from the spin drift effect, the vertical drift can still be measured in inches at long and extreme ranges. However, as the strength of this effect relates directly to the profile shape of the projectile in question, it is very difficult to compensate for.

## THE POISSON EFFECT

The Poisson effect relates to the axis of rotation of the projectile being either above or below the direction of flight. This effect is rarely experienced and has far less effect on shot place than does spin drift. The Poisson effect is created by a high-pressure air zone forming on the top of the tip of the projectile (if the axis is below the direction of flight), vice versa if the axis is above the direction of flight. This high-pressure zone, in conjunction with the rotation of the projectile, causes an extra sideways force in the direction of rotation, as the projectile effectively "rolls" away from the high-pressure zone.

While knowledge of the Poisson effect is sensible, compensating for it is nearly impossible, due in part to its weak effect on rifle trajectories, and also because it's nearly impossible to determine if and when it is occurring.

## THE CORIOLIS EFFECT

The Coriolis effect relates to the rotation of Earth's surface while the projectile is in flight. The Coriolis effect affects projectiles, because the position of the shooter on the Earth's rotating surface does not provide a straight line to the target, but rather a curved line, as the target is, essentially, a moving target.

The result of the Coriolis effect is dependent on the latitude of the shooter and the direction the shooter

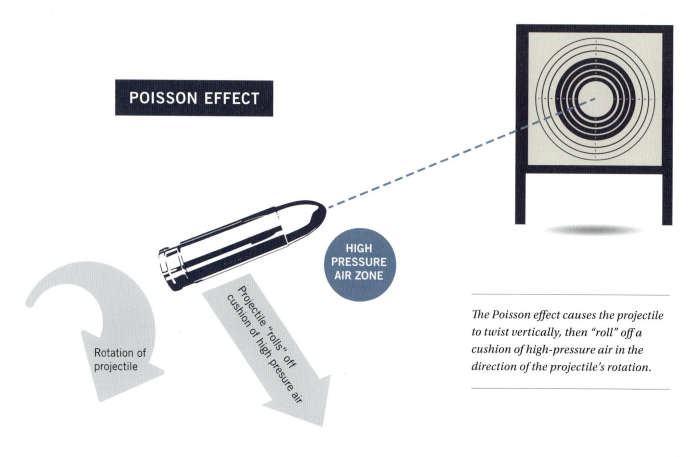

**POISSON EFFECT**

HIGH PRESSURE AIR ZONE

Projectile "rolls" off cushion of high pressure air

Rotation of projectile

*The Poisson effect causes the projectile to twist vertically, then "roll" off a cushion of high-pressure air in the direction of the projectile's rotation.*

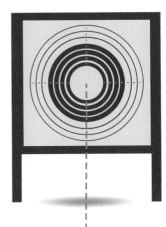

Target moves
while projectile
is in flight

*The Coriolis effect
causes windage, due
to the rotation of the
Earth's surface.*

SKETCH COURTESY ALLY ROLLS PHOTOGRAPHY

*On a clear night during a hunt, the effect of the earth
spinning is obvious!*

is shooting in. If the shooter is in the Northern Hemisphere shooting perfectly North/South, the projectile will appear to drift to the right (from the shooter's perspective), vice versa in the Southern Hemisphere. If the shooter is shooting perfectly East/West, there is no change in the rotational velocity of the Earth's surface between the firing point and the target, but the left or right drift will remain the same for that latitude due to the curvature of the Earth's surface. If the shot is towards the East, the projectile will impact high, because Earth is rotating towards the firing point. If the shooter is shooting to the West, the projectile will impact low, because Earth is rotating away from the firing point.

To calculate the vertical and lateral drift due to the Coriolis effect, the shooter needs only their latitude and direction of the shot. This data can be input into good quality ballistics software and the result accounted for in the ballistics solution. Manual calculation of the Coriolis effect goes well beyond the needs of most shooters and the scope of this book.

The Coriolis effect need only be considered at long to extreme ranges. As an example, a .308 fired North/South will experience drift in the order of three inches or so at 1,000 yards— *significant* drift for this kind of distance. In most shooting situations, the drift caused by the Coriolis effect over shorter ranges, although present, is too small to compensate for or notice.

**CHAPTER 14**

# Safe Firearms Handling

The first principle of accurate shooting is to ensure the shooter is operating the rifle and ammunition correctly, consistently, and reliably. To achieve this, it is best to start at a grass roots level. The human body, like a rifle, is a machine. It must be maintained properly in order to carry out whatever tasks we ask of it. Ask yourself, how many times have you made it to the firing line or to your favorite hunting stand and are jittery and have a headache because you missed your morning coffee, or are out of breath and can't hold good aim after hiking to the top of a saddle or back from the 300m line? I'll expand more on how to tune the shooter's body at the end of this Part III, so let's backtrack for a moment and address the numerous factors that go into perfecting the act of shooting.

As much as it is about the rifle and the ammunition in their individual idealization, accurate shooting is also about how the human body interacts with the

*Diamonds in the rough. Any shooter can benefit from tuning their own body.*

rifle. From the choice of shooting position to breathing control, heartbeat timing, trigger control, and correct sight picture, good accuracy can be ensured and gains achieved long before the shooter squeezes the trigger. By following a few simple rules, you, the shooter, can avoid trigger flinch, hold your rifle steadily, choose a firing position appropriately for your target and shooting location, and know when to allow that round to leave the barrel, all so that your rifle and ammunition become the limiting factor for accuracy, instead of you.

## FIREARMS SAFETY

Firearms safety is everybody's responsibility. The shooter needs to be aware of the safety of their own firearm, the location they are in relation to others and their firearms, and the area they are shooting into. The golden rule of firearms safety is to treat every firearm as though it is loaded and ready to fire. This is applicable at all times and applies to all firearms, whether they belong to you or not. If this basic rule is followed, no dangerous situations should develop and no mishaps occur. There are many other layers of safety, of course, and it is the responsibility of the shooter to determine which should apply to them and when and where.

## DEGREES OF FIREARM READINESS

The degrees of firearm readiness form a framework for the shooter to understand how to utilize their firearm in a safe manner. This framework is an excellent model for safe operations of all types of firearms and ensures that a firearm is capable of being fired only when the shooter is ready to shoot.

The first degree of firearm readiness is "unload." In this state, the firearm has no rounds in the chamber, no rounds in the magazine, and the magazine is detached (if possible).

The second degree is "load." Here, there are rounds in the magazine and, if detachable, the magazine is fitted to the rifle.

The third degree is "action." Now there is a round in the chamber, regardless whether a magazine is fitted. Also, the cocking piece or striker is held rearward by the trigger mechanism and the safety is engaged.

The fourth and final degree of firearm readiness is "instant." In this capacity, there is a round in the chamber, irrespective of whether a magazine is fitted, the cocking piece or striker is held rearward by the trigger mechanism, and the safety is disengaged. In other words, the firearm is capable of being fired.

Moving from one degree to the other, this framework should be practiced until it is second nature. Real-world application of this safety framework could take the following form, as an example.

The shooter travels by car to the range (or hunting area), with all firearms in the "unload" condition. Once arrived and set up at the range, the shooter moves to the shooting bay when authorized and proceeds to the "load" condition; in the case of a hunting afield, when the shooter arrives in the hunting area and is ready to commence hunting, they also proceed to the "load" condition.

## DEGREES OF FIREARM READINESS
*The degrees of firearm readiness—a simple plan for safety!*

| DEGREE OF WEAPON READINESS | ROUNDS IN THE MAGAZINE | ROUNDS IN THE CHAMBER | SAFETY ENGAGED |
|---|---|---|---|
| UNLOAD | ✗ | ✗ | ✓ |
| LOAD | ✓ | ✗ | ✓ |
| ACTION | ✓ | ✓ | ✓ |
| INSTANT | ✓ | ✓ | ✗ |

*Unload, load, action, and instant. All shooters should always know the condition of their firearm, for safety's sake and to ensure they don't miss a shot due to firing on an empty chamber or pulling a trigger while the gun's on safe!*

Back at the range, the shooter now has targets to their front, but with no authorization given to fire, the shooter may proceed only to the "action" condition. For the hunter reaching their hunting stand or a specific area they intend to hunt, this is the point where they, too, may proceed to the "action" condition.

At the range again, the green flags are flying, indicating that it is safe to shoot, so the shooter proceeds to the "instant" condition and proceeds to engage targets. The hunter, seeing the big buck they've tracked has appeared from behind some bushes, will likewise proceed to "instant" and engage the animal.

Finally, at the range, once the shooting serial has concluded, the shooter would proceed back to the "unload" condition and withdraw from the shooting mound, likewise for the hunt concluded with the taking of the buck.

Of course there are caveats to this particular scenario. For instance, the shooter may be shooting a second serial, and the hunter may be hunting dangerous game—in either case, the shooter should choose their degrees of firearm readiness based on the environment and activities. Most important of all, know what degree of firearm readiness your firearm is in at all times!

## HANDLING OF FIREARMS

The term "handling of firearms" refers to the basic manner in which firearms are held and ensuring that they are never pointed in a direction that could harm anyone, including the shooter. It bears repeating that firearms should always be handled as though they are loaded and ready to fire.

Holding a firearm, the shooter should always be aware of where it is pointed. If removing a firearm from a safe at home or out of the trunk of a car at the range, the shooter should always make sure the arc they swing the firearm through to remove it from the these places is clear of people. While walking on a hunt, the shooter should ensure that the firearm is never pointed at fellow hunters. This is particularly important when hunting as a group and the group is single file or in an otherwise extended line. Also, when cleaning a firearm, the shooter must ensure the firearm is never pointed at anyone, remembering that a partially dismantled firearm may still be capable of being fired.

## FIREARMS CARRIAGE

First and foremost, when a firearm is picked up, it must be picked up in such a way that it can be determined if the safety is engaged and, in doing so, that the firearm cannot be accidentally fired.

When carrying firearms, the shooter must grip the firearm correctly, to ensure the firearm isn't inadvertently dropped nor pointed in a direction that may harm a bystander or the shooter. During carry, the primary hand (the hand that operates the trigger), must never leave the pistol grip or wrist of the stock. Too, the trigger finger must never touch the trigger until the shooter is ready to shoot and the firearm is at the "instant" condition. The secondary hand should grip the forearm of the stock, provided the shooter is not carrying out some other task with that hand. It is always the secondary hand that is used to move bushes aside or cushion the body as the shooter lies down to shoot. Finally, the butt of the firearm should be held near the biceps of the arm of the primary hand and the firearm positioned across the body. Firearms should never be carried by the muzzle and the stock over the shoulder, nor should they be carried by the forearm with the butt balancing on the hip.

In slinging a firearm, the firearm needs to be slung in such a manner that not only is the rifle pointing in a safe direction when slung, but also that the firearm is pointed in a safe direction *as* it is slung. To do

*Carrying a firearm properly is a balance between safety, comfort, and function. A poorly carried firearm will be uncomfortable to bear, as well as unsafe, and it will also be slow to bring to the shoulder and aim.*

this, the firearm is held by the sling (having ensured that the sling is correctly fitted and secure), by the secondary hand, with the muzzle pointed towards the ground. The primary hand and head are then passed through the loop of the sling and the firearm is rotated onto the back of the shooter. This process concludes (for a right-handed shooter), with the firearms butt behind the left shoulder and the muzzle pointed at the ground to the right of the shooter.

## TRANSFER OF FIREARMS

When passing a firearm from one person to another, it is easy for lapses in safety to occur. These lapses can occur for many reasons, the simplest being that different shooters may have different ideas on what a safe situation is, while others may be ignorant of the degree of firearm readiness that the firearm is at.

Firearms should always be transferred from one person to another in the "unload" condition with the action open. There is no reason this cannot occur. It allows the person receiving the firearm to see that it is unloaded and also adopt their own degree of firearm readiness from the base of a safe condition.

When transferring a firearm from one person to another, the person giving up control of the firearm should grip the firearm about its forearm with the secondary hand and place the primary hand on the butt of the firearm. This allows the person receiving the firearm to grip initially with the primary hand on the pistol grip or about the wrist of the stock and then grip the forearm of the firearm with the secondary hand to take control. Having received the firearm safely, the receiving shooter then must clear the firearm, once again ensuring that it is safe and unloaded, and then adopt his or her own degree of firearm readiness.

With the physics of transferring firearms from shooter to shooter safely out of the way, the next question is when would all of this occur? The simple rule for determining this is when handling or possessing the firearm may create a dangerous situation and a fellow shooter is available to take carriage of the firearm. For instance, when a pair of hunters have come across a

*Fences claim lives every year in shooting accidents. Use common sense when crossing a fence or transferring any firearm from one person to another.*

fence, the first hunter hands their firearm to the second hunter using the process detailed above, and then negotiates the fence. Next, the second hunter hands both firearms one by one to the first hunter, again using the same process, the hunter receiving the firearms placing the first flat on the ground and holding the second until the second hunter has negotiated the fence. Once the second hunter has crossed, the second firearm is handed back to the second hunter using the process above, and the first hunter picks up their own firearm using the safe process for doing so. In an alternate case that might happen at the range, a shooter may be handing his or her firearm to a range safety officer or competition adjudicator for inspection. The same process of handing the firearm to the second person and receiving it back is so followed.

Simple structure such as this adds a significant amount of safety to an otherwise potentially unsafe situation. Further, it allows the shooter to gain confidence in the handling of their own firearm and permits others to gain confidence in and feel comfortable with the shooter and their handling skills.

# Misfires

Misfires occur, even with modern firearms and ammunition, and it is extremely important that the shooter knows what to do in the event of one. The shooter must be able to identify the misfire, carry out a clearing of it, and return the firearm to a safe state from any degree of firearm readiness.

Misfires can be categorized in the following terms: feeding failures that will result in the firearm not chambering a round; firing failures that result in the chambered round not firing; and extraction and ejection failures, which will result in the expended round not being extracted and ejected from the firearm. The first two failures are the most dangerous, as the firearm may well be in a fireable condition in either case.

In the case of a feeding failure, the shooter actions the rifle, but the top round in the magazine fails to strip from the magazine, resulting in the bolt closing on an empty chamber. The shooter pulls the trigger and is rewarded with an oddly loud click. Here, the shooter is not aware that there is no round in the chamber (and the symptoms described are the same for a "hang-fire" which will be discussed in a bit). When this happens, the shooter must remain in the shooting position, with the firearm pointed downrange for at least 30 seconds. Having waited the 30 seconds, the shooter keeps the firearm pointed downrange and the safety is then engaged. The shooter then tips the rifle onto its side with the ejection port pointed to the ground, and then the firearm is returned to the load state with the opening of the bolt. This helps to ensure that any obstructions fall free from the firearm, and also that, if there is some kind of chamber explosion while the bolt is open, the blast is directed down and away from the shooter and anybody else on the firing line.

With the opening of the bolt, the shooter is able to observe the empty chamber and plainly see that a round had not been extracted and ejected. Having next ensured that there is no obstruction in the chamber, the shooter can identify the misfire as a failure to feed and can then return the firearm to the action or load state and continue firing, or return the firearm to the unload state.

In the case of a failure to fire, the shooter actions the rifle, but pulls the trigger to no effect. As in the previous case, the shooter must remain in the shooting position, with the firearm pointed downrange for at least 30 seconds. In the case of a failure to fire, the problem is either with the firing mechanism of the firearm not applying enough pressure to the primer to produce solid ignition, or the primer of the particular round in the chamber is defective or seated too far into the primer pocket of the case, causing the striker and firing pin to fail to apply enough pressure to the primer to achieve ignition. In either case, a particular type of misfire known as a "hang-fire" can result.

A hang-fire is a delayed or retarded ignition of the primer. This results in the round actually firing some time after the trigger is pulled, that time ranging from several tenths of a second to *many* seconds. This is the primary reason the shooter must remain in the shooting position with the firearm pointed downrange for at least 30 seconds.

Having waited the 30 seconds and ensuring the firearm is pointed downrange and the safety is engaged, the shooter tips the rifle onto its side with the ejection port pointed to the ground, then the firearm is returned to the load state and the bolt opened. The unfired round is extracted and ejected, the shooter can observe the chamber is now empty, and the shooter can return the firearm to either the action, load, or unload state.

Once the firearm is made safe, the shooter can observe the base of the unfired round, in particular the primer. One of several different scenarios may have occurred.

A small firing pin mark on the primer, known as a "soft strike," is indicative of a faulty firing mechanism of the firearm, either that of not containing enough

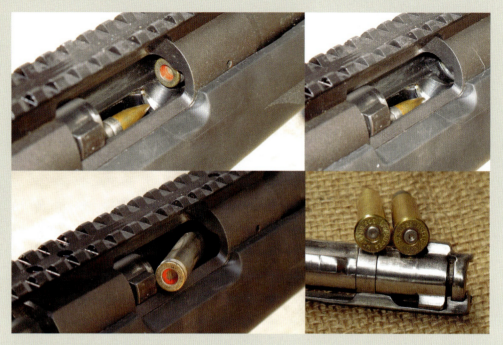

spring energy to adequately strike the primer with the firing pin, or that of the firing pin being too short, in which case the primer has not received adequate spring energy from the firing mechanism. Alternately, the primer can have been seated too deeply into the primer pocket within the case, thus preventing the striker and firing pin from supplying sufficient pressure to the primer to achieve ignition.

The shooter may see a heavy firing pin mark on the primer. This is indicative of a faulty primer. Although this is rare in modern commercial ammunition, it is a common occurrence in surplus military ammunition. It can also occur with handloaded ammunition, where contaminants have found their way into the primer during the manufacture of the handload. Case lubricant is usually the culprit, it getting into the primer and degrading the small charge contained there.

In the case of a failure to extract and eject, the shooter actions the firearm, pulls the trigger, fires the round in the chamber, and opens the bolt. When they attempt to chamber a new round, the shooter discovers the bolt won't close. Since the round in the chamber has been fired, the shooter need not wait 30 seconds before ensuring the firearm is pointed downrange and the safety is engaged, before tipping the rifle onto its side with the ejection port pointed to the ground. Next, the shooter removes the magazine or opens the floor plate on the firearm. The shooter then pulls the bolt rearward and inspects the chamber, noting that there will be a loose round in the receiver (this will normally fall free when the bolt is pulled rearwards). With the firearm at the unload state, the shooter can now remove the empty case in the chamber. Normally, closing and reopening the bolt will extract and eject the case, but, if that doesn't work, a cleaning rod will need to be inserted from the muzzle end of the barrel. With the rod in place, a light tapping of the hand on the rod will knock the case out of the chamber.

Failure to extract and eject is normally caused by a weak extractor spring or claw, a damaged or rebated rim on the case, or by a dirty case or chamber. A repair may be needed in the first instance, ammo replacement in the second, and cleaning in the third.

While the misfires and clearing actions so described provide guidelines on what to do in the case of one, they do not cover all possibilities of the different types of misfires and the different clearing actions required. The shooter must also recognize that different types of firearm are susceptible to different types of misfire, therefore the shooter must develop a very good operating knowledge of their own firearm and circumstances and develop their own clearing actions based on these guidelines.

# CHAPTER 15

# Shooting Positions and Locations

The choice of shooting position and the location of the shot go hand in hand. The first principle of both is that they must provide a solid and stable platform for the shooter and the rifle. For instance, in a range setting, shooting mounds would be the correct height and length to facilitate a good prone position, and they should be firm and dry. Shooting benches should be free from wobble and fitted with a steady chair at the right height.

Both the shooting position and location must offer adequate sighting of the target, plus sufficient ground in front, behind, and beside the target and *en route* to it, to ensure good visibility and a safe shot. In its simplest terms, if the shooter cannot see his target, the shot will be futile and potentially dangerous.

Both the shooting position and location must complement the characteristics of both the rifle and the shooter. If a rifle is set up for stalking and close-range shooting, it will most likely be unsuited to a prone, long-range shot at a varmint target. Likewise, a long-range rig with a heavy barrel and 50x benchrest scope would equally be unsuited to a standing shot on a moving target at close range. Taking this to another level, choosing a shooting location at the top of a hill or high in the mountains

for an unfit person may lead to an extended period of increased heart rate and respiration, potentially making immediate shots on arrival inaccurate. If a shooter knows themselves, in terms of capabilities and limitations, and knows their rifle, in terms of characteristics, capabilities, and limitations, they are well on the path to accurate shooting.

## SHOULDERING ARMS

There are many ways to "shoulder" a rifle, the placing the butt of the rifle into the shoulder to achieve a firing position and sighting on the target. Unfortunately, most methods are incorrect. Many lead to goose-necking behind the scope or iron sights. Others lack provision for a consistent "cheek weld," or the point at which the cheek touches and is pressed onto the stock to prevent movement of the neck and head relative to the scope and rifle before, during, and directly after the shot. Such bad shouldering will result in the shooter jiggling around to get comfortable and twisting the rifle around to get the rifle and scope vertically aligned so that the crosshair runs straight up and down. Incorrect shouldering also fails to provide a solid rest for the rifle before, during, and directly after firing, and it does not provide for repeatable shouldering of the rifle.

*1. Hold the firearm 45 degrees to the right and 45 degrees up. 2. Pull the rifle into the shoulder.*
*3. Swing the rifle down to a straight and level position.*

If a person asks the average shooter to shoulder his or her rifle 10 times using their own method or "what feels right," there will be 10 different results in terms of angles, pressures, grip, sight alignment, trigger reach, etc. All of these will have significant effects on the point of aim and the point of impact.

The most important aspects of shouldering a rifle are consistency and repeatability. If the shooter holds the rifle before, during, and directly after firing in exactly the same way, variation in trigger pull, eye relief, and alignment behind the scope or iron sights, stock twist, rigidity of grip, and cheek weld will be minimized. Having an ingrained and repeatable process for achieving this is paramount.

The best process to use is to hold the rifle 45 degrees up and 45 degrees to the right (if the shooter is

right-handed), with the butt just lightly touching the shoulder and the right elbow horizontal to the arm, with the left hand gripping the fore-end of the stock as normal. With the arms in this position, a natural "pocket" or shoulder cavity will form and the butt of the rifle is placed into it. Then the rifle is swung down 45 degrees and left 45 degrees at the same time, while pulling the rifle firmly into the shoulder cavity. When this movement is complete, the rifle should be firmly in the shoulder cavity, the eye correctly positioned behind the scope or iron sights, and a good solid cheek weld on the stock that falls into position and holds the head firmly behind the scope or iron sights. The trigger finger should come to the correct distance past the trigger shoe for a comfortable trigger pull, the rifle should be aligned straight up and down, and the entire grip should feel comfortable, firm, and solid.

How do you know you have this right? A good test is to go through this process with the eyes closed. When the rifle is position, the shooter opens their eyes and should be presented with a perfect sight picture. If this doesn't occur, the shooter should consider adjusting the scope's position or the stock configuration.

A correctly shouldered rifle will integrate the rifle so closely to the body that the rifle will become part of the body. This is the level of support that the rifle and shooter need to achieve for accurate shooting.

## THE PRONE UNSUPPORTED POSITION

There are two prone positions: supported and unsupported. The prone unsupported position is very similar to the prone supported position, with the exception that the rifle is entirely supported by the shooter in the unsupported variant. This position offers the advantages of greater flexibility over the prone supported position in that the shooter can more easily change or track targets.

In prone unsupported, the rifle is at a slightly greater height off the ground than in the supported. This allows for better vision over vegetation or obstacles. This variation is slightly faster to adopt than the prone supported position, and it is one less affected by heart rate and respiration, because the upper body is supported off the ground to a greater degree. This position also allows for fast adjustment of the elbows, to level the rifle for the shot on otherwise uneven ground, as well as for elevation and declination of the rifle.

Prone unsupported has the disadvantages of providing a less stable platform for the rifle than the prone supported position. Actioning of the rifle and changing magazines is more cumbersome and, in many cases, will require the shooter to shift out of the shooting position and then readopt it for the following shot. Too, by elevating the firing position, any movement of the body will be magnified when it reaches the rifle. The prone unsupported position can be enhanced by the use of a properly adjusted sling, which creates a forth point of contact between the rifle and the shooter.

THE PRONE UNSUPPORTED POSITION

The prone unsupported position is suited to particular range matches where bipods and rests are disallowed. It's likewise appropriate for hunting when an opportunity presents itself that needs be addressed in perhaps half a minute or less, or when ambushing a moving target.

To adopt the prone unsupported position, the rifle is gripped by the primary hand and the secondary hand is used to help lower the body to the ground. The secondary hand is then used to steady the fore-end of the rifle, while the upper part of the body is supported by the tips of the elbows contacting the ground. The shooter's legs are extended behind their body, with the feet about 30 centimeters apart and facing outwards. There are several variations on the prone unsupported position, including the most frequently used method of folding one leg at the knee inwards and placing the ankle behind the knee of the other leg.

## THE PRONE SUPPORTED POSITION

The prone supported position is considered to be the most stable firing position available. It involves the shooter lying down behind the rifle, with the rifle's weight being supported by a bipod, shooting bags, or a natural rest. This position offers the advantages of being the most stable for the shooter in that there are many points of contact between the shooter and the ground, and very few of the shooter's muscles are required to adopt or hold this shooting position. The rifle may also be supported by another bag under the butt, as well as being gripped by the shooter.

The prone supported position has the disadvantages of being very low to the ground, limiting the shooter's view, particularly when there is vegetation above grass level. The rifle must be aligned closely to the target before the position is adopted, so changing or tracking targets is difficult, due to the style of hold on the rifle and the fact that the shooter is lying down. It is not a position favorable for uphill or downhill shots. In an uphill shot, the rifle needs to be elevated higher off the ground to achieve a good sight picture. In a downhill shot, the shooter will have blood begin to rush to their head, generally making the shot uncomfortable. The prone supported position can be enhanced by the use of a properly adjusted sling to create a forth point of contact between the rifle and the shooter.

## THE PRONE SUPPORTED POSITION

This position is most suited to a predetermined or setup shot, and it has great applicability at the range and for ambush hunting in the field. It offers maximum accuracy potential for the shot, even though it also greatly limits the ability to track or change targets.

To adopt the prone supported position, the shooter lays the rifle on the bags or bipod so that it is roughly in alignment with the target. The shooter then lowers their body down to the ground behind the rifle, supporting the upper body on the inside of the elbows and extending the legs behind the body with the feet about 30 centimeters apart and facing outwards. The primary hand grips the rifle about the wrist or pistol grip, and the secondary hand grips the rifle about the fore-end. There are several variations on the prone supported position, including folding one leg at the knee inwards and placing the ankle behind the knee of the other leg. Too, the shooter's secondary hand can be placed underneath the butt of the rifle, palm up or down, to effect small changes in elevation of the point of aim. This technique generally utilizes equipment such as a rear shooting bag or sand sock.

## THE SITTING UNSUPPORTED POSITION

The sitting position bridges the gap between the prone and standing positions. The sitting position involves two variations. In the first, the shooter sits cross-legged at a 45-degree angle to the target, supporting the rifle with the arms only. In the second, the shooter sits facing the target with the legs comfortably apart and the knees bent. This position is really only used when the prone positions are inviable, such as with high vegetation, uneven or rocky surfaces, or when there simply isn't any space on which to lie down.

The sitting positions offer the advantages of a greater field of view and target tracking capabilities than the prone positions and allow the shooter to see over obstacles that would block the line of sight in the prone positions. Too, this position is a fairly natural shape for the body to conform to and, as such, is less fatiguing to maintain for an extended period, is faster to adopt than the prone positions, and allows for easier actioning of the rifle, because the shooter's elbows and forearms are free.

This position has the disadvantages of being less stable than either the prone or sitting supported positions. As the upper body isn't supported, movement from respiration and heart rate is greatly magnified when it reaches the rifle. The sitting unsupported position can be enhanced by the use of a properly adjusted sling to create a forth point of contact between the rifle and the shooter. Stability can be improved by the shooter leaning their side or back against a solid object, such as a tree, large rock, or a wall or fence.

**THE SITTING UNSUPPORTED POSITION**

To adopt the sitting position at 45 degrees to the target, the rifle is gripped about the pistol grip with the primary hand and about the fore-end with the secondary hand. The shooter then sits and crosses their legs with the left leg over the right for right-handed shooters, vice-versa for left-handed. (Note that having the legs crossed in the wrong direction will cause the shooter to tip over with the weight of the rifle.) The elbows are then drawn in towards each other and the shooter hunches over the rifle.

In the alternate variation, the rifle is gripped in the same manner, but the shooter faces the target when sitting and keeps the legs extended with a 45 degree bend at the knees. A fairly unique variation on this has the shooter gripping the rifle in the normal way and sitting, but here the left knee is brought hard up into the chest, with the sole of the left foot flat on the ground. The right knee is kept level with the ground and the right foot is wrapped around the ankle of the left leg. This allows the left knee and thigh to act as a post that the shooter can lean forward onto, providing an excellent shooting rest.

## THE SITTING SUPPORTED POSITION

The sitting supported position is the preferred approach, when either lying prone or standing aren't possible. The sitting supported position is identical to the sitting unsupported position, with the exception that the elbows are supported by the knees. This has the effect of stabilizing the entire upper body, providing a more stable platform for the rifle. This position is really only used when the prone positions are not viable, due to high vegetation, an uneven or rocky surface, or when there simply isn't any space on which to lie down. It is, however, excellent for varmint and stand hunters, given the flexibility and comfort of the position coupled with field of view and the addition of equipment such as shooting sticks.

This position offers the advantages of a greater field of view and target tracking capabilities than the prone positions and allows the shooter to see over obstacles that would block line of sight in the prone positions. Further, this position is a fairly natural shape for the body to conform to and, as such, is less fatiguing to maintain for an extended period, particularly given that the upper body is supported by the knees. This position is faster to adopt than the prone positions and allows for easier actioning of the rifle, because the shooter's elbows and forearms are unrestricted.

This position has the disadvantages of being less stable than both the prone positions. Too, in most cases, a sling cannot be used effectively in the sitting supported position, because the elbows are drawn in so far and also contact the knees.

This position is perfect for the use of shooting sticks. Stability can be improved by the shooter leaning or backing against a solid object such as a tree, large rock, or a wall or fence.

## THE SITTING SUPPORTED POSITION

PHOTOS COURTESY ALLY ROLLS PHOTOGRAPHY

To adopt the sitting position, the rifle is gripped about the pistol grip with the primary hand and about the fore-end with the secondary hand. The shooter then sits and crosses their legs with the left leg over the right for right-handed shooters and vice-versa for left-handed shooters. (Note that having the legs crossed in the wrong direction will cause the shooter to tip over with the weight of the rifle.) The elbows are then drawn in towards each other and the shooter hunches over the rifle. In an alternate variation, the rifle is gripped in the same manner, but the shooter faces the target when sitting and keeps the legs extended with a 45-degree bend at the knees. It is important to note that the elbows are supported by the fleshy insides of the knees—any other bone-to-bone support will result in an unstable firing position.

A unique variation on this position involves the shooter gripping the rifle in the normal way and sitting, but the left knee is brought hard up into the chest, with the sole of the left foot flat on the ground. The right knee is kept level with the ground and the right foot is wrapped around the ankle of the left leg. This allows the left knee and thigh to act as a post that the shooter can lean forward onto, providing an excellent shooting rest.

## THE KNEELING UNSUPPORTED POSITION

Kneeling is the preferable position to adopt when on the move and engaging a target of opportunity on the hunt. It is also a well-known military competition position and can be used in specific competitions. This position combines the advantages of sitting and standing positions, in that the shooter can quickly adopt a relatively stable position, while still having excellent visibility, target tracking, and ease of rifle operation.

This position has the disadvantages of being less stable than either the sitting or prone positions. It is a highly fatiguing position to adopt and hold, requiring good body core strength to endure, and it relies on suitable ground on which to kneel. Stability can be improved by the shooter leaning the sides of the body or back against a solid object, such as a tree, large rock, or a wall or fence. This position is greatly assisted by the use of a sling and/or shooting sticks. This position is suited to snap shooting when a couple seconds can be taken for preparation.

To adopt the kneeling unsupported position, the rifle is gripped about the pistol grip with the primary hand and about the fore-end with the secondary hand. The shooter then kneels with the left knee up and the right knee down for a right-handed shooter (vice versa for a left-handed shooter). The right knee will be at 90 degrees (or as close to that angle as comfortable) to the point of aim, while the left knee faces the point of aim. The elbows are then drawn in towards each other and the shooter hunches over the rifle.

## THE KNEELING SUPPORTED POSITION

The kneeling supported position is the most flexible, stable, and adaptable position available to the hunter. It also has place in many modern tactical shooting competitions, as well as military competitions. It offers the advantages of the unsupported kneeling position—it is relatively stable, provides excellent visibility and target tracking, and is fast to adopt—and it couples them with greater accuracy through improved stability of the rifle and shooter. This position is suited to snap shooting, when there is time for preparation, when lying prone or sitting is unsuitable due to tall grass or topography, and when it is disallowed by competition rules.

This position has the same disadvantages as the kneeling unsupported position: it is highly fatiguing, requires good body core strength, and requires suitable kneeling ground. It also takes slightly longer to adopt and requires the shooter to move out of

the supported aspect of the position to operate the firearm. Although this position is supported, leaning against a solid object, such as a tree, large rock, or a wall or fence, will improve stability.

To adopt the kneeling supported position, the rifle is gripped about the pistol grip with the primary hand and about the fore-end with the secondary hand. The shooter then kneels with the left knee up and the right knee down for a right-handed shooter (or vice versa for a left-handed shooter), with the right knee at 90 degrees (or as close as comfortable) to the point of aim and the left knee facing the point of aim. The left elbow is then placed on top of the left knee, ensuring that the bony part of the elbow never touches the bony part of the knee; the elbow itself must either go in front or behind the knee. The right elbow is drawn into the side of the body and the shooter hunches over the rifle.

## THE STANDING UNSUPPORTED POSITION

The standing position is the fastest position to adopt, while standing or on the move. The standing position is used by many hunters worldwide, as it is the quickest way to get rounds on target while backpack hunting. The standing position is also used in service rifle and tactical competitions, as well as

### THE KNEELING SUPPORTED POSITION

PHOTOS COURTESY ALLY ROLLS PHOTOGRAPHY

western action and other competitions. The standing position offers the advantages of extreme speed to adopt, extreme flexibility, and the ability to change targets or scan an area. It offers the best viewing conditions of the target area and the best opportunity to clear obstacles between the shooter and the target. This position also provides the shooter the ability to view other possible shooting sites, as well as time to assess and consider other shooting positions, while deciding whether or not to take the shot. Truly, this position exists to let the hunter cover ground and get the sights on target, all the while having the option to consider the situation and assess if there is a better one available.

This position does have significant disadvantages. It is the most unstable and inaccurate position that can be adopted. This position requires the shooter to yield hunting advantages, such as cover and concealment, in favor of mobility and flexibility, and it effectively puts the hunter on display to the prey. This position is highly fatiguing to maintain and highly susceptible to any movement on the part of the shooter; even the environmental effects of a light gust can easily throw of aim. This position, due to its inherent instability, will benefit from any external support possible, such as long shooting sticks, a sling, or a natural rest such as a tree branch.

To adopt the standing position, the shooter stands with the left foot forward and the right foot back (for a right-handed shooter). The left foot should point towards the target and the right foot should be at 90 degrees (or as close as possible) to the target. The left leg should carry about 60 percent of the shooter's body weight, and the shooter should lean forward towards the target with the knees slightly bent and with a straight back. The shooter grips with the primary hand around the wrist or pistol grip of the stock and at the fore-end with the secondary hand. The rifle butt is then placed in the shoulder. Once the rifle is in the shoulder, the left elbow should be almost in line vertically with the body, while the right elbow should be almost parallel to the ground. A variation on this position is to have the weight distribution on the feet reversed and bend the knees more, lowering the body slightly. This variation allows for a more stable shot in some circumstances.

## THE STANDING SUPPORTED POSITION

The standing supported position is a natural progression of the standing position, one that hunters and competition shooters should strive to maintain, when attempting a standing shot. The advantages of the standing supported position are the same as the normal standing position, though it takes slightly

PHOTOS COURTESY ALLY ROLLS PHOTOGRAPHY

**THE STANDING UNSUPPORTED POSITION**

longer to adopt, but becomes more stable for doing so. The standing position can be supported by long shooting sticks or a walking stick, a sling, or standing behind a medium-height wall, rocks, or parts of a car. The position can be supported by hanging the rifle sling from a tree branch or by placing the secondary hand on a tree trunk, creating a "V"-shape between the index finger and thumb in which the fore-end of the rifle can rest. In reverse, the shooter places the flat of the secondary hand against a tree trunk and cradles the fore-end of the rifle in the "V" between the index finger and thumb, or even by resting the fore-end of the rifle on another (trusting) shooter's shoulder (with their permission, of course, and hearing protection on their part).

To adopt the standing supported position, the shooter stands with the left foot forward and the right foot back (for a right-handed shooter). The left foot should point towards the target and the right foot should be at 90 degrees (or as close as possible) to the target. The left leg should carry about 60 percent of the body weight, and the shooter should lean forward towards the target with the knees slightly bent and with a straight back. The shooter grips with the primary hand around the wrist or pistol grip of the stock and about the fore-end with the secondary hand. The rifle butt is then placed in the shoulder. Once the rifle is in the shoulder, the left elbow should be almost vertically in line with the body and the right elbow should be almost parallel to the ground. A variation on this position is to have the weight distribution on the feet reversed and the knees bent more, lowering the body slightly. This variation allows for a more stable shot in some circumstances.

## THE HAWKINS POSITION

The Hawkins position is similar to a prone supported position, and is the first of our special positions. Originally conceived for military sniping purposes, this particular position has limited use in a hunting situation and almost no application at all in a competition situation. It is, however, a unique position that may give a shooter options and assist in developing a stable platform for their rifle. It offers the advantages of the prone supported position, along with an extremely stable platform that is as low to the ground as possible. This position is supported by the shooter and the ground at the same time and does not require a bipod, rest, shooting sticks, or other environmental support.

This position offers the disadvantages of the prone supported position and it is also difficult to adopt correctly. The position hampers operation of the rifle, is not flexible, and requires the shooter to crane their neck for correct sighting through a scope.

## THE STANDING SUPPORTED POSITION

This position can be considered a form of the prone supported position; however, in something like a stalking situation, where the hunter needs to "tiger crawl"—a very low crawl with the body on the ground—into position or needs to clear the crest of a hill without being seen by game or silhouetted by the skyline, the rifle is already grasped correctly. In this manner, a fast and stable sight picture can be achieved. It should be noted that elements of the Hawkins position can be adapted to other firing positions, and it is especially useful when the shooter is trying to incorporate environmental support into their shooting position.

To adopt the Hawkins position, the shooter, while lying flat on the ground, grasps the rifle about the wrist or pistol grip with the right hand (for a right-handed shooter) and the secondary hand grasps the forward most part of the rifle sling and sling swivel in a fist like grip. The fist made by the secondary hand is then allowed to rest on the ground and can be used to achieve elevation changes of the rifle's sight picture. The stock is *not* placed into the shoulder, being allowed, instead, to ride under the armpit and

dig slightly into the ground (a small hollow can be made in the ground with the fingertips prior to taking up the position). The armpit is then lowered down on top of the stock and the head is allowed to roll over the stock comb to achieve a full sight picture. Some shooters may find that extending the secondary arm so that the elbow is straight may assist with getting a full sight picture and reducing recoil. This position is difficult to adopt correctly and should be practiced at the range prior to hunting use.

## THE BACK POSITION

The back position is essentially a prone supported position, but one in which the shooter is in a supine (lying on their back) position. It is the second of our special positions. Originally conceived for military sniping purposes, this particular position has limited use in a hunting situation and almost no application at all in a competition situation. It is, however, a unique position that may give a shooter options and assist in developing a stable platform for the rifle.

This position offers the advantages of the prone supported position and can be adopted without

THE HAWKINS POSITION

PHOTOS COURTESY ALLY ROLLS PHOTOGRAPHY

the need of a bipod, rest, shooting sticks, or other environmental support. It is very fast to adopt and is particularly suited to downhill shooting in a steep environment. This position offers the disadvantages of the prone supported position and is difficult to adopt correctly. It hampers operation of the rifle, the position is not flexible, and it is most suited to a rifle of considerable length and/or fully wooded, such as a 1903 Springfield, 98 Mauser, or a Lee Enfield, though it can be used with any rifle in any configuration, if the shooter is careful.

To adopt the back position, the shooter grasps the rifle about the pistol grip of the stock with the primary hand and lies down on their back. The shooter then rolls over mostly onto their right side (for a right-handed shooter), the right leg is bent to about 90 degrees at the knee, the left leg is placed on top of the right leg and with the knees together, and the left knee is bent to about 45 degrees. The secondary hand is then placed on top of the stock, and the butt of the rifle is pulled into the armpit, with the fore-end of the stock lying over the side of the left thigh, just above the knee. The head is then placed to achieve a sight picture, noting that the sight picture achieved will most likely not be full, but can be maintained evenly from side to side and top to bottom. It should be noted that the head itself is unsupported and held in an awkward and fatiguing position.

This position can be enhanced and made extremely comfortable by either placing a rucksack or similar object behind the head or, if the rifle is fitted with a sling, the sling can be lengthened and looped behind the head, thus supporting the head very effectively and in a relative manner to the rifle and scope, achieving a very stable sight picture.

## USE OF ENVIRONMENTAL SUPPORT

Correct use of environmental support, coupled with common sense and some simple equipment, can make the difference between an awkward and inaccurate shot and a stable and accurate shot from an unfavorable position.

THE BACK POSITION

PHOTOS COURTESY ALLY ROLLS PHOTOGRAPHY

*The use of environmental support is limited only by the shooter's imagination and the rules of environmental support.*

The first rule of environmental support is to never allow the rifle to contact a hard surface. This, for instance, would include things like laying a fore-end directly onto a stone wall. When the rifle contacts hard against hard, any slight movement on the part of the shooter will be amplified by the hard surface and lead to a wandering point of aim. Further, recoil will make the rifle buck wildly, and the shooter will not be able to spot their shot.

The second rule of environmental support is that the shooter must think laterally in its application. An unfavorable position can be adopted with environmental support over a more favorable (accuracy) position, to achieve a better point of aim and accuracy solution. A good example of this would be choosing a standing position with the rifle supported by a tree branch from a sling, rather than a kneeling position on rocky ground.

The third rule of environmental support is going equipped to make use of environmental support and knowing how to make use of it to its greatest potential. It's quite easy to pack a sling, tree hook, a set of shooting sticks, or a sock capable of being filled with sand into a backpack ready for a hunt. These items are lightweight, small and, in most cases, multi-purpose. For instance, a set of shooting sticks can be made to form the one walking stick, a sling can also be used as a belt (and vice-versa), and a tree hook can be clipped onto a belt or back pack.

Returning to rule No. 2, think laterally: If a backpack were hooked onto a broken branch stem by its center hang loop and the fore-end of the rifle slipped through the shoulder loops of the back pack, the shooter has just utilized the one piece of equipment for more than three different purposes.

When considering using environmental support, the shooter needs to take their current shooting position and analyze the surroundings at rifle height. By doing this, the shooter will be able to assess possible environmental support and then correlate that with the equipment at hand and the shooting position required for the shot. The shooter can then set about employing the best available environmental support for the shot.

The shooter may discover that they are not carrying any equipment suitable for the environment around them. Should this occur, we refer again to rule No. 2 of environmental support, and that is to think laterally. Small tree stems or branches can be cut and lashed with a shoe lace (spare or otherwise), or even held with the hand, to make a standing tripod with which to cradle the fore-end of the rifle for a standing shot. A small to medium-sized tree can be "hugged" to stabilize a standing or kneeling position. A small mound of dirt can be piled up under the fore-end of the rifle to enable a prone supported position. Ultimately, the use of environmental support is limited only by the imagination and ingenuity of the shooter. The only caveat is that the shooter must not use environment support that is less stable than the shooter. A pile of soft dry sand is not so good, and neither is a flimsy sapling or a stretchy sling.

# CHAPTER 16

# Hand Position and Trigger Operation

Appropriate trigger control is a challenge for all shooters and all firearms. Many sources will discuss ways to achieve smooth, clean, and crisp trigger technique, but, in reality, how the trigger breaks relies on far more than just how the shooter pulls the trigger.

When pulling the trigger, the motion begins with the muscles in the shoulder contracting against bones in the upper arm and torso. This pressure gets transmitted through various ligaments, tendons, muscles, and bones, down through the arm to the wrist, hand and, finally, the trigger finger. Here the pressure moves up through the bones, changing direction at the knuckles and, finally, focusing on the pad of the trigger finger. Then the pressure can go to work on the trigger mechanism itself, while all the bones, muscles, tendons, and ligaments continue to move, applying pressure to the trigger.

All these activities need to be coordinated and controlled down to the microseconds, when the trigger actually breaks and the firing pin flies forward. This is truly a complicated issue, but, assuming the shooter has a correct grip on the rifle, trigger control can be broken down into the position of the primary hand on the rifle, the finger position on the trigger itself, and the way in which pressure is applied to the

trigger. If these three points can be suitably addressed and a correct grip is used, then most trigger control issues can be resolved.

It must be noted that the use of the techniques here relies on the trigger mechanism of the rifle being correctly maintained and adjusted. It will be very difficult to achieve good results with a worn or heavy trigger that exhibits excessive take-up, let-off, and creep. On a final note, good trigger control requires a lot of practice, and it will deteriorate without practice. So, if the shooter is a large-caliber practitioner, by all means practice with small-caliber rifles; even a .22 LR or an air rifle will assist the shooter in keeping their trigger control in check. It's the *process* that's important in trigger control.

## HAND POSITION

The correct positioning of the hand for the purpose of trigger control relies on several factors. First is the style of the stock and grip, whether it be a near vertical pistol grip, thumbhole, or a conventional long arm wrist stock. Second is the body position the shooter has adopted for the shot; there is a difference to the particulars of the hand position if the shooter is standing versus lying down. Finally, the position of the thumb can have a great effect on the hand position, and although it is mostly a matter of personal preference (within certain limitations), the position of the thumb must be trained to work complimentary to the rest of the hand.

To illustrate correct hand position in general terms, we will look at a conventional long arm wrist-styled stock, as seen from various shooting positions. Having grasped the stock about the wrist, the position on the middle, ring, and little fingers should be lightly pressed together as a group and wrapped around the wrist in such a way that the trigger finger contacts the trigger half way between the end-most knuckle and the tip of the finger. Most shooters will find that this spacing and position of the fingers on the wrist will force the hand to move to a more rearward position on the stock. This is perfectly fine and, in fact, on some stocks, the little finger may well position itself under the bottom of the grip.

The position of the thumb varies based on the shooting position chosen by the shooter. Most shooters will find that the thumb position will change as the position of the elbow on the primary hand changes. For instance, in a standing position, where the elbow and arm are predominantly in a horizontal position, so, too, the thumb will wrap itself around the wrist like a ring. In the case of a prone position, where the elbow is predominantly vertical to the body, the thumb will tend to straighten in line with the stock.

It should be noted that these are not hard and fast rules. The correct method for the individual will rely on their own physiology. A better gauge of the correct thumb position for a particular shot is whether or not the hand is relaxed or if the natural pressure of the thumb "fights" the natural pressure of the fingers. Any imbalance here will affect the natural point of aim.

*The position of the hand must conform to the style of the stock, while not adversely influencing the position of the stock (i.e., canting), the natural point of aim, or the position of the trigger finger.*

Looking at pistol grip or thumbhole-styled stocks, the type of hand position and how it changes based on the chosen shooting position is far more limited. Many shooters find a pistol grip that is near vertical to be quite uncomfortable in the prone position, due to the angle the pistol grip imposes on the wrist. Typically a pistol grip-type stock is gripped with the middle, ring, and little fingers grouped together. Again, there is little room for the hand to be moved rearward and bring the middle of the tip of the trigger finger into contact with the trigger, just as in most cases the thumb is restricted to wrapping itself about the wrist of the stock in a ring shape.

A common fault with regards to the hand position on the grip of the stock, whether it be a conventional stock or a pistol grip-type, is not applying hand pressure directly rearward. This will result in the rifle being canted. Another problem occurs when the trigger finger protrudes a long way past the trigger,

*The position of the trigger finger is critical. It must not touch anything but the trigger, and it must apply pressure to the trigger only in a rearward direction.*

thereby incorrectly applying pressure to the trigger during firing. Last, there can be too much grip pressure exerted, with the primary hand degrading stability, by introducing muscular shaking. A good way of detecting whether or not you are gripping the rifle too hard is to look for telltale "white knuckles."

## FINGER POSITION

As previously discussed, appropriate trigger control relies, in part, on correct positioning of the trigger finger. While the trigger finger is extended, the trigger should lay midway between the front-most knuckle of the trigger finger and that finger's tip. Getting this position right has as much to do with the length of the stock as it does the hand position, though, as I've said, there is room to maneuver the hand to achieve the appropriate position.

Further to the position of the trigger finger in relation to the trigger, we also must look at the location of that entire finger in relation to the stock, whether it be a conventional long arm stock, a pistol grip, or thumbhole stock. The critical factor here is that the trigger finger, from below the first knuckle to the tip, must not contact the stock (or anything else) aside from the trigger, when ready to fire—this is a hard and fast

rule. If the trigger finger contacts, for instance, the palm-swell in the grip or the top or side of the trigger guard when pressure is applied to the trigger, the finger will naturally lever off these obstructions. This changes the pressure that reaches the trigger and the angle of the pressure, resulting in the trigger being pulled in a manner that is not straight backwards.

## TRIGGER PRESSURE

Trigger pressure and the way it is applied to the trigger is the final culmination of all the shooter's preparations and draws upon everything the shooter has done and achieved up to this point. We all know that trigger pressure application needs to be smooth, slowly increasing, and clean. Few people know that the trigger must also be pulled perfectly rearwards and without changing any other pressures in the grip of either hand. If the trigger is allowed to be pulled at an angle, it will force the various pins and levers inside the trigger mechanism to bind and run off axis, ruining the pull of the trigger by introducing creep and a greater trigger weight to overcome. This is the critical point of the application of trigger pressure.

Looking at the physiology of the hand, in order for the tip of the trigger finger to move perfectly rearwards, the second knuckle of the trigger finger (on a right-handed shooter) must move laterally to the right. If the second knuckle remains in its position or moves to the left, the tip of the trigger finger will move through an arc, which, in turn, will apply pressure to the trigger at an angle and degrade the pull. There are no special hints or tips to overcome this. The only true method for ensuring correct trigger pressure and application is one of vigilance and practice.

## FOLLOW-THROUGH

Many shooters believe that the principles of trigger control cease to make a difference as soon as the firearm fires. This is not the case. Follow-through, or the act of maintaining the principles of trigger control after the firearm has fired, is an often overlooked skill. That said, follow-through is simple to implement.

To maintain follow-through, the shooter need only maintain their finger position, hand position, grip, and shooting position as the firearm fires. This ensures the firearm recoils in the same way each time it is fired, by maintaining the same pressures on the stock and limiting variations between shots. Beyond this, correct application of follow-through will allow, in most cases, the firearm to settle back onto the aiming point after the recoil has subsided. Not only does this allow the shooter to be in position to take a follow-up shot at the target, but also to spot their fall of shot (especially at longer ranges), and then correct if necessary.

A secondary effect of a good follow-through is that it allows the shooter the opportunity to ease out of the shooting position, rather than immediately release all the tension that builds up in the body as the firearm is discharged. Although follow-through on the surface appears unnecessary, because the firearm has already been fired, a wise shooter will understand that there is always a benefit to seeing the effect of the first shot and being ready for the second!

## FLINCH AND TRIGGER CONTROL TRAINING

Flinching, or sudden, almost involuntary movement just before the trigger breaks, is the body and subconscious preempting the blast, noise, and recoil of a rifle discharging. The flinching results in the body slightly tightening directly before the round is fired—even the pupils will dilate and contract slightly. The effects of flinching vary, but the result is the same: the point of aim changes just before the round is fired, the projectiles go where the shooter points the rifle and, the projectiles will go anywhere but at the target!

Flinching is nothing to be ashamed of. All shooters flinch at varying times, and shooters who have once flinched and cured it have begun to flinch again. Moreover, many shooters will be flinch free for the first 20 or 30 rounds in a session, then, as the body and mind tire, flinching will return.

The key to prevention is practice. The body and the subconscious both need to be trained to not flinch. Fortunately, the training techniques used to curb and eliminate flinch are also useful for practicing appropriate trigger control. Likewise, once appropriate trigger control for a particular rifle has been learned and integrated into muscle memory, the shooter will be less likely to flinch with that particular rifle.

The most useful training technique in eliminating flinching is regular (at least weekly) practice with a light-caliber rifle such as a .22 LR, while being consciously aware of trigger control and maintaining a stable shooting platform. A non-shooting observer is highly useful here, as sometimes the shooter can be genuinely oblivious to slight flinching movements.

If regular live-firing practice is unavailable due to weather or location, dry-firing is an excellent alternative. It should be stated here that dry-firing rifles of conventional design, with a snap cap, whether it be homemade or purchased, is perfectly safe for the mechanism of the rifle, and though no live ammunition is involved, it is important that full safety precautions be followed.

When dry-firing, the shooter should follow the exact same firing procedure as if they were firing a live round. Again, an observer is useful to detect movement. If an observer is not available, then place a pencil along the barrel near the muzzle. As the shooter dry-fires, the pencil may rock or fall off. This would indicate some movement on the part of the shooter. Once the shooter can dry-fire without moving the pencil, proceed to placing the pencil across the tip of the muzzle, as that will register even finer movements on the part of the shooter.

The final technique for eliminating flinch and practicing appropriate trigger control is to have an assistant load the magazine of the shooter's rifle, either at the range or in the field, with snap caps or dummy rounds, but also with one live round somewhere in the magazine. Then, the shooter proceeds to fire at a target. Not knowing whether the round in the chamber is live or not will allow the shooter to critically analyze their technique. Many shooters have reported that the tightening of flinching can be easily felt when a dummy round is triggered upon, though the shooter believed a live round was in the chamber.

# CHAPTER 17

# Breathing

Breathing is an integrated act, one utilizing many aspects of the body, and, since it is an involuntary bodily function, it is generally taken for granted. The simple act of drawing breath requires the use of the brain, central nervous system, ribs, spine, and most of the muscles found between the navel and the nose. A breath can change the volume of the chest cavity by up to six liters, or 1½ gallons. It is little wonder, then, that breathing can have a large effect on the shooter's point of aim and point of impact.

Of course, not breathing isn't a viable solution to the problems of bodily movement associated with breath, but there are several techniques available to limit the effects of breathing. Furthermore, these techniques can limit the effects of other involuntary movements by the body, such as the heartbeat.

Before looking at techniques, it is important for the shooter to understand the process of breathing. Take a moment now to look at your own breathing. You inhale, the chest and stomach both rise, air enters the lungs to a comfortable point, everything slows down, then reverses, and the chest and stomach both fall to another comfortable point. It is important to notice that the lungs are neither full nor empty when the body decides to exhale or inhale. Also, when a breath is let out, there is a short pause before the next breath begins (when the body is at rest). Ultimately, there is an inhalation, slowing to a short pause of a couple seconds, and then an exhalation resulting in another short pause. Now, take a one-third breath and hold it while focusing on a distant point. You will notice that,

after about 10 seconds, your ability to focus on the target and keep your eyes steady begins to fail. This is due to the very early stages of oxygen deprivation and carbon dioxide saturation on the brain.

The pause components of the breathing cycle and the timing and length of breath holds are how we deal with breathing and its effects on shooting. The techniques used to stabilize the breathing cycle for an accurate shot are the full breath hold method and the natural respiratory pause method. Once learned and internalized, these techniques will allow the shooter to achieve greater accuracy and, due to the simplicity of the techniques, will be applied without the shooter realizing it!

## FULL BREATH HOLD

The full breath hold is exactly as it suggests. In this method, the shooter takes a comfortably full (or near full) breath in the seconds prior to taking the shot.

This method has two distinct advantages. The first is that, given a large volume of air taken into the lungs, the effects of oxygen deprivation (hypoxia) are put off for slightly longer. (It is important to note though that the feeling of needing to breathe is not derived from a lack of oxygen, but actually a build up of carbon dioxide within the body.) The second advantage is particular to a hunter's situation, in that the body, due to a long walk or other physically stressing activity that has the shooter at a lack of oxygen, experiences a higher heart rate and deep, fast breathing. If a shot were to be attempted in this condition and the natural respiratory pause method was used, the shooter would

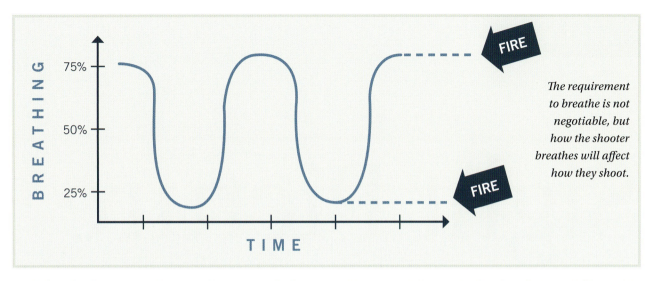

The requirement to breathe is not negotiable, but how the shooter breathes will affect how they shoot.

quickly suffer the effects of oxygen deprivation, leading to a poor point of aim. In this same situation, if the shooter were to use the full breath hold method, they would buy some more time for the shot, by having an excess of oxygen in the lungs.

Further advantages of this method include the fact that, as the chest cavity is enlarged and pressurized, the torso will become more rigid (particularly when in the standing, kneeling, or sitting positions), and so produces a more stable shooting platform. Further, as the chest cavity is enlarged and the stomach is pulled downwards, the pressure of the body (particularly in the prone position), will be taken off the heart and major arteries in the torso, leading to less heartbeat-induced movement on the body.

Of course, with the advantages come disadvantages. The greatest of these is that many people find the full breath hold method to be uncomfortable when coupled with some shooting positions. Further, particularly in the prone position or when using environmental support across the front of the chest or torso, it can be difficult to get the body down low and flat behind the rifle, and there will be rocking of the torso left and right due to the shape of the enlarged rib cage.

## NATURAL RESPIRATORY PAUSE HOLD

The natural respiratory pause method of breathing control utilizes the several seconds between breaths where the lungs are neither inhaling nor exhaling and the lungs are predominantly empty. The primary

advantage of this method is that the body is "at rest;" the muscles that are used in breathing are relaxed, the chest cavity is collapsed and flat, and the body is sufficiently oxygenated. All these factors help to provide a stable shooting platform.

The disadvantages of this method are predominantly around the subject of timing. The shooter needs to be able to time their aiming and shot to coincide with the natural respiratory pause. This might sound easy, but it requires a large amount of practice to coordinate the entire process within a two-second time frame. Further disadvantages include the fact that as the shooter's lungs are near to empty, the amount of time before oxygen deprivation sets in is reduced. Where a shooter could rely on no ill effects for up to 10 seconds with the full breath hold method, use of the natural respiratory pause method will halve that time frame, further if the shooter is breathing heavily or otherwise physically stressed after exertion.

This method is most effectively employed in a stand or ambush hunting situation or in competition. Normally, the shooter would "pre-breathe," with several deep breaths, while assessing the target and environment, achieving a good scope picture, and getting comfortable behind the rifle. Then the shooter will release the last deep breath until the body naturally stops exhaling. At this point, final aiming is completed and the rifle is fired. The body then resumes breathing as part of the follow-through of the shot.

# CHAPTER 18

# Sight Picture

The sight picture is the image presented to the shooter through their telescopic or iron sights. Maintaining a consistent and correct sight picture during not just individual firings, but across all firings, is a critical component of accuracy. Failure to achieve a consistent sight picture will result in varying points of aim. Likewise, failure to achieve a correct sight picture (noting the difference between consistent and correct), will result in an offset point of aim.

Achieving a correct and consistent sight picture is a function of four components. First is maintaining the correct eye relief—the distance between the eyepiece and eye—for the shooter's scope and chosen magnification (if a variable magnification scope is used). Second is maintaining a full sight picture (complete image) that fills the eyepiece of the scope, by making sure the shooter's eye is placed laterally and vertically in the correct position behind the scope. Third is ensuring that the shooter has the correct eyepiece and objective lens sun shade or other device installed on the scope for the particular environmental conditions. Finally, the shooter must ensure the correct parallax setting and adjustment are set on the scope, which allow the sight picture and crosshairs to both be in focus at the same time. If these key points are addressed and corrected

where necessary, the shooter will be able to adopt and maintain a consistent and correct sight picture.

## EYE RELIEF

Eye relief is the distance between the eyepiece lens of the scope and the shooter's eye. Eye relief is normally set when the scope is mounted to the shooter's rifle. It is important to note that, on variable magnification scopes, the correct eye relief distance actually forms a range, due to the fact that the correct eye relief distance will change with different magnification settings. When the correct eye relief distance is used, the shooter's eye will be presented with a full image that fills the scope's eyepiece, without the shooter needing to crane his or her neck back and forth. The picture will also present immediately, allowing fast target acquisition.

Symptoms of incorrect eye relief include an image that is blurred at the edges (eye relief too long), or an image that appears as if the shooter is looking through a keyhole (eye relief too short). To rectify a scope that has the wrong eye relief, all that needs to occur is loosening of the scope rings and either moving the scope forward or rearward, depending on the problem. Once the scope is set—for the shooter's eye, not the gunsmith's—the scope is leveled to remove any canting of the scope and the rings are tightened. With the eye

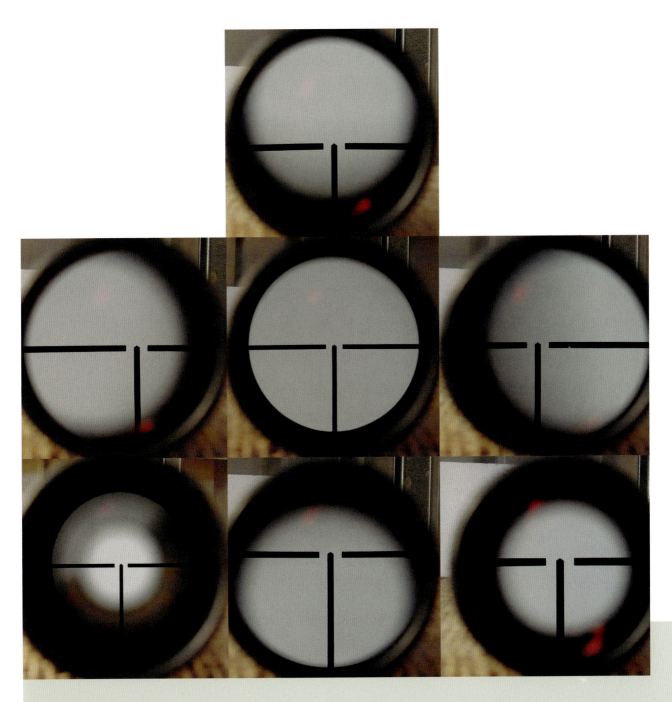

*Correct sight picture (center, center row), versus left, right, almost right, and far sight pictures. Only the correct sight picture will deliver accuracy.*

*Correct eye relief will not just give you the correct sight picture, it will also save you from an embarrassing and dangerous bruise or cut around your eye!*

relief correctly set, not only will the shooter and rifle be capable of greater accuracy, the issues of general fatigue, muscle tension, and eyestrain will be reduced.

## FULL SIGHT PICTURE

A full sight picture is achieved by the shooter positioning their head directly behind the scope, so that the image viewed through the scope is, first, a focused perfect circle that fills the eyepiece. Second, it is one that is also free from dark crescents, which would indicate a minor misalignment between the eyepiece and the shooter's eye.

Misalignment can occur in both the vertical and horizontal planes, and it has more to do with the design of the stock than it will be a "fault" of the shooter. Suffice it to say, while gripping the rifle in the correct manner, if the shooter's eye is too low (dark crescent in the top of the field of view), then a cheek rest should be added or lower scope rings used. Conversely, if the eye is too high (dark crescent in the bottom of the field of view), either the cheek rest should be lowered or slightly higher scope rings used. If there is a horizontal misalignment, the shooter need only reposition the head so that the eye is directly behind the scope. In severe cases of misalignment, a cutout in the stock may be appropriate; a horizontally adjustable butt plate may also be of benefit.

## PARALLAX

"Parallax" is a complicated optical term defining a rather simple principle. The parallax setting on a scope sets the distance at which both the image of the crosshair and the image of the target are on the same focal plane at the same time. In layman's terms, if the shooter's parallax setting is correct, they will be able to view both images, focused at the same time, without having to focus the eye, for instance, on the target first and then on the crosshair. A parallax-induced error (in terms of accuracy) results from the images being on different focal plans and, if there is a misalignment between the images, the shooter will not be able to detect it.

A simple test for parallax error at the shooter's chosen distance is to sight the rifle on the target. Then the shooter moves their head ever so slightly left and right while still looking through the scope. If there is parallax error, the crosshair will "wander" over the target. If there's no parallax error, the entire image of both the target and the crosshair will move sideways, but not change in relation to each other.

Most scopes have a parallax setting from the factory, and hunting-type scopes are generally set at 150 yards. But a lot of scopes these days are adjustable and come fitted with an adjustable objective (AO) or a side focus knob. Both adjusters come with range hash marks indicating at what range the parallax setting will be correct. Still, the best method for testing the correct setting is to carry out the parallax error test already outlined.

As a note, some will also advocate that parallax adjusters can be used to estimate range. This is somewhat haphazard and inaccurate, but can, with practice, be a useful adaptation of a tool to remember.

As to whether an adjustable objective is better or worse than a side focusing knob, it is mostly a matter of personal preference. It should be noted that a side focusing knob on a rifle scope allows the shooter to continue looking through the scope while the shooter employs the knob, so its usage does not interfere with the shooting position. The same cannot be said of adjustable objectives, unless the shooter has very long arms.

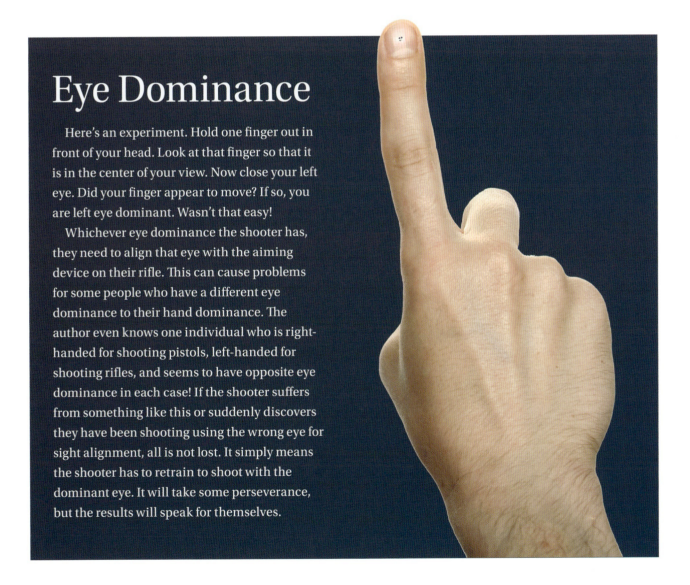

# Eye Dominance

Here's an experiment. Hold one finger out in front of your head. Look at that finger so that it is in the center of your view. Now close your left eye. Did your finger appear to move? If so, you are left eye dominant. Wasn't that easy!

Whichever eye dominance the shooter has, they need to align that eye with the aiming device on their rifle. This can cause problems for some people who have a different eye dominance to their hand dominance. The author even knows one individual who is right-handed for shooting pistols, left-handed for shooting rifles, and seems to have opposite eye dominance in each case! If the shooter suffers from something like this or suddenly discovers they have been shooting using the wrong eye for sight alignment, all is not lost. It simply means the shooter has to retrain to shoot with the dominant eye. It will take some perseverance, but the results will speak for themselves.

## CHAPTER 19

# Rifles for Every Occasion

In this highly over-commercialized world, there is a bewildering array for firearms available, and each manufacturer will have absolute and perfect reasoning as to why its is guns are better than any other on the market. On the other side, public perception, in this all so disposable world, suggests that anything old is not new and, as such, to achieve performance, new firearms are required. In this section, I will take the shooter through various types of rifles, old and new, and their shooting and maintenance that will fulfill those shooting needs, without breaking the bank.

### TRAINING RIFLES

Typically, a training rifle is a small-caliber rifle that the shooter can use to learn on, practice with, and reinforce the principles of marksmanship such as trigger control, breathing, and shooting positions. Training rifles are also meant to be fun, cheap to shoot, easy to maintain, and convenient to carry and use. Training rifles are "range-based" rifles, set up to mimic larger calibers. A side benefit is that, due to

their size and weight, there are no real problems with taking a training rifle into the field to hunt small game.

Ideally, the training rifle should be a .22 LR bolt-action and have a heavy barrel, an adjustable trigger, and a rifle scope of at least 3-10x. A variable scope is preferable, to allow the shooter to practice various shooting scenarios, such as standing snap shots and prone deliberate shots. The training rifle can also be fitted with a lightweight bipod and some sort of cheekpiece. The shooter needn't worry about changing stocks or modifying the barreled action, as the standard setup should be perfectly sufficient. In this configuration, the shooter can conduct long-range shooting in a short-range context. By firing at ranges in excess of 100 yards/meters, the shooter will be forced to utilize ballistics data and adjust for windage and elevation in the normal manner they'd have to for a larger centerfire rifle over longer ranges.

Good examples of a training rifle are the Savage Mk2 FV, either TR or TRR, fitted with a Simmons, Tasco, or Bushnell scope, an inexpensive bipod, and

*Small-caliber training rifles allow the shooter to practice and hone their skills for larger calibers, without breaking the bank.*

*Fast, light, and entertaining are the hallmarks of a good "fun gun!"*

a soft, wraparound cheekpiece. Offerings from Ruger and Mossberg also fills this niche well. A high-value .22 LR, such as those from Walther, Anschütz, or Brno, needn't be used, and no real training advantage will be obtained in terms of a *training* rifle.

It should be noted that .22 LR rifles really don't wear out, unless they are abused. As such, secondhand rifles in this category can fulfill the purpose of a training rifle just as well as a new offering. A training rifle is the perfect way for the shooter to hone their skills across the full spectrum required for the accurate shooter, in an affordable manner, while also having a bucket-load of fun!

## SHORT-RANGE FUN GUNS

A short-range fun gun is a rifle that the shooter can use for plinking, short-range hunting, and also some short-range competition. A short-range fun gun needs to be convenient, light, and capable of both very close-range shooting and longer, more challenging shots. A short-range fun gun needs to have an amount

of stopping power suited to cola can busting (a fun visual pastime, when the cans are full!) and capable of humanely killing small and even medium game.

A lever-action rifle fits this bill perfectly. In calibers such as .30-30 or .44-40 (or, more commonly these days, .357 Magnum and .44 Magnum), these rifles are perfectly capable of taking small deer at shorter ranges. Further, western action competition is a niche, but highly entertaining sport that uses such guns.

When discussing lever-action rifles, Winchester, Marlin, and Browning make good rifles in a variety of calibers. The shooter needn't worry about mounting a scope on these rifles, as the iron sights are perfectly sufficient and will also teach the shooter a lot about snap shooting and the kneeling and standing shooting positions.

As it is with a designated training rifle, the shooter shouldn't be concerned with buying a brand new rifle for this purpose. There are almost limitless numbers of secondhand lever-action rifles available to the shooter, some of which have varying degrees of collectable

*Short- to medium-range hunting rifles need to be light and comfortable to carry. They also require a caliber good for a variety of small to medium-sized game species.*

value, if the shooter is inclined to consider this rifle an investment. Lever-action rifles, when cared for properly, are also long lasting and lots of fun.

## SHORT- AND MEDIUM-RANGE CENTERFIRE HUNTING RIFLES

This type of rifle should have sufficient stopping power at the 300-yard/-meter range to humanely kill medium-sized game, yet, at the same time, should be convenient and light enough for backpack hunting. The rifle should have a variable scope, possibly fitted with a bullet drop compensator, but magnification of more than 10x. A medium-weight barrel is suitable, although lightweight barrels are fine, if the shooter intends to use this rifle as a stalking or purely backpack hunting rifle. Accessories such as a bipod, sling, and shooting sticks are advisable and will address nearly all shooting positions.

In terms of caliber, .243 and above are suitable for all medium-sized game, though the rifle may become unmanageable, in terms of recoil, if cartridges such as .300 Winchester Magnum and larger are used. The rifle should have an adjustable trigger, and a wooden stock will work just as well as a composite or synthetic stock.

The shooter can look towards new rifles such as the Ruger 77 series or the Remington 700 series. There are also a miscellany of Mauser 98-based sporting rifles from the 1960s through the '80s that will fit this niche well, while also adding an amount

of "old world" class that new rifles cannot match. Rifles made by Parker Hale and BSA are other excellent examples that have adjustable triggers and some of the best barrels ever made; when found in good condition, are an excellent addition to the shooter's safe. Moreover, they can often be had for a few hundred dollars and are available in all the major calibers from .22-250 to .300 Winchester Magnum.

Rifles such as these will teach the shooter to shoot from many different shooting positions using different aspects of environmental support, and they are very much a multipurpose hunting rifle that can transform the shooter into a well-rounded rifleman.

## LONG-RANGE HUNTING RIFLES

A long-range hunting rifle is a purpose-built piece of equipment. This type of rifle is intended for the hunting of medium to large game in excess of 600 yards/meters and possibly beyond 1,200. This type of rifle is characterized by a 26-inch barrel of a heavy profile, but can be as much as 30 inches. The stock is optimized for being shot off the bench or a bipod and should be equipped with an adjustable cheekpiece. The scope in this case should not be any less than 10x, and a variable up to 36x is quite appropriate. This type of rifle is suited to the .300 Winchester Magnum and larger, though .308 is sometimes applicable at 800 to 1,000 yards/meters, depending on the shooter and the game species. The shooter should have access to ballistics software and an accurate

*Long-range hunting rifles are characterized by heavy barrels, stout cartridges, and adjustable stocks. These rifles can deliver excellent long-range accuracy, but usually at the cost of mobility.*

method of measuring the range and environmental forces, for this type of shooting.

In terms of suitable rifles, the shooter can consider offerings from all the major manufacturers. A good example would be the Remington 700 Sendero series of rifles. The shooter is not restricted to new rifles and can certainly consider (with some modifications) older benchrest rifles with long, heavy-profile barrels. These rifles can be retrofitted with appropriate scopes, and they nearly always already have adjustable triggers and stocks. Good examples would be the Omark 44 series and the miscellany of Mauser 98 and P14/M17 rifles that have been turned into range rifles.

Shooting at extended range is really just benchrest shooting in the field. Given the lack of range flags and known ranges, it will require the shooter to have a good understanding of ballistics and how to apply ballistic theory to their shooting. It will also require the shooter to understand and apply their

marksmanship skills to the limit and exercise ethical decision making, when assessing possible shots.

## BENCHREST ON A BUDGET

Benchrest rifles, much like long-range hunting rifles, are purpose-built and intended for competition ranging from 100 yards/meters to 1,000 yards/meters and beyond. These rifles are characterized by heavyweight barrels, sometimes as long as 33 inches. Calibers range from .308 and up, and there really is no limit to where the shooter can go to—even the .50 BMG is used in some competitions!

The stocks on these rifles are generally very heavy and can be either adjustable or fixed, but will be customized to the particular shooter. These rifles rarely have detachable magazines, normally being single-shots. Scopes of 36x and above are used, though the reticles are normally very simple crosshairs, so as to avoid making the sight picture "busy" at long range.

*A competitive benchrest rifle does not have to cost the Earth! Older rifles, with good handloads and correct shooting technique, can still make the "X"-ring.*

*Tactical rifle configurations are limited only by the imagination of the shooter.*

Quite often, these rifles are fitted with an integral bipod or are shot off shooting rests positioned at both the fore-end and butt.

These rifles are mostly custom built with a particular set of competition parameters in mind, as it is difficult to formulate a rifle that will perform well in all competitions. Commercial manufacturers really don't cater to this market, but building a benchrest rifle does not need to be an extremely expensive process. The shooter can opt to utilize an off-the-shelf action with a custom barrel and other alterations/improvements performed. Of course, the shooter can look to secondhand benchrest rifles; they can certainly still be competitive with older Mauser 98-based benchrest rifles from the 1970s on, with correct attention being paid to handloading and shooter skills. A top of the line benchrest rifle can be beaten by a less accurate and older model, if the shooter of the latter has a better understanding of windage and ballistics at long range!

## TACTICAL RIFLES

Tactical rifles are a modern style of rifle that tends to bridge the gap between short-range and long-range rifles. Tactical rifles tend to operate in the 100 to 800 yard/meter bracket and are generally styled or tailored towards military or law enforcement applications. These rifles offer convenient lengths and weights, coupled with heavy barrels and longer-range capability. They are suited to most types of hunting, and are accurate enough to be competitive in many types of competition. Still, they are not geared to any specific capability, except that of being multipurpose.

These rifles tend to mount either 3-10x variable or 10x and beyond variable scopes. Reticles tend to be derivatives of the Mil-Dot, for the ease of elevation, wind holdover, and ranging capabilities.

Tactical rifles are generally built around the .308 Winchester cartridge, due to its multipurpose capability. The .223 Remington also features heavily in this class.

Tactical rifles generally have permanently fitted accessories such as extended bolt handles, muzzle brakes, and suppressors that add to their consumer appeal. Due to the modern styling of this type of rifle, shooters are usually forced to look at new rifles. Notably, Remington produces its Tactical and Police lines of rifles, Savage offers its own lines of Law Enforcement rifles, and Ruger has a line of Tactical M77s. Still, with those and others frequently in short supply in shifting political climates, older barreled actions, particularly from varmint-styled rifles, can be used with an aftermarket stock.

Putting aside the consumer appeal of tactical rifles, the actual underlying philosophy behind their construction and usage is very sound. If a shooter could own only one rifle, this style would offer the greatest potential for multiple uses.

# CHAPTER 20

# New Rifle Setup

This section of the book takes the shooter through the setup, running in, shooting, cleaning, and basic maintenance of a brand-new, off-the-shelf rifle. For the purposes of this discussion, the reader can consider this rifle to be one that is multi-purpose, suited to hunting medium game and the occasional club competition shoot. The reader can consider this rifle to be any rifle from the major manufacturers in a centerfire cartridge of .243 to .300 or so.

The sequence of events described here can be applied to any firearm, with any style action, including auto-loaders. By following this sequence of events, the reader will make the most of their purchase and their ammunition.

## OUT OF THE BOX

Having taken the rifle home, the very first task for the shooter is to leave the rifle in the box and reach for the owner's manual. The owner's manual will contain, right up front, safety documentation and operating instructions for the gun. The manual will also contain the necessary instructions for stripping the firearm, which the shooter will need to draw on soon enough.

Having read the safety and operating instructions, the next task for the shooter is to clear the firearm and ensure it is safe, with no rounds in the magazine or chamber and with the action decocked and the safety on. Having completed this task, the shooter can now begin to experiment with shouldering and different shooting positions, along with looking at the length of pull for the stock, or perhaps examining the firearm for transit damage or defects.

Satisfied with their purchase, the shooter can begin readying the rifle for use. Many shooters believe that, when a new firearm is purchased, it can be taken straight from the box, loaded, and fired. Although the shooter certainly can do this, in most cases, the new rifle will benefit from a good going over of many of its technical aspects. This will let the rifle perform at its best from the outset, and will enable the shooter to make the most of their ammunition and truly enjoy and become familiar with their new investment.

*So, you've taken your new rifle home! Always read the manual before taking the rifle out of the box.*

The first job for the shooter is to remove the barreled action from the stock by removing the bolt and undoing the action screws. *The shooter should take note of the level of tension on the action screws.* Having removed the barreled action, the shooter can inspect the various surfaces that would otherwise be invisible when the action is attached to the stock. In particular, the shooter is looking for dirt and grease that can be cleaned out and defects or obstructions that may impact the performance of the rifle. Examples would be loose plastic flashing from the stock that may have made its way into the action, or small metal burrs around the action screw holes.

The shooter should next field strip the bolt, leaving it in (normally) two parts, those consisting of the bolt body and the firing mechanism. Again, there should be an inspection here to locate possible obstructions or defects.

Now the shooter can really get down to business! The task next on the list is degreasing the barrel, action, bolt, and trigger mechanism. Degreasing of these components is very important. As new from the manufacturer, these parts are generally encased in a heavy, persistent grease, which, contrary to popular belief, is *not* intended as a lubricant, but, rather, as an anti-corrosive agent, to prevent rust while the rifle is sitting in its box unsold at the factory or at the dealer's shop. This grease does work as a lubricant, but, due to the sheer amount involved when using it as a packing/shipping grease, it can cause immediate

problems, particularly in cold climates, as the grease seizes up. Too, over time, the grease will act as a dust and grime magnet. Eventually this will form into a hard paste that might seriously foul the working parts and cause the rifle to stop functioning, (or at least accelerate the wear on the working parts).

To remove the factory lubricant, a spray such as carburetor or brake parts cleaner is perfect, and there are plenty of commercial, gun-specific degreasers available. In fact, any degreaser spray should work well. The shooter needs to spray out the entire bolt and action, paying particular attention to the firing pin spring and the extractor/ejector mechanism. The shooter also needs to spray out the trigger mechanism to ensure the factory lubricant is removed from the small parts and spaces inside. When done, the shooter can set the parts aside to dry. As a last task at this stage, it's a good idea to rinse the parts with alcohol prior to setting them aside to dry, to ensure that no residue from the degreasers remains.

Once the parts have dried off, they can be re-lubricated. There are two options for this: the shooter can choose a dry lubricant such as graphite or Teflon (in the form of a spray that dries), or they can use one of the approved gun oil products readily available on the market, with one exception. In the case of the trigger mechanism, this part must *only* be dry lubricated; if dry lubrication is not an option, then no lubricant whatsoever should be used on the trigger mechanism.

When lubricating the bolt, particular attention must be paid to the cocking piece, to ensure it can move in and out with the firing pin smoothly, and also any camming surfaces that force the firing pin to move from un-cocked to cocked. These surfaces are subjected to fairly heavy loads and "grinding," as parts ride up on each other under the compression of the firing pin spring.

Looking next at the bolt body, the only parts that need to be lubricated here are the backsides of the locking lugs with a small amount of lubricant, and perhaps the ejector and extractor mechanism with a light lubricating spray. Ensure the excess is removed. Likewise, on the action itself, the locking lugs require some light lubrication. That said, the first time the bolt is returned to the action, the excess on the lugs will rub off on the lugs in the action, achieving the same results. Having re-lubricated the rifle, the bolt can be reassembled and fitted back into the action.

The next step is looking at the interface between the barreled action and the stock. Ideally, the only places an action should touch the stock are at the recoil lug, the bottom of the action (if a Remington action is used), or the action flat (if a Ruger or Winchester action is used). In some cases, the tip of the fore-end should contact the underside of the barrel. The shooter should ensure that the tang or rearmost part of the action is not butting up against the edge of the action recess in the stock (particularly important in Winchester actions), and that the barrel only contacts the stock at the tip of the fore-end when fitted, assuming that the barrel is not intended to be free-floating from the factory. The shooter should also inspect the functioning of the bolt, ensuring that the bolt handle doesn't touch the stock in the closed position, and that the safety and bolt release still function when the action is fitted into the stock.

Having confirmed that the stock is free from obstructions, the shooter can torque the barreled action into the stock. This is done by first tightening the front action screw to finger tight, then following with the rear action screw. It is also a good idea to do the tightening with the butt firmly placed on a workbench and the muzzle pointing straight up. Both processes ensure that the action is pulled down and back onto the recoil abutments in the stock. Once this is completed, the shooter can go ahead and torque the front screw down to 45 in-lbs for a wooden stock or 65 in-lbs for a composite stock or a stock with an aluminum bedding block.

Having refit the barreled action to the stock, the shooter can then consider their sighting devices for the rifle. For the purposes of this discussion, the shooter intends to fit a medium-power rifle scope.

The key to fitting rifle scopes is keeping everything level. Starting with the receiver pads or rail, the shooter should begin by leveling the action and stock on a solid surface and checking that they are level with a spirit level. Then the shooter can fit the pads or rail to the top of the action, with the screws provided. (Know that, occasionally, the screw holes can be filled with a greasy mess of dust and particles. This can be blasted out with degreaser or removed with the correct tap.) The screws should be tightened to 25 in-lbs of torque and locked with Loctite or another similar compound. Then the shooter can check to ensure that the pads or rail are level to the action with the spirit level. If there is a misalignment (generally the case with pads, but rarely with a rail), the shooter can cut shims from brass or aluminum and place these underneath the pads to level them to the action. At the same time, the pads may not be level to each other and, so, the shimming process may be required to correct this, as well.

Once the pads or rail have been leveled, the shooter can then install the scope ring bottoms on the pads or rail, ensuring they are square to the rail or pads and also level to the pads. Check this with the spirit level.

Just before placing the scope in the cradle of the bottom rings, check that the scope reticle is mechanically centered within the scope tube by placing the objective lens against a mirror and then looking through the scope and aligning the two images of crosshairs over each other. Next, the shooter should check to see that the ring bottoms aren't twisted to the axis of the scope and that the eye relief is correct. Place the scope in the cradle of the bottom rings, then the ring caps can then be lowered into position and the screws tightened in an opposite and alternate manner—front left screw, then rear right, and so on—to 15 in-lbs. It is also a good idea to match the gaps (if any) between the ring halves left to right. It's not good to have the left side pinched up and the right side with a large gap, as this will apply uneven pressure to the scope's tube, plus it also looks messy!

Last, the shooter can attach any accessories to the rifle, such as a sling or a bipod. Doing this, the shooter should return to their shooting positions and ensure that, when a shooting position is adopted with a bipod or a sling, there are no extra forces on the fore-end that could cause pressure against the barrel prior to firing.

The rifle can now be considered as assembled and ready for the next stages of preparation prior to range testing. To that end, before the shooter heads to the range for the first time with the new rifle, there are several things the shooter needs to do to get the most out of their purchase. First up is a pre-firing cleaning. Next, the shooter will need to bore-sight the rifle. Finally, the shooter needs a checklist to ensure all the equipment they need is available at their fingertips and so they can make the most of their first day out. Let's look more closely at each of these steps.

## PRE-FIRING CLEANING

A pre-firing cleaning can take two forms. The first for a new rifle, the second for any firearm that has been correctly cleaned, but placed in storage.

Looking first at the pre-firing cleaning for new rifles, the shooter needs to place the firearm in a gun vice with the muzzle pointing downward on a steep angle. Once so established, apply a good quality bore solvent such as Sweets 7.62 to a clean and dry patch and pass this patch through the bore in the direction the projectile flies. Many shooters only dampen the patch with solvent and then pass it through the bore. This is insufficient. The patch needs to be *saturated* with solvent, so much so that, once the patch as gone through, drops should come out of the muzzle.

Having passed the patch through the bore, the shooter needs to wait the full amount of time specified on the solvent's label, normally 15 minutes, before passing a clean dry patch through the bore to remove any dissolved fouling and excess bore solvent. If insufficient solvent is used, little or no fouling will be removed from the bore, and the shooter will mistakenly believe their bore is clean.

A good way to check for any fouling left in the bore is to examine the rifling just inside the muzzle with a very bright light. If orange streaks are seen, there is still fouling in the bore. Normally, patches and solvent are enough to remove all the fouling, particularly in a new bore, but, if there is stubborn fouling present, one pass from chamber to muzzle only (no reversing), with a bronze phosphor cleaning brush, should enable the last of the fouling to be removed with a further patch saturated with solvent.

Having completely removed all the fouling from the bore, the shooter needs to pass through several clean and dry patches to ensure that no solvent remains. Once this is complete, a final patch saturated with acetone should be passed through the bore, being careful to ensure there are no spills of the acetone into the action or other parts. The acetone will remove any final oils, anti-corrosive agents, solvents, etc., from the corners of the lands and grooves in the rifling and the chamber. This ensures that the case will correctly grip the chamber walls and that the rifling is absolutely free of any obstructions, and so limits the effects and deviation of the cold-bore first shot. The acetone will dry off in a couple minutes and the bore is then ready for shooting!

If a firearm is absolutely clean but has come from storage, it is only necessary to patch out the bore with a clean and dry patch, and then patch again with acetone for the same reasons stated for a new-in-box rifle.

## BORE SIGHTING

The next task for the shooter is to bore sight their rifle scope. Bore sighting is a very rudimentary system of zeroing that will result in easier true zeroing with live ammunition.

In order to bore sight the rifle, the shooter simply clears the rifle, removes the bolt, and positions the rifle

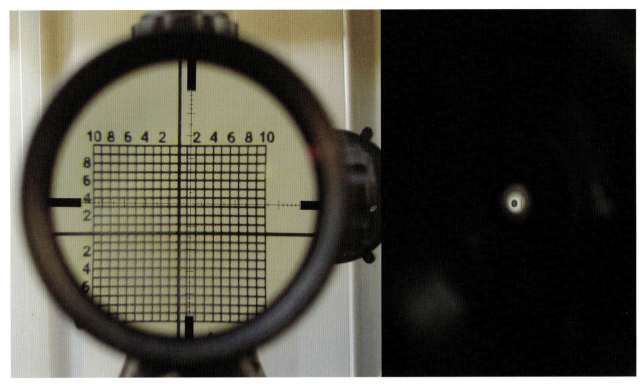

*Bore sighting can be done either with an optical bore sighter or by simply looking down the bore at a target and lining up the optic's crosshairs on it.*

so the shooter can look through the bore at a target 100 yards/meters away. Once the bore of the rifle is lined up with the target, the shooter simply looks through the scope (or other sighting system) and adjusts the scope's reticle so that it aims at the target. This must be done carefully, as any bumping of the rifle that moves it from its natural point of aim will ruin the bore sighting. It is important to note that given that the scope has been mechanically centered, the bore sighting adjustments should be input via the mount, if possible.

Most ring and base combinations allow for a coarse adjustment of windage via a pair of screws; one screw is loosened and the other tightened, resulting in a shift in point of aim. The shooter should take care to ensure that the screws are done up tightly. Some shooters even lock the screws by striking the area next to the screw with a punch, preventing the screw from being moved further. The elevation adjustment can be carried out as normal on the scope's elevation turret.

In another method used to bore sight the rifle, the shooter can invest in a tool known by the same name. A bore sight is a lens system with a crosshair in it. It fits to a mandrel and is placed in the muzzle of the rifle. The shooter then simply looks through the scope and lines up the reticle in the scope with the reticle in the bore sight. This system technically is no more accurate than the traditional method, but it is quicker and easier.

Once bore sighted, the rifle should put the first rounds onto the target at 100 yards/meters, though fine adjustment with live ammunition will be required.

## EQUIPMENT CHECKLIST

Although an equipment checklist sounds terribly mundane, there are some pieces of equipment and tools the shooter needs to have access to for that first trip to the range. Possessing these tools and equipment will not only allow the shooter to get more out of their day, but also to troubleshoot problems and fine-tune their rifle.

First, the shooter must take their cleaning gear with them, that consisting of a rod, a jag or loop for cotton patches, a bronze phosphor brush, and a quality bore

*Having the right tools for the first day at the range with a new rifle makes all the difference, when problems crop up!*

solvent. This gear will allow the shooter to clean and run in their rifle correctly, as well as knock loose any stuck cases from the chamber.

Second, the shooter needs to take a full set of screwdrivers and/or Allen keys, along with their torque wrench, so that action screws and others can be tightened as the shoot progresses. It is quite common for the action screws to loosen as the stock settles down on a new rifle, and accuracy will improve if the shooter checks the tension on the action screws and ensures the correct tension is retained at all times.

Third, the shooter needs to take a notebook and pen to record group sizes, ammunition velocities, weather conditions, and any other relevant information the shooter may gather when setting up the rifle at the range.

Finally, the shooter should make note of any other accessories or equipment that may come in handy. Examples would be a spotting scope or binocular, so that the shooter doesn't have to walk up to the targets as often; a laser rangefinder to confirm the exact length of the range, important when zeroing a scope the has a bullet drop compensator or is going to be used with ballistics data; and even a packed lunch and a drink is important, given that most ranges are out in the sun and the shooter will quickly dehydrate and get hungry, ruining their mood and ability to shoot well.

# CHAPTER 21

# First Shots

## THE FIRST FOULING SHOT

The first fouling shot is the first round the shooter puts through a freshly cleaned bore, whether the rifle is brand new or not. The first fouling shot will nearly always maintain a point of impact that is different to the normal zero point of impact for the firearm, yet it is also consistent. Some firearms require two rounds to complete the first fouling (both of which are predictable in their points of impact), before the normal point of impact is achieved by subsequent rounds. This is because, as a projectile travels down the bore, not only does it burn off excess oils, solvents, and dust from previous storage or cleaning, it leaves a trail, however small, of copper fouling. This fouling effectively bridges the microscopic gaps between the rifling and the projectile at the surface of the rifling. Once the trail has been laid on the surface of the bore, only a very small amount of further fouling is deposited by subsequent projectiles, which allows them to maintain the same points of impact.

Because the first projectile down the clean bore interacts differently with the rifling (because more of the copper jacket is being left in the bore), that projectile would react differently when it exits the bore. Still, the firearm has "lost" little of its accuracy from the first fouling shot. The impact from the first fouling shot is *highly* predictable in nearly all

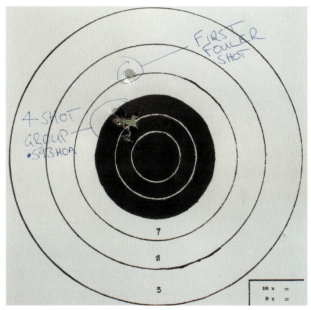

*The impact point of first fouling shots is common and predictable in most rifles. Knowing where your fouler is going to land is an asset!*

firearms. The lesson to take away from this is that the shooter needs to be aware and even log the point of impact for the first fouling shot. At the same time, the shooter should not fear the first fouling shot—nor should they fire a bullet just for the *sake* of fouling the rifle! If a shooter is on a hunt, the first fouling shot can be used, so long as the shooter knows where it is going to impact.

## RUN-IN

The first critical process the shooter must carry out on a new rifle—or, more correctly, a new *barrel*—at the range is a "run-in." Even a secondhand rifle that has seen extensive use can benefit from a correctly conducted run-in.

The run-in for a new barrel is a wearing-in process, much like with a new set of hiking boots or a new car engine. The run-in process effectively polishes the bore, removing microscopic burrs, tool marks, and any uneven edges. The "tool" used to do this polishing is the projectile the shooter intends to use the most in this rifle. The end result is a bore free of small inconsistencies and match-polished to suit the projectile the shooter will use. Rifles that have been run-in correctly will exhibit less fouling, more stable velocities, and potentially enhanced accuracy. All that is required of the shooter is patience and attention to detail.

In order to run-in a rifle correctly, the shooter must ensure that the rifle is absolutely clean of all fouling. The best solvent to use for this, in my opinion, is Sweets 7.62. When no more copper fouling is removed and no persistent fouling can be seen just inside the muzzle with a light, the shooter can proceed. From here, the shooter fires a round. Next, the shooter cleans the bore back to its previous, nearly sterile condition, then fires another round. This process is repeated until at least 20 rounds have been fired, each time ensuring the bore is absolutely clean after a round has been fired. Up to 30 rounds can be fired in this manner, but it is rarely necessary to proceed past this number, as the polishing will be complete or nearly there and can be finished with normal shooting.

Many shooters dispute whether run-in is necessary and if any gains can be made. Ultimately, this comes down to the quality of the new barrel. For instance, an off-the-shelf factory rifle may see great benefits in a properly conducted run-in, but a hand-lapped custom barrel may not. Ultimately, it certainly doesn't hurt the rifle, so why not run-in the barrel and eliminate a possible compromise to accuracy, especially when the process can be combined with coarse zeroing?

## GROUPING

Grouping, or the firing of three to five rounds at the same point of aim, allows the shooter to gauge their rifle's accuracy, in terms of consistency, by repeatedly hitting the same point. Grouping also allows the shooter to fine zero their rifle.

Looking first at gauging accuracy, the shooter fires three to five rounds at the target, preferably at 100 yards/meters so that any crosswind effect will be minimized, and then measures the group size from the centers of the furthest holes in the target. It is important for the shooter, while shooting groups, to allow the barrel to cool between shots.

Group sizes are generally expressed in minutes of angle (MOA), remembering that 1 MOA equals 1.145 inches at 100 meters and 1.047 inches at 100 yards, and that it is an angular measurement; at 200 meters, 1 MOA equals 2.290 inches.

Sometimes during group firing there can be fliers, or individual impacts that are well outside the rest of the group. These can be ignored and eliminated from measurement. Fliers are generally caused by external factors, such as flinching on the part of the shooter or some sort of inconsistency with that particular round of ammunition. Fliers can also be symptomatic of a bedding problem, so keep track of their occurrences as you proceed.

By the time five rounds have been fired, the bore most likely will be at least blood warm; it can heat up rapidly in the sun. Shooting an overheated barrel will affect the point of aim and accuracy and can lead to accelerated wear and damage to the throat and rifling. The best way to cool a barrel is to simply leave the bolt open. The barrel, being warm, will suck cold air through the chamber via convection and allow warm air to escape out of the muzzle, thereby cooling the bore from the inside. Placing a damp rag on the bore is not advisable, because this will only effectively cool that section of the barrel that contacts the damp rag. Placing the rifle in the shade or, even better, shooting from a shaded location, will help keep barrel temperatures down.

Looking at grouping as a means to achieving fine zero, the shooter again needs to fire three- or five-round groups. Then, when measuring the group sizes, the shooter needs to calculate the "mean point of impact" (MPI), or the average point on the target around which the holes are clustered. (Note that the MPI itself is rarely a hole in the target.) There is computer software the shooter can use to accurately determine the MPI. In this, the shooter will take a photo and upload it into the software. For most purposes, an estimated point of impact is fine. Once the MPI is established, the shooter simply measures the distance vertically and horizontally from the MPI to the point of aim on the target. These two distances comprise the elevation and windage adjustment the shooter needs to input into their scope to achieve a fine zero. The three- to five-round group should then be fired again, to either confirm the zero is correct or make any further small adjustments. If further adjustments are made, the shooter should reconfirm the zero.

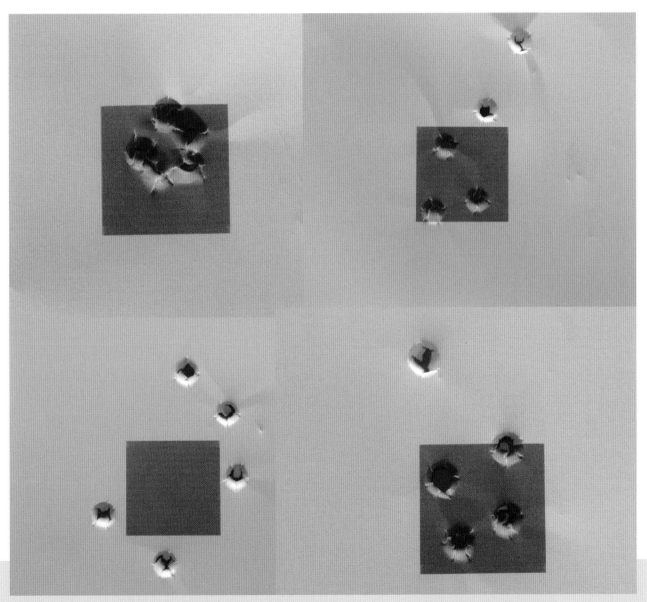

*Groups can vary a lot, but much information is available for the shooter to study, if they look carefully. Top left we have a good group, a wide group at lower left, a stringing group at top right, and a group with a flier at lower right.*

This process ensures that, from then on, the groups the shooter fires will cluster about the point of aim, creating consistency, accuracy and on the part of the shooter, and confidence in their rifle.

It is important that the shooter record their results in a data book, logging the range, atmospheric data, load, and points of impact. This will allow the shooter to log the performance of their firearm and ammunition and will assist in creating accurate rifle/ammunition package and ballistic solutions.

## BALLISTIC SETUP

Setting up a rifle for use with a ballistic table or ballistic software is a two-stage process. First, the shooter calculates a ballistic table for the ammunition they're using and some specific details on the rifle. Second, the shooter needs to synchronize their rifle to the table.

For the ballistics table, the shooter needs to know the projectile weight, ballistic coefficient, and the velocity this ammunition achieves out of the shooter's rifle. An approximation of velocity is good, but an exact measurement from a chronograph is best. The shooter also needs the height of the center axis of the scope from the axis of the bore line. This can be measured by carefully using a steel ruler to line up the center point between the scope ring base and cap, and the center point at the chamber or firing pin hole. This information is either fed into a ballistic software program or cross-referenced with a ballistic data table, normally supplied by the manufacturer of the projectile.

In the case of the ballistics table supplied by the projectile manufacturer, the table will require the shooter to zero their rifle, normally at 100 yards/meters, on a "standard day" (in terms of temperature, barometric pressure, humidity, and altitude), to synchronize the rifle to the supplied table. Having done this, the table will generally supply the correct elevation adjustments in increments of 100 yards/meters out to 500 yards/meters. The table will generally also supply the windage adjustments for five-, 10-, and 15-mph direct three or nine o'clock crosswinds

at the same range increments. This completed table forms the shooter's ballistics data, enabling the shooter to input the approximately correct windage and elevation adjustments in varying conditions out to medium range.

It should be noted that using the method that employs the manufacturer's table does not take into account the height of the scope axis above the bore axis, and it also uses an approximation of velocity to the closest 100 fps. The lack of both these factors combine to decrease the effectiveness of the table; the actual accuracy of the rifle isn't affected, but the discrepancies between the point of aim and the point of impact will be larger and increase with range, due to the use of approximations.

Ballistic software *does* take into account the height between the scope and the bore line, and the exact velocity of the projectile can be input. In this case, the shooter can allow the ballistics software to create a table tailored for their rifle, or the shooter can calculate individual shots using current atmospheric data from a Kestrel or other similar tool.

A tailored ballistics table is a very good idea no matter what method the shooter prefers to use, and one can be kept with the rifle. The tailored ballistics table will be far more accurate than the table produced by the ammunition manufacturer and will serve as an excellent backup or quick reference chart that can be taped to the side of the butt of the shooter's rifle, good for shots that don't permit the use of a PDA, due to time constraints. The shooter is also able to determine the range increments instead of using increments of 100 yards/meters. Generally, for a tailored ballistics table, 50-yard/meter increments are accurate enough for the task and are not so small that the shooter will get lost in the numbers, when looking up an adjustment in the field. If it can be managed, 25-yard/meter increments are the best for precision.

When using a tailored ballistics table, it's a good idea to calculate the windage for a one mile per hour three or nine o'clock crosswind. This will allow the shooter to lookup the crosswind adjustment and simply multiply it by the measured or estimated wind strength. This is far more accurate than simply using preset adjustments for five-, 10-, and 15-mph crosswinds.

When using ballistics software in the field, perhaps on a PDA or smartphone, the shooter can generate perfect ballistic solutions based on the exact range, projectile velocity, atmospheric data and crosswind, instead of using estimations and approximations. This type of ballistic calculation forms the pinnacle of ballistic solutions and will allow the shooter to achieve the best results.

Looking at the table below as an example, the shooter has generated a ballistics solution for a shot using all three methods. The first solution uses the basic data provided by the projectile manufacturer, the second uses a tailored ballistics table, and the third uses exact data and is generated from ballistics software on a PDA. As the reader can easily see, at this range, the difference in solutions is staggering.

In this case, a large difference can be seen between the manufacturers' solution and that of a tailored ballistics table. That said, the tailored ballistics table comes quite close to the "perfect" ballistics solution supplied by the software, though the gap would open up with increasing range. So, the manufacturer's data table is probably sufficient out to 300 yards/meters. Beyond that point, the shooter requires a tailored table, but it has to be remembered that at ranges beyond about 600 yards/meters, the tailored table becomes significantly inaccurate in its solution and full ballistics calculations will be necessary.

Having calculated the ballistics table or setup the ballistics software, the shooter must ensure that their rifle is synchronized to the table or software. Synchronizing is also carried out as a two-stage process.

Initially, the shooter simply ensures that the zero defined by the ballistics table or data is the same as the zero for which the rifle is currently set. This calibrates the rifle to the table and vice versa. The second stage requires the shooter to go to the range and actually shoot at each specified distance or at certain distances on the ballistics table or data, using the adjustments specified, and then note any differences between the ballistics solution and the real-world result. The shooter can then combine this information and adjust the ballistics table or data to show the correction.

Some ballistics software have a function whereby the shooter can shoot using the adjustment specified at one distance beyond the zero of the rifle (preferably mid-range in the table or data), input the correction, if any, and the software will take this information and adjust its calculation accordingly for all the specified ranges in the table or data. By coupling both the predicted ballistic solutions and real-world data, the shooter has perfected their ballistic solutions.

---

**Ammunition:** .243 firing 85-grain Sierra HPBT Matchking (BC 0.311) at 3,167 fps
**Rifle:** 1.5-inch distance between bore axis and scope axis
**Range:** 463 meters
**Atmospheric Data:** Temp: 86 F, Relative Humidity 86%, Barometric Pressure 28.27 inches Hg, Altitude 1500 feet Atmospheric Surface Layer
**Crosswind:**
  Seven mph at seven o'clock (calculated at 50-percent strength, due to angle)

## Firing Solutions:

### Manufacturer Produced Table:
  **Elevation:** 48.97 inches drop (8.55 MOA Up)
  **Windage:** 14.775 inches right (2.5 MOA Left)

### Tailored Ballistics Table:
  **Elevation:** 67.51 inches drop (11.79 MOA Up)
  **Windage:** 13.65 inches right (2.38 MOA Left)

### Ballistic Software Calculation:
  **Elevation:** 63.31 inches drop (10.88 MOA Up)
  **Windage:** 13.01 inches right (2.23 MOA Left)

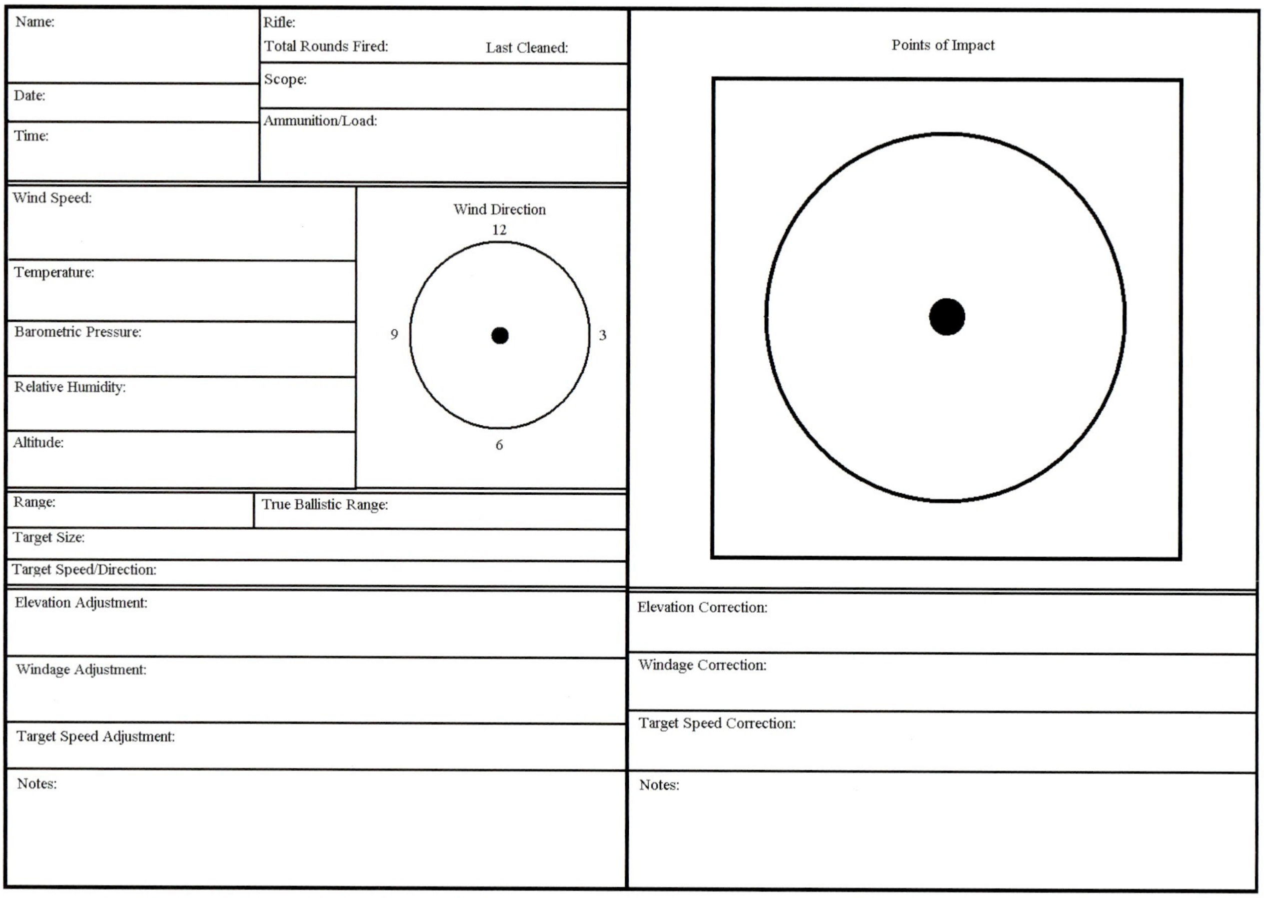

| | | | Points of Impact |
|---|---|---|---|
| Name: | Rifle: | | |
| | Total Rounds Fired: | Last Cleaned: | |
| Date: | Scope: | | |
| | Ammunition/Load: | | |
| Time: | | | |

Wind Speed:

Temperature:

Barometric Pressure:

Relative Humidity:

Altitude:

Wind Direction
12
9    3
6

Range:    True Ballistic Range:

Target Size:

Target Speed/Direction:

Elevation Adjustment:

Windage Adjustment:

Target Speed Adjustment:

Notes:

Elevation Correction:

Windage Correction:

Target Speed Correction:

Notes:

*This data book page can be reproduced by the shooter to keep track of their rifle and progress.*

## POST-SHOOT CLEANING

Post-shoot cleaning is a very important, but regularly overlooked task. The shooter should expect to spend at least half an hour conducting a normal post-shoot clean on one rifle.

The focus of this dedicated clean is twofold. First, the barrel should be absolutely cleaned, using appropriate solvents, until it's free of all copper fouling and powder glaze; the bolt and action should also be cleaned to this standard. Second, the screws on the rifle need to be checked to ensure none have come loose during the shoot.

In cleaning the bore, the shooter needs an appropriate cleaning rod, preferably one that's of a one-piece design and with a plastic coating and swivel handle (to allow the rod to rotate freely with the rifling). Also needed are a cleaning jag or loop to hold pieces of cleaning cloth, cleaning cloth in abundance, and solvent. As described before, the shooter simply places a small piece of cleaning cloth or patch (enough to ensure a tight fit in the bore) on the jag or through the loop, saturates the cloth with bore solvent, passes it through the bore from chamber to muzzle with the muzzle being lower so any excess does not drip into the action, and then waits the full specified time on the solvent's label. Once this time period has elapsed, the shooter must pass a clean and dry patch through the bore, then repeat the process until all the copper fouling is removed.

Many shooters make a series of mistakes in this process, which leads them to the false belief that their rifle is clean.

First is not using enough cleaning cloth for a tight fit with the bore. The cleaning rod should firmly resist the shooter when an appropriate amount of cloth is used, though the shooter shouldn't be required to exert *too* much force.

Second, many shooters don't use enough solvent on their patches. They just smear a little on the patch, pass it down the bore, and wonder why it comes out clean again. The cleaning patch should be *saturated*, almost *dripping* with solvent, to ensure all surfaces within the barrel are coated. When the clean and dry second patch is passed down the bore, a thick, rich, blue gooey liquid will come out ahead of the patch. This is a good sign of the use of a proper amount of solvent.

Third, many shooters do not use an *appropriate* solvent. The two layers of fouling that need to be removed are the copper fouling that gets directly deposited on the steel of the bore, and then a powder glaze that gets deposited over the top of the copper fouling. Most solvents on the commercial market are not up to this task. The shooter needs to understand that this metal and glass-like mixture is deposited under *thousands* of pounds of pressure and *hundreds to thousands* degrees of heat. This sort of fouling is not going to be removed by glorified window cleaner. A solvent such as Sweets 7.62 is appropriate for this task, though the shooter must be cautious when cleaning stainless steel firearms with it, because the solvent will attack stainless steel much faster than 4140 gun steel.

Finally, the shooter should always clean their rifle from the chamber to the muzzle and never reverse the direction of the patch or the rod. When the shooter takes the time to clean a rifle barrel using tight patches and good solvent, they will discover they seldom require the services of a bronze phosphor brush to help break free the fouling. The end result is less wear and a cleaner bore.

Once the bore is clean, the shooter can put a single patch through the bore with a small amount of an anti-corrosive agent, such as a simple gun oil, to ensure that the bore is protected between shoots.

Putting the bore aside, the shooter must also clean the bolt face. During firing, the bolt face will attract brass shavings, carbon, and other contaminants that must be removed. To clean the bolt face, the shooter

*Fouling builds up with every round. The post-shoot cleaning needs to remove this fouling. Here, the removed fouling is characterized as a thick blue (copper) goop—remove it all!*

need only apply a very small amount of bore solvent to a Q-tip and wipe it over the bolt face. This will dissolve the carbon and brass, and another wipe with a clean Q-tip with remove the solvent. The bolt should then be wiped over with a clean and dry cloth and re-lubricated. After this, the extractor and ejector can be sprayed out with high-pressure air, to ensure no other contaminants remain.

The second aspect of the post-shoot clean is to ensure that all the screws on the rifle are still at the correct torque levels. New rifles in particular tend to loosen up during the course of the first few groups, and the action screws require checking and tightening almost on a between-group basis.

Once the shooter has finished shooting for the day, they should also check the tension on the scope ring screws and those on any accessories. There are small, adjustable, screwdriver-like torque wrenches available that fulfill this task perfectly. As an aside, the shooter may also like to clean the lenses of their optics at this time. There are many self-contained lens-cleaning devices available from camera shops that will be perfect for this task. Finally, the shooter can wipe over the exterior of their rifle with a light, anti-corrosive agent for the metalwork and, perhaps, a small amount of beeswax for a wooden stock or a damp cloth for a composite or synthetic stock. The rifle is now clean and ready to return to the safe or the range!

# Shot Checklist

*This checklist can be used by the shooter, to make sure all bases are covered before pulling the trigger.*

| | | |
|---|---|---|
| | **Shooting Location** | Clear view of target and surrounding area. |
| | **Shooting Position** | Suitable to shooting location and affords adequate view for shot and safety. |
| | **Range** | Measured or estimated; laser rangefinder or rangefinding reticle; map and compass; known distance; estimation/bracketing. |
| | **Wind** | Direction and strength; visual clues; measurement; felt; mirage; flags; dust. |
| | **Altitude/Temperature/ Humidity/Barometric Pressure** | Height above zero height; temp change/humidity change/pressure change; measurement; map. |
| | **Uphill/Downhill** | Determine angle to target. |
| | **Data Corrections** | Correct data for altitude/temp/humidity/pressure. |
| | **Range Correction** | Correct range for uphill/downhill. |
| | **Windage Correction** | Adjust wind strength for crosswind direction. |
| | **Determine Elevation Adjustment** | Refer to ballistic table or software and input into scope. |
| | **Determine Windage Adjustment** | Refer to ballistics table or software and input into scope. |
| | **Final Shooting Position** | Shooter locks into their shooting position. |
| | **Aim** | Shooter takes aim on target. |
| | **Final Checks** | Shooter ensures that wind strength and direction have not changed or waits until the conditions are the same as when measured; shooter ensures that it is safe to take the shot. |

## FIRE

| | | |
|---|---|---|
| | **Follow-through** | Shooter remains focused on the target and takes one normal breath without moving. |
| | **Spot the Fall of the Shot** | Shooter spots the effects of the shot to determine if a follow-up shot is necessary. |

# CHAPTER 22

# Regular Firearm Maintenance

Periodic firearms maintenance takes the basic principles of a post-shoot clean and expands on them. This form of maintenance and cleaning could be considered "spring cleaning" for the shooter's firearm. Further, this form of maintenance and cleaning should be carried out any time the firearm is exposed to rain or large amounts of water, filled with dust or mud (perhaps from being dropped or left in a dusty environment), or when the point of impact characteristics of the rifle suddenly change.

In such maintenance, the action screws are taken out and the barreled action is removed from the stock. Aside from the normal cleaning of the bore and bolt face, the bolt should be stripped and cleaned as if the bolt were new, as previously detailed. Any persistent carbon inside the bolt or extractor or ejector mechanism can be dislodged with the end of a paperclip. On the subject of persistent carbon, .22 LR-chambered rifles are subject to the phenomenon of the "carbon ring." This is a ring of carbon and other contaminants such as wax and lead that collect at the very end of .22 LR chambers. Removal of this ring can greatly improve accuracy, by allowing the projectile to move into the throat and rifling without interference. Removal of the carbon ring is generally achieved with a pin or needle, and this area should be checked at every cleaning.

Having cleaned out the bolt internals, the shooter can then inspect the parts, looking for any abnormalities or sudden and unexpected wear. Some wear is perfectly normal and will, in fact, improve the performance of the rifle. But any wear that is more severe should be referred to a qualified gunsmith.

Having completed this, the shooter can look at the trigger mechanism and clean it in the same way a new trigger mechanism is cleaned. The shooter need not go any further than this with the trigger mechanism. In most cases, the working surfaces inside the trigger mechanism are not visible unless the mechanism is disassembled.

The shooter can inspect the various adjustment screws in the trigger mechanism and ensure they are still locked. If the shooter feels the trigger mechanism adjustments have changed, they can refer to the owner's manual of their firearm for information on adjusting the trigger mechanism, or take the barreled action to a qualified gunsmith for adjustment.

*Maintenance is important. The rifle will only work as well as its weakest part.*

The stock is next inspected. The shooter must take particular note of the recoil lug abutments in the stock and the action screw holes. Here the shooter is looking for hammered surfaces or cracks, either of which are symptomatic of incorrect action screw tension.

The shooter should ensure that the correct relief gaps between the stock and the action still exist and that the barrel touches the fore-end of the stock in the correct places. The shooter should also inspect the magazine recess to ensure that detachable magazines aren't binding on the stock and that internal magazine guides don't bottom out on the bottom of the action and inside of the magazine recess when the action screws are tensioned.

If the interior of the stock is dirty, it must be cleaned. This can be as simple as wiping it out with a clean, damp rag. Many things can collect inside stocks, from moisture and dust to mud and excess bore solvent.

From this point, the shooter can inspect their scope, clean the lenses, and ensure all the scope mounting hardware screws are correctly torqued. It is not uncommon for some of these small screws to loosen over the course of a hunting season.

Finally, all the parts are reassembled and every screw on the rifle checked for the correct torque setting. Having completed this, the shooter can give the firearm a quick wipe with an anti-corrosive agent to remove the finger prints and protect the metalwork, and return the firearm to the safe.

# Part V: Shooter Maintenance

## CHAPTER 23

# Shooter Diet

Though this chapter starts the final section of the book, its subject matter is really the first principle of accurate shooting. To ensure the shooter is operating the rifle and ammunition correctly, consistently, and reliably, it's best to start at a grassroots level, and that's the human body.

The human body, like a rifle, is a machine. It must be maintained properly in order to carry out whatever tasks we ask of it. Ask yourself, how many times have you made it to the firing line or to your favorite hunting stand and are jittery and have a headache because you missed your morning coffee, or are out of breath and can't hold aim after hiking to the top of a saddle or back from the 300 meter line? These are the signs of a poorly tuned body, whether it be general fitness, dehydration, hunger, or a lack of sleep. With any of these things in place, you will have started on the path to taking a shot and already be on the wrong foot. To take a note from the last chapter, the shooter can clean their gun until it could be considered near-sterile, but, without the shooter also being in top physical form, the shooter can never expect to wring the best effort from their time at the range or afield.

Body conditioning encompasses the simple steps that we can all take to get our bodies functioning properly. Diet, sleep, hydration, general fitness, and eyesight are key in ensuring that the rounds that leave the shooter's rifle end up at the destination they have chosen. It's important to note that the shooter doesn't have to be a health food nut or be able to run a half marathon without breaking a sweat to achieve good body conditioning. It's as simple as eating good quality food, going for a walk or bicycle ride each day, and getting a good night's sleep after a good day's work. These simple steps, when applied appropriately, will give the shooter a significant and noticeable edge in as little as a week and, once part of a normal daily routine, after a couple weeks, will seem effortless.

### DIET

Diet is the single most important aspect of body conditioning and can be broken down into two important parts. First, there is the general diet, or what the shooter eats in a normal week. Second, there is the immediate diet, or what the shooter eats when they are out hunting or between serials when shooting at the range. The two differ greatly for the simple fact that the needs of the shooter's body change, based on what they're doing with it. A well-balanced diet at home simply doesn't give your body the

*Natural foods supply the shooter with the greatest advantage in terms of nutrients, vitamins, and energy.*

energy it needs out in the field, and a heavy meal just before lying down on the firing line at the range is catastrophic, when compared to the intake of a couple fruit and nut bars. The following will give the shooter a guide as to what is appropriate both for healthy eating and healthy shooting.

## GENERAL DIET

We have all heard about the healthy eating food pyramid, which contains five layers or groups of foods and the percentage that each group should occupy in a daily diet. The bottom of the pyramid is the carbohydrate group containing foods such as pasta, rice, breads, and grains. The carbohydrate group supplies the body with energy in varying forms. The next layer is the vegetable group of potatoes, carrots, peas, etc. This group supplies the body with vitamins and minerals and some energy. The third layer is the fruit group of berries, apples, oranges, etc. The fruit group supplies the body with vitamins and minerals, as well as complex fruit sugars and fiber. The fourth layer is the dairy group, which includes milk, cheese, and yogurt. This group supplies the body with calcium, protein, and complex sugars, as well as fat (which is essential, in small quantities, for healthy eating). The fifth and final layer of the healthy eating food pyramid is the protein group, which includes meat, eggs, and fish. These foods provide the body with protein, amino acids, iron, sodium, and fat.

The idea of the food pyramid is to structure the shooter's diet to conform to the ratios set by the sizes of each layer. While this method of determining a suitable diet is a definite step in the right direction, it is a little simplistic. For instance, as a refinement, a good rule of thumb is to avoid processed foods. Processing of foods tends to strip vitamins and minerals, concentrate fats and salts, and alter the glycemic index of the food, allowing the body to absorb and digest faster, which is not desirable. A good way of applying this rule of thumb is by asking, "What is our body designed to eat?" If the shooter ate the diets of their forebears from, perhaps, 1,000 years ago, they can see that the foods consumed were simple, essentially unaltered from how they were hunted, grown, or farmed.

Another good rule of thumb is never to eat until you feel full. Most people forget or don't know that the body is designed to feel hungry for a reasonable portion of the day. If the shooter eats until they feel full, they are likely to experience lethargy and sleepiness about half an hour after eating, as their body goes about digesting the volume of food they've consumed. If, on the other hand, the shooter restricts eating to predetermined times of the day, it will assist them in keeping to a pathway of healthy eating.

The final rule of thumb is that energy in must equal energy out. If the shooter consumes food in excess of their body's requirements, an amount of it will end up as fat.

## ON THE HUNT/AT THE RANGE DIET

We have all been there, at the range or in the field, cold and hungry and no one is having any fun. It doesn't have to be like that!

Looking food intake, in terms of breakfast, lunch and dinner, light meals with regular snacking are the best way to go.

For breakfast, a meal providing a small amount of energy in the form of complex sugars, protein, and carbohydrates is the best way to start the day. A small amount of oats or muesli early in the morning will give the shooter all the energy they need to get going, without all that energy being expended at once. It will help the shooter to feel less hungry for longer, and also has the benefit of being quick and easy to prepare before heading out for the pre-dawn hunt or travel to the range. If such fare isn't to the shooter's taste, toast with a simple topping and/or fruit is perfectly acceptable alternative. For the shooter in the field who doesn't want to start up a source of heat for fear of scent and smoke, but still wants a substantial kick start, why not do what the Europeans do and have a miniature lunch consisting of cheese, meat, or sausage and a thick slice of a heavy bread? Pumpernickel is excellent for this purpose. On the other side of the coin, a big plate of eggs, bacon, mushrooms, and sausages, while alluring on a cold morning, will do far more damage than good and set the shooter's body off on the wrong path.

*Good diets are built on a solid plan. (Courtesy USDA)*

Food in the field—
the good, the bad,
and the ugly!

Lunch, ideally, is something the shooter can take with them, without having to prepare to any great degree. Preferably, it can be eaten either on the move or in stages, so that the shooter doesn't have to start and finish in the one sitting. Sandwiches, cereal bars, and fruit are an excellent solution that provide nutrition, a small amount of protein and salt (in the case of a meat- and/or cheese-based sandwich), carbohydrates from oats and seeds, energy from a wide variety of complex sugars, and the simplicity of little preparation and cleanup.

Off-the-shelf products such as spaghetti in a can or noodles in a cup require preparation and normally a source of heat (yes, these can be eaten cold—been there, done that!). More importantly, they are of questionable nutritional value, and given the high glycemic index (rate at which sugars are absorbed by the body), of highly processed foods, will result in carbohydrate poisoning of varying degrees. Carbohydrate poisoning will cause the shooter to become lethargic and tired, will result in increased blood pressure and heart rate and, due to the fats and salt concentration present, will increase the water requirements of the shooter.

Dinner is a time of rest and recuperation in anticipation of the next day's shooting or hunting. It is the body' opportunity to repair damage, replenish sugars and salts, take in protein, and restore water balance. Likewise, it is the shooter's opportunity to consume those heavier foods that require preparation and require the shooter be off their feet while the food is being digested.

Ideally, the body requires a good source of (preferably) red meat for protein (white meat is also acceptable in good quantities), while potatoes, pasta, or rice are excellent sources of carbohydrates. Sauces and ketchups can be used to provide a source for simple sugars and salts. Vegetables such as broccoli, Brussels sprouts, and spinach provide essential vitamins and aid in digestion overnight.

If the shooter is backpack hunting, couscous, dehydrated mashed potato, and polenta provide many of the benefits of fresh potatoes, pasta, and rice, but in a very packable and easy to prepare format. Couple this with a big handful of beef jerky in the pot and some freeze-dried peas and carrots, and you can have a stew going in a matter of minutes in one cooking vessel, over one heat source. If the shooter plans well ahead, they can pre-mix the ingredients into zip lock bags at home, then, when ready to cook in the field, add the predetermined amount of water to the bag of ingredients, seal it up, and drop in into boiling water for a few minutes. Hot meal, a cup of coffee with the leftover boiling water, no washing up, and just the flames of the campfire or the stars of the night sky as nature's television make for a good way to end the day.

We've discussed what's good to eat, but now lets look at fluids to drink on the range or in the field. Ideally, we drink fluids to maintain water balance in our bodies. Humans, however, are fussy creatures and like flavorings, colors, and sugar. As a rule, good things to drink can be consumed through the entire day, while food is more closely tied to the activities before and after each meal.

The best drink of all, at any time of day, is unaltered water. Pure water is tasteless, scentless, and is readily absorbed by the body. But, for most people, drinking unaltered water isn't exciting. So what other options are available?

Fruit juice that is good quality, preferably a fresh bottled type diluted 50 percent with water, is an excellent drink. It contains the flavors we all like, coupled with complex fruit sugars and an amount of simple sugars (depending on quality) that can provide fast energy; cordials or concentrated fruit juices are less desirable. Heavier milk-based drinks are also good; although the water content and absorbability are reduced, they are a good source of protein magnesium, and complex sugar, plus milk contains and tryptophan, an essential amino acid that, among other things, has a calming effect on the muscles of the body and can limit or reduce movement in the sight picture through the scope and assist in a steadier aim.

Tea is an excellent drink that provides excellent water content and the natural properties of the particular tea used. Tea also has a cleansing effect on the mouth (good in the morning), and can limit scent that game may detect on a hunt.

Now, I can't stand tea—I'd rather drink dishwater. My drink of choice is coffee and, I admit, it's a very poor choice. Coffee does about everything we *don't* want, either at the range or on a hunt. It increases the heart rate and blood pressure, it can make the body jittery, it increases intestinal activity and, possibly worst of all, it is a diuretic, causing the body and kidneys to work overtime to get rid of water the shooter may need.

Soft drinks are also not a desirable option. They are extremely rich in simple sugars, have diuretic properties, are low in straight water content and, in some cases, contain additives (colors, flavors, and preservatives), that are difficult for the body to break down. Sports drinks tend to fall into the same category. Although these drinks are marketed as containing all the salts, sugars, and fancy packaging you will ever need, the simple fact remains that, if it's not in a format the body can absorb, then it will go in one hole and out the other and stress the body on the way through. The human body is designed to absorb salts and sugars from *natural* foods at a *natural* rate.

As a final note, it must be mentioned that alcohol and firearms don't mix. Although alcohol in its various forms can provide excellent medicinal effects, it is also a diuretic, impairs judgment, impairs vision, reduces the effectiveness of all the senses, and stresses the body during digestion. If the shooter intends to drink, they must secure their firearms and drink at the bar!

I'm a great believer in having something up your sleeve or, in this case, in your pocket. I always carry with me, either in the field or at the range, several good quality hard candies and a few strips of homemade beef jerky. Sometimes you need some energy and other times a quick burst of salt. These cover both bases and can come in handy when you're behind your sights and need a little something to tide you over until you're out of the hunting stand or off the range.

# CHAPTER 24

# Sleep

The lack of quality sleep affects just about everyone these days. There are a huge number of scientific studies that have looked at various forms of sleep deprivation, both in terms of quality and quantity of sleep. All tend to show that sleep deprivation of any kind has a marked effect on the human body.

Many studies have looked at remedies for sleep deprivation, for instance, a 20-minute catnap every four hours after the first 24 hours of being awake. But even utilizing these techniques, mental and physical capacity suffers greatly. In some cases, sleep deprivation has the same effect on the body as being drunk. It's important for the shooter to understand the reasons for sleep deprivation, its effects, and how to counter or make allowances for those effects. It is important

*Sleep is mandatory; quality sleep is a must for accuracy.*

to note that, if the shooter should ever feel that safety is being compromised, due to sleep deprivation or tiredness, it's time to unload, pack up, and go home. A good shooter knows that safety comes first.

## GOOD SLEEP

Sleep is made up of five stages that form a cycle, according to brain activity, and the stages can be determined and measured through brain wave analysis. The cycle occurs several times per night.

Stage one, lasting as little as 10 minutes, is categorized as a near-awake state, where a person can be easily woken and can experience a falling sensation. This stage of sleep is only experienced once per night.

Stage two is a continuation of stage one involving a drop in heart rate and body temperature and is considered a forerunner to actual deep sleep.

Stages three and four are considered to be deep sleep, where brain activity, temperature, and heart rate are at their minimum. During these stages, it is difficult to awaken the sleeper.

The fifth stage is categorized by rapid eye movement (REM) and brain activity that is close to that of being awake. Temperature and respiration will increase, and it is during this stage of sleep that most dreaming occurs.

This cycle of sleep reoccurs several times during the night, progressing in stages one to four, then backwards from four to two, and finishing with stage five (REM).

In terms of body chemistry, the sleep cycle is very different. Most people know that old adages that sleep before midnight is better than sleep after, and early to bed is early to rise. Never have these been more true! Body chemistry during sleep is driven by the cortisol cycle. Cortisol is a hormone released by the body, based on a daily cycle and determined by the amount of light that enters the eye. Levels increase through the morning, peaking at midday and tapering off during the afternoon, with the minimum levels being recorded during the night.

During sleep, cortisol levels decrease in two stages. The first stage, lasting about four hours (during an eight-hour sleep state), is geared for cell repair and production of new cells. The second stage, again lasting the next four hours, is when the body's immune system is at its peak and damaged cells, viruses, and bacteria are eliminated.

It's all very well to have an understanding of brain activity and body chemistry during sleep, but how can we use it to our advantage?

Let's first look at quantity. It's no good snatching a few hours here and a few hours there during the day and night. The processes described above dictate that, in order for the objectives of sleep to be met, the framework of *regular* sleep needs to be adhered to. For instance, getting four hours sleep in the middle of the night is going to be far more beneficial than the same amount through the middle of the day—and the rule of thumb for quantity of sleep is eight hours per day. In reality, this figure is highly dependent on the activities and health of the individual. In reality, six to seven hours is generally sufficient for an adult in good health, in an unstressed state.

Quality of sleep pertains to the types of sleep achieved and how the sleep fits into a natural pattern. For the objectives of sleep to be met, the body and brain must drift through all the stages of sleep, allowing sufficient time for cell repair and renewal and full immune system activity to occur. It is no good to sleep, wake early in the morning, and drift back to sleep. Not only does this promote bad sleeping habits, when the sleeper awakes, their brain activity

and body chemistry will have changed to that of a different stage. Ultimately, the sleeper will awake and feel tired and lethargic.

If the shooter wakes early, it is better to get up and start the day early. If the shooter intends to sleep, it is better to take a minimum of three to four hours during the night. Better still, if the shooter can take the three to four hours sleep before two a.m., at the latest, the sleep he or she does achieve will maximize the amount of cell repair and renewal that can occur. If, for some reason, the shooter cannot allocate that amount of time, it is better to remain awake or cat nap for 20 minutes every four hours until the shooter can allocate an appropriate amount of time to sleep.

## SLEEP DEPRIVATION

The effects of sleep deprivation vary from individual to individual and also the environmental circumstances the individual is in. In general terms, an individual who is sleep deprived will experience lapses in memory, impaired cognitive function, increase in production of stress hormones, impaired concentration, lower reaction times, lower energy levels, impaired moral judgment, and headaches, watering eyes, muscle cramping, and physical fatigue or weakness. In severe cases, confusion, hallucinations, aggressive behavior, and symptoms of general psychosis may result.

As the shooter can see, sleep deprivation won't just harm accuracy in shooting, but will harm every aspect of every task the shooter performs. Most insidiously of all is the fact that, in minor cases, the human psyche will underrate the actual level of sleep deprivation that the body and mind is experiencing, thereby exposing the shooter and anyone in the area to an extra level of danger.

Knowing the signs of sleep deprivation in one's self is the first step to combating the effects and ensuring your shooting situation is safe for everybody. By the same token, a good shooting buddy, spotter, or hunting partner will recognize the signs in you. Learn to trust each other's judgment. If you feel sleep deprived, you shouldn't be shooting, period.

# CHAPTER 25

# Hydration

Hydration is a simple term that describes a complex set of biochemical reactions in the body. Specifically, hydration deals with maintaining the correct concentration of water and salt within the body. Failure to maintain this equilibrium will result in poor scores on the bench or missing that big buck in the field.

## WATER INTAKE

The average person, in a rested state, in temperate conditions, requires a minimum of one liter of water per day. Where a person is undergoing normal daily activities with some exertion, this figure can easy rise to three to five liters per day, even more under extreme conditions and on a per-hour basis. Of course, due to the constraints of modern life, few people actually take the time to hydrate appropriately or to the correct level.

The effects of dehydration initially include lethargy, lack of concentration, and headaches, leading to blurred vision and difficulty with simple arithmetic. It is important to note that a feeling of thirst is a reactionary response to dehydration. If the shooter feels thirsty, they are already suffering the initial effects of dehydration.

The best way to avoid dehydration while in the field or on the range is to regularly sip fresh water from a water bottle or backpack-mounted carrier. The shooter must be preemptive with water consumption

and base intake on temperature, exertion, and perspiration. It is important not to gulp water. Gulping tends to waste water, as the body cannot absorb the water fast enough, plus, an overload of water in the stomach causes discomfort such as "stitches."

*In some climates, this glass of water may only be one-fifty-fourth of the shooter's daily requirements.*

*The reality of sweat is salt loss, as seen on these salt-encrusted boots.*

## SALT BALANCE

In hand with water intake is salt balance. When a person perspires, not only are they loosing moisture from the body, they are also loosing salts. The effects of salt imbalance are far more difficult to detect, as they mirror the effects of dehydration except for a feeling of thirst. The key symptoms of mild salt imbalance separate to those of dehydration include muscle cramping, a need to urinate almost directly after consuming water, and a general weakness of the body. In particular to shooters, one will have difficulty in achieving shake-free sight pictures through scopes or iron sights, stiffening of the muscles, and difficulty in concentrating.

The best way to avoid salt imbalance is preemptive salt balance monitoring and manipulation. As it is with water consumption, more is *not* better. Salt absorption is best achieved with small amounts dissolved in large amounts of water, then regularly sipped. A concentration of no more than one-quarter metric teaspoon of good quality sea salt per liter of fresh water is the requirement. The water should taste barely tainted by the salt and should be easy to consume.

There are many electrolyte solutions commercially available that contain the relevant salts, along with sugars and flavorings, in both a liquid and powder forms. These products tend to stress the body by placing many complex molecules into the stomach, requiring the body's organs to work hard to digest and absorb the necessary salts and sugars. As such, this can lead to increased heart rate and breathing, which is not desirable.

# Fitness

*Daily exercise will tune the body for accuracy.*

The art and science of accurate shooting requires the shooter to maintain a solid and repeatable platform for the rifle. Factors such as a high heart rate, breathing, and general fitness levels can impact the stability and repeatability of the rifle during and between shots. A good example of this is taking an offhand shot in the field after coming over the crest of a hill and being out of breath. As another example, the shooter may be at the range and the excitement of competition has got the shooter's blood up and their heart pumping fast.

General fitness applicable to accurate shooting in any discipline doesn't necessarily require the shooter to be a fitness guru or work out several times a week at the gym. Of course, a higher level of physical fitness can only do you good, but it does tend to offer diminishing returns for effort. So, what does all this mean for the shooter?

When we talk about physical fitness, we are talking about cardiovascular and pulmonary fitness, or how efficiently the shooter's heart and lungs work. Fortunately, heart and lung fitness pretty well go hand in hand, and the same exercise, will address both areas.

Two other points of interest for shooters are weight versus height, and flexibility. Excess weight is not desirable for any kind of shooting. That and the often accompanying lack of flexibility can make adopting

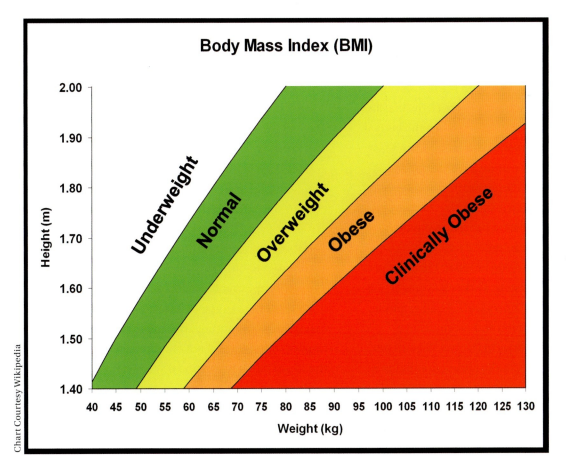

*The Body Mass Index (BMI) table is a useful guide for assessing the shooter's condition.*

and changing firing positions difficult and slow, interfere in correct shouldering of the rifle, and prevent achieving appropriate and repeatable cheek welds and eye relief.

## BODY MASS INDEX (BMI)

Body Mass Index (BMI) is a graphical scale comparing weight versus height. It breaks down the result into five categories: emaciated, underweight, average, overweight, and obese. BMI is simplistic in its design and does not take into account a body shape that is not "average," nor does it account medical factors affecting the results. It is, however, a good guide to determining the shooter's status, as to whether they are overweight, underweight, or about right, and can give the shooter an idea of goals and where they might need to be on the scale of BMI.

## HEART RATE AND RESPIRATION

Heart rate and respiration rate can be a good measure of cardiovascular and pulmonary fitness. Heart rate is broken down into two main categories, resting heart rate and normal exertion heart rate.

A resting heart rate can be taken when the body is at rest, relaxed, and generally with the feet raised, for instance, in a seated position on a couch or sofa. The normal exertion heart rate is taken when the body is stressed to a medium level, for instance, after a fast lap in a pool, a long walk, or medium-length jog. A good indicator of normal exertion is the presence of sweat and an overheating response by the body.

In average terms, a resting heart rate should be about 60 to 80 beats per minute. An exerted heart rate is normally in the region of 120 to 140 beats per minute. Because this system works on averages, it can be inaccurate for some individuals. As an example, many champion sportsmen and -women have recorded resting heart rates in the low 30 beats per minute region. Conversely, the author maintains a resting heart rate of over 80 beats per minute and, on occasion, as high as 90 beats per minute, yet has an optimum body mass index ratio and good health with an active lifestyle. See? Averages.

Respiration rate generally goes hand in hand with heart rate and will improve as general fitness improves, helping to remove the feeling of running out of breath as exertion is experienced, and lessening the feeling of muscles tiring during exertion.

## A SIMPLE FITNESS PLAN

A fitness plan for healthy shooting and, indeed, healthy living, doesn't have to be a tough grind every day. A short amount of exercise of medium intensity every day or at least every two days in three, is an excellent framework for building a good level of fitness. If possible, the plan should be combined with daily living and activities. Of course, for the first week or so of a new exercise regimen, it will seem like an uphill battle, but, by the end of the first week, the activities will be noticeably easier. Inside of three weeks, the body will have adjusted to the new routine of exercise, and not only will it have become relatively easy, psychologically it won't be perceived as a negative activity in the mind. In fact, after a short time, perhaps a month, the body will be so used to the endorphins being released in the brain during exercise and getting outside in the sunshine and fresh air, that the shooter will begin to miss exercising on off days or on a layoff.

And there end-eth the pep talk. Now, let's look at good exercise, tailored to the activities of shooting and hunting.

Walking, cycling, and swimming are all low-impact exercises that mimic what our bodies experience in the natural environment. These exercises are all high repetition, low power exercises that tend to improve cardiovascular and pulmonary fitness, as opposed to building muscle. Exercises such as weightlifting, squats, and treadmill/jogging exercise don't achieve the type of fitness required for all the disciplines of shooting. Moreover, they are high-impact exercises and not conducive to prolonging the life of joints in the body.

So, where's a good place to start? Take simple walking, for an example. We walk in everyday life. Heck, our bodies are *designed* for walking. For most people, walking is a simple, low-impact exercise.

# Basic Fitness Plan

| SUNDAY | MONDAY | TUESDAY | WEDNESDAY | THURSDAY | FRIDAY | SATURDAY |
|---|---|---|---|---|---|---|
| Morning bicycle ride | Walk to and from work | Take the kids swimming | Take the dog for a walk | Football practice | Evening walk with partner | Walk up and down the range |
| *25 minutes* | *30 minutes* | *45 minutes* | *25 minutes* | *90 minutes* | *30 minutes* | *30 minutes* |

*Fitness plans don't have to be about dedicated time at the gym. The smart shooter uses their daily activities to exercise.*

What better way to start on the path to a good fitness plan than walking down a path!

Initially, the shooter needs to do less than they think they should. If the shooter goes out and walks too much to begin with, they will end up with sore muscles, a lethargic state, and sore feet. The shooter should start off with small steps, perhaps take a walk at a medium pace around the equivalent of two city blocks, or for 15 minutes. Take some music along as company. When the shooter has finished, they will feel warm, slightly out of breath, but will recover well over a further 15 to 30 minutes. The shooter needs to do this for a week; by the end of the week they, will be covering the same distance faster and with less effort.

The start of week two is the time to start stepping up the intensity and distance. Try to walk around the equivalent of four city blocks or for 30 minutes at a medium pace. Again, you will probably end up sweating slightly and be a little out of breath.

The start of week three will have the shooter in an established routine on an established route and getting used to the exercise. Any soreness the shooter may have felt when starting the exercise plan will have faded and the walking the shooter does now will have become to feel fairly effortless. Now is the time to step up the pace to medium-fast. Most people walk at roughly four miles per hour. This is slow. Try to aim for six to seven miles per hour. If the shooter can maintain this pace for a full 30 minutes, every day, they have set an excellent routine that will see their cardio vascular and pulmonary fitness improve quickly and significantly. The shooter will also develop a wide band of muscles that are directly useful, whether the shooter is on the range or in the field.

It is important to address that the shooter is changing the energy and hydration requirements of their body as they become fit. In doing so, they must address their diet and water intake to suit the activity. Also, know that this system can be equally applied to swimming or cycling. Perhaps try cycling to work or stopping at a public pool on the way home. Exercise itself is easy. It's possessing the psychology to carry through with exercise and be firm with one's self that is hard.

# CHAPTER 27

# Eyesight

Good eyesight and understanding how the shooter's eyes function with the rest of their body is key to accurate shooting. Small imperfections in sight, such as short sightedness (myopia) or long sightedness (hyperopia) or even astigmatism (slight double vision due to misshapen eyeball or lens), can have drastic effects on the ability to achieve a correct and repeatable sight picture. Even a simple lack of understanding of eye dominance can lead to error in sight picture. Fortunately, with the exception of a degenerative eye condition, all these issues can be resolved by a trip to an optometrist or ophthalmologist. In the event that the shooter believes their eyes are perfectly fine, small gains can generally be made for those over the age of 30 through slight augmentation with glasses or contact lenses.

Quality of eyesight, or "visual acuity" (VA), is a measure of how well one sees, in terms of the sharpness and clarity of an image. This test is usually carried out by looking at the Snellen chart of letters or numbers, commonly found in an optometrist's office as viewed from a known distance, usually 20 feet. The result of the VA test is given in the form of a fraction, namely, 20/20 for someone who can resolve the same sharpness and clarity of an image at 20

*The eye is a precision instrument that needs to be well maintained.*

feet, as well as an average person can at that same distance. For a fraction of 20/40, a person can only resolve the same sharpness and clarity of an image at 20 feet that the average person would see at 40 feet, and so on. This is the primary test used to determine

| | |
|---|---|
| A | 20/200 |
| D F | 20/100 |
| H Z P | 20/70 |
| T X U D | 20/50 |
| Z A D N H | 20/40 |
| P N T U H X | 20/30 |
| U A Z N F D T | 20/25 |
| N P H T A F X U | 20/20 |
| X D F H P T Z A N | 20/15 |
| F A X T D N H U P Z | 20/10 |

*Hold this table (reduced in size for use in this book), seven feet away and see what you can see!*

whether corrective augmentation of vision or glasses or contact lenses are required to generate a 20/20 Snellen chart result, or average acuity.

## EYESIGHT AUGMENTATION

If, after examination, one's eyesight is found to be deficient, augmentation through glasses or contact lenses may be required to achieve average vision capabilities.

Myopia, or nearsightedness, is the most common form of natural vision degeneration and is common in adults over the age of 40. Myopia is a defect in either the lens or structure of the eyeball and causes the individual to see a blurry image at distances, while objects close up appear to be in focus. There are several different types of myopia, but the effects and treatment are generally the same. Concave glasses or contact lenses can be proscribed that will correct the focus within the eye to achieve 20/20 vision.

Hyperopia, or long sightedness, is the reverse condition of myopia. The individual is unable to achieve focus on objects that are close up, while objects at 20 feet or greater are generally easily seen. Contact lenses or glasses with a convex lens can be prescribed to treat this condition. It should be noted that those with varying degrees of both conditions can have their vision corrected with the use of bifocal glasses that have a section in the lens for close focus and another for far focus.

Astigmatism is a condition whereby the lens or surface of the eyeball is slightly out of round, causing a double or overlapping image. Of note is that the function of the muscles and lens within the eye may be perfect (aside for the imperfection itself, and this distinguishes astigmatism from myopia and hyperopia. This condition also manifests in those over the age of 20, and the condition generally stabilizes and does not degenerate further from the mid-thirties onward. Again, this condition can be corrected with glasses or contact lenses, and laser surgery is now available to permanently correct astigmatism.

Interestingly, astigmatism has the capacity to affect only one eye, as in the author's case. The author's dominant right eye maintains 20/10 un-augmented visual acuity, while the left eye suffers from a mild astigmatism. Some might say that no augmentation is necessary, due to the fact that the eye used for aiming is functioning properly, but the author tends to disagree on the grounds that both eyes should be open during shooting and, therefore, both eyes need to be functioning properly.

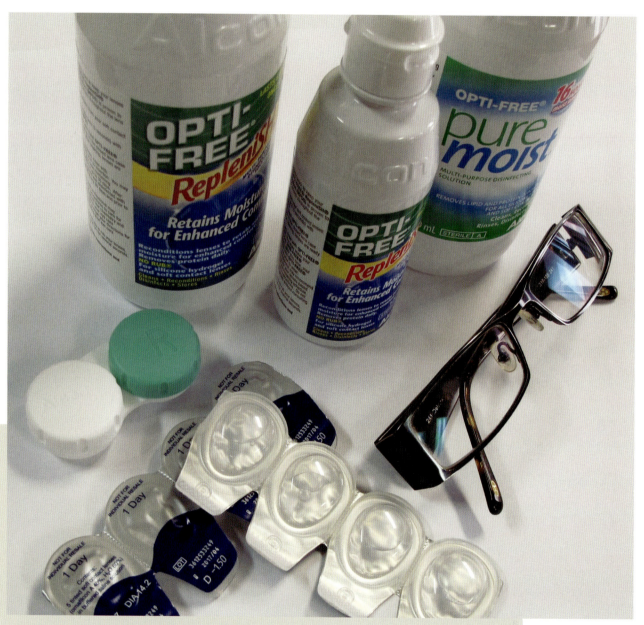

*Augmenting the shooter's eyesight through the use of prescription glasses or contact lenses is a simple process that pays big dividends.*

# CHAPTER 28

# Clothing and Eyewear

Clothing is as much a matter of personal preference as it is functionality, with regards to the shooter's purpose. For competition, there are many custom-made garments, some with built-in pads and braces. Likewise, there are camouflage garments for all types of seasons, weather, and terrain. Both styles of shooting apparel go far beyond the general purpose of clothing. In reality, providing certain rules are followed, most clothing comfortable to the shooter and suitable for the environment is suitable for shooting, whether it be for competition or hunting.

Following the axiom "form following function," it can be easily seen that, as the body must hold various shooting positions, the shooter's clothing must allow the shooter to achieve these positions, i.e., the shooter requires flexibility in the clothing. This can stem from flexible fabrics that conform to the shapes the shooter requires, or there must be a bulk of inflexible fabric to allow the shooter to be flexible within their garments.

Synthetic fabrics such as fleece provide excellent thermal protection, while also being exceptionally flexible. Likewise, a long-sleeve shirt with a thermal vest over it provides core warmth, while allowing arm movement. Loose-fitting cargo-type trousers are excellent for ventilation in arid and hot conditions, and they are also very flexible. Denim jeans, on the other hand, are not a good choice, due to their constricting nature and poor thermal properties (in any environment).

A large brimmed hat offers advantages in sunny and hot conditions and can also act as an eyepiece shade—easy, right? The subject of gloves is more difficult. Gloves need to be tight fitting and thin in terms of the material used in their construction. It is critically important that the shooter can "feel" the rifle in their hands. At the same time, "buffer" (glove material) between the skin of the shooter's hands and the stock of the rifle is a point of possible instability and would require the shooter to grip harder than necessary. Further, the skin of the trigger finger should be exposed to the trigger. This can mean that the finger of the glove is cut off or, on a tight-fitting glove, just the pad of the trigger fingers finger can be removed from the glove, thereby allowing the pad of the trigger finger to directly contact the trigger. In contrast, a poor choice would be a pair of mittens!

Looking briefly at eyewear, the primary purpose of it is safety in the event of a destructive misfire. Another benefit is that various filters can be used on eyewear to improve vision in certain circumstances, for instance, yellow-tinted eyewear improves the view in foggy conditions. Further, darkly tinted eyewear will enhance the shooter's light sensitivity before taking a low-light shot, while some tints in today's modern eyewear amplify colors of the spectrum that relate to the shooter's target, whether on the hunt or in competition.

# End Note

The shooter has now come full circle and discovered how they interact with their firearm and ammunition. The shooter has learned what is required in order to achieve the most out of themselves and they equipment they have. Now that the lessons have been preached, it is time to put them into practice.

It is ego—more than bad weather, more than poor ammunition, more than any other factor—that will defeat the shooter, when all things come together in that spontaneous moment when the striker drops and the target shows a hit or a miss. If the shooter is capable of taking in the information and advice in this book, assimilating, assessing, and employing it, they will have overcome the greatest impediment to progressing in the realm of shooting—their own ego.

Good shooting, everyone, good shooting to you one and all!

*Good hunting!—The Author*